THE RISE OF ISLAMIC POLITICAL MOVEMENTS AND PARTIES

Morocco, Turkey and Jordan

Esen Kirdiş

EDINBURGH
University Press

Edinburgh University Press is one of the leading university presses in the UK. We publish academic books and journals in our selected subject areas across the humanities and social sciences, combining cutting-edge scholarship with high editorial and production values to produce academic works of lasting importance. For more information visit our website: edinburghuniversitypress.com

© Esen Kirdiş, 2019, 2021

First published in hardback by Edinburgh University Press 2019

Edinburgh University Press Ltd
The Tun – Holyrood Road
12 (2f) Jackson's Entry
Edinburgh EH8 8PJ

Typeset in 11/15 Adobe Garamond by
Servis Filmsetting Ltd, Stockport, Cheshire

A CIP record for this book is available from the British Library

ISBN 978 1 4744 5067 6 (hardback)
ISBN 978 1 4744 5068 3 (paperback)
ISBN 978 1 4744 5069 0 (webready PDF)
ISBN 978 1 4744 5070 6 (epub)

The right of Esen Kirdiş to be identified as author of this work has been asserted in accordance with the Copyright, Designs and Patents Act 1988 and the Copyright and Related Rights Regulations 2003 (SI No. 2498).

CONTENTS

List of Figures and Tables   iv
Acknowledgements   v

1 Introduction: Between Movement and Party   1
2 Form a Party or Stay a Movement? Structures and the Menu of Options   31
3 Islamic Movements Take Agency: The Decision over Participation   54
4 Two Paths, Six Different Outcomes, Three New Political Centres   121
5 Conclusion: The Rise of Islamic Political Movements and Parties   166

Bibliography   188
Interviews   216
A Note   219
Index   221

FIGURES AND TABLES

Figures

1.1	A Visual Representation of the Three Propositions	21
2.1	Urban Population (Results from Morocco)	38
2.2	School Enrolment (Results from Morocco)	39
2.3	Urban Population (Results from Turkey)	42
2.4	School Enrolment (Results from Turkey)	43
2.5	Urban Population (Results from Jordan)	46
2.6	School Enrolment (Results from Jordan)	47
4.1	Evolution of Islamic Movement–Regime Relations	127

Tables

1.1	Comparative Method	10
1.2	Within-case Comparison	11
2.1	The Menu of Options	36
3.1	Independent Variables and Expectations	59
4.1	PJD's Electoral Performance	128
4.2	Parties Related to the NOM	136
4.3	NOM Related Parties' Electoral Performance	137
4.4	IAF's Electoral Performance	145

ACKNOWLEDGEMENTS

This book started out as a dissertation during my PhD studies at the University of Minnesota Political Science Department. I feel especially privileged and honoured to have had the chance to work closely with and to be mentored by, two brilliant advisors, David Samuels and Kathleen Collins. It was in David's 'Political Parties and Party Systems' seminar that I started researching Islamic political parties, and under Kathleen's guidance, I embarked on fieldwork. I am also indebted to the other members of my dissertation and prospectus committees, Abdi Samatar, Michael Barnett, and Kathryn Sikkink, for their enthusiastic support and inspiration. Special thanks must also go to my undergraduate advisor, Ziya Öniş, at Koç University, from whom I learned the fundamentals of the field.

I owe a big debt of gratitude to many people and agencies for their moral and financial support. I could not have gone through with my studies without the financial scholarships provided by Koç University and the University of Minnesota. My fieldwork would also have not been possible without the generous help of the Andrew Dickinson Fellowship at the University of Minnesota, and the J. S. Seidman Fellowship at Rhodes College. I was lucky to have been surrounded by exceptional fellow graduate students at the University of Minnesota, who continue to provide precious camaraderie. Graduate school would have not been the same without the friendships of Giovanni Mantilla, Azer Binnet, Erica Owen, Darrah McCracken, and

Çiğdem Çıdam. My colleagues at Rhodes College International Studies Department have also supported me by providing an encouraging environment in the last seven years. I am also indebted to all the people who have helped me tremendously during my fieldwork. I was also particularly lucky to receive guidance and accommodation from two institutes during my fieldwork: the American Center for Oriental Research in Jordan (ACOR) and the Dutch Institute in Morocco (NIMAR). I am also thankful to all those who have taken the time to be interviewed by me for this project. I would also like to thank everyone at Edinburgh University Press who helped in the publication of this book.

I was very fortunate to have been surrounded by family and a close group of friends along the way. Hence, I owe a big thank you to my big family, to my aunts, uncles, and cousins, who made home always feel home, and to my friends Sonya Özbey, Gülçe Cin, Gülis Zengin and Vanessa Mongey.

Words cannot describe the gratitude I feel towards my amazing parents, Nesrin and Halis Kirdiş. They are and have always been my rocks. The only reason I could brave the world and could stand firmly on my feet throughout the years is the knowledge that I always had an embracing home to return to even if everything went wrong. I consider myself fortunate and proud that I had the privilege of being born as their daughter. It is to them that I dedicate this book.

For my parents, Nesrin and Halis Kirdiş

1

INTRODUCTION: BETWEEN MOVEMENT AND PARTY

At the Istanbul Modern Art Museum, there is a video installation by Kutluğ Ataman titled 'Women Who Wear Wigs', which documents four women who discuss the reasons why they have had to wear wigs. The first woman is a left-wing radical in disguise forced to hide her real identity by wearing a wig, while the second woman is a secular journalist and a cancer patient who wears a wig to hide her hair loss due to chemotherapy. The third woman is a pious Muslim university student who wears a wig to the classroom instead of her veil, which was forbidden under the laic[1] laws of Turkey until 2013. And the fourth woman is a transgender sex worker, whose hair was forcefully shaved by the police when she was arrested. All of these women are wearing wigs, but for different reasons, while also forming a community of 'women who wear wigs'.

Islamic movements are similar to the 'women who wear wigs' in that they are also thrown into a forced community of 'Islamists' and yet have vast differences within this so-called 'community'. Take Islamic movements in Turkey for instance. On 15 July 2016, Turkey witnessed a violent coup attempt wherein more than 300 people died overnight. Soon after that, the governing Justice and Development Party, a party with roots in the Islamic National Outlook Movement, accused the Gülen Movement, the country's most-known Islamic movement, of orchestrating the coup attempt. The coup attempt was a shocking development because these two Islamic movements had no history of violence. While the Gülen Movement (at least publicly) had worked as an informal social movement focused on education, the Justice and Development Party and its predecessors under the National Outlook Movement had chosen to participate in party politics by running in elections. Hence, the coup attempt had made it clear that these two Islamic movements, although both categorised as 'Islamists', nevertheless had vital differences between them, such that they were now clashing publicly.

The National Outlook parties and the Gülen Movement today have more in common with their counterparts in other parts of the world, who face drastically different socio-political contexts, than with each other. Like the National Outlook Movement in Turkey, the Movement for Unity and Reform in Morocco and the Muslim Brotherhood in Jordan both pursue party politics under the banner of the Party for Justice and Development and the Islamic Action Front Party respectively. Meanwhile, their counterparts, the Justice and Spirituality Movement in Morocco and the Quietist Salafis in Jordan, like the Gülen Movement in Turkey and yet unlike their 'colleagues' in Morocco and Jordan, stay out of party politics and instead focus their energies on social movement mobilisation outside of institutional channels.

To understand such variation and similarities amongst Islamic movements, this book asks why some Islamic movements facing the same socio-political structures pursue different political paths, while their counterparts in diverse contexts make similar political choices? Within this general framework, this study tackles one particular difference within political Islam, between Islamic parties which run in elections and Islamic movements which don't, and asks why some Islamic movements in contexts as varied as Morocco, Turkey, and Jordan all form political parties, while their counterparts within the same country, facing the same socio-political structures, reject doing so and instead engage in political activism as a social movement through more informal channels? This book also asks what the consequences of such varying political paths are for Islamic movements themselves and for the regimes under which they operate. In doing so, this study questions the motivations, successes, and failures of Islamic actors, and looks at how Islamic movements make strategic decisions and how these strategic decisions impact their political evolution. Within this framework, this book, following McAdam, Tarrow and Tilly,[2] studies the shifting relationship between

Islamic movements and the regime, and the processes and mechanisms of this relationship. The following pages of this chapter will start addressing these questions by discussing the definitions, research design, and theoretical framework of this study.

Islamic Movements and Islamic Political Parties

Egyptian theologian Nasr Abu Zayd once stated,

> The Quran is at the mercy of the ideology of its interpreter. For a communist, the Quran would thus reveal communism, for a fundamentalist it would be a highly fundamentalist text, for a feminist it would be a feminist text.[3]

As such, different Islamic movements have derived different meanings out of Islam's holy text. Consequently, Islamic movements today do not share many commonalities other than referencing Islam as the source of their political identity and behaviour.

To define such diversity within political Islam, this study will, foremost, use the term 'Islamic' rather than 'Islamist'. Firstly, the term 'Islamist' is often used as a term describing groups with a fundamentalist political agenda based on literal interpretations of Islam. Nonetheless, many Islamic groups are not fundamentalists and instead bring new and non-literal interpretations to Islam. Hence, using the term 'Islamic' recognises the multiplicity of the interpretations of Islam used by these groups. Secondly, this study uses the term 'Islamic' to reference how these groups' ideology is loosely based on Islam. Although these groups start out as organisations claiming to derive their political agenda from Islam, over time some become secular organisations with religious origins, while others continue to seek religious revival. The term 'Islamist' is often used to describe the latter situation, while terms such as 'Muslim democrats' or 'moderate Islamists' have been used to describe the former situation. Thus, to cover such diverse transformations, this study uses the term 'Islamic' instead. Thirdly, the term 'Islamist' is often used as a term for those Islamic movements targeting the state. In this, it fails to account for Islamic movements that aim at societal transformations. By using the term 'Islamic' instead, this study accounts for an understanding of politics beyond formal institutions.

In order to study such multiplicity within political Islam, this study will focus on Islamic movements and parties because, despite being lumped together under the category of 'Islamists', they diverge in crucial ways. Whereas 'Islamic movements' are collective, non-violent, and rational organisations that promote Islam, through sustained competition, opposition, or cooperation with 'elites, opponents, and authorities',[4] 'Islamic political parties' are organisations which seek political influence by running in elections[5] with the aim of winning votes, office and/or seats.[6] Differently from other political parties, Islamic political parties have 'clearly identifiable' 'religious values in [their] manifesto', make 'explicit appeals to religious constituencies', and/or have 'significant religious factions [...] within the party'.[7] As a result, Islamic parties differ from Islamic movements in that the former 'focus their energies on participation in an existing political system within the rules and boundaries set by that system'[8] in order to represent 'aggregate interests'[9] within the institutional boundaries of the regime, while the latter work outside institutional channels to voice demands that are unrepresented by formal institutions. Hence, Islamic movements and Islamic political parties diverge in both their means (utilising informal versus formal channels) and goals (voicing unrepresented demands versus representing interests) and thus have different impacts on the regime (challenge to the regime versus working within the regime). Organisationally, since Islamic political parties often need to make concessions to accommodate other parties in the party system, they are expected to be more pragmatic in their quest to become part of decision-making and thus to be more open to change.[10] Within this understanding, the inclusion-moderation literature, for instance, addresses the 'moderation' of Islamic parties 'from a relatively closed and rigid worldview to one more open and tolerant of alternative perspectives'[11] after their 'inclusion' (participation) in the party system as 'electoral contestants'.[12] Meanwhile, since Islamic movements, as social movements, seek to provide an alternative to formal institutions and consist of informal networks based on shared beliefs,[13] they are expected to be more idealistic in their quest to challenge formal institutions and thus to be more likely to resist change.[14] Consequently, the decision to form a political party (or not) is a critical juncture point for Islamic movements and their possible transformations.

By utilising different means, goals, and organisations, Islamic movements and Islamic political parties also embody various opportunities for and challenges to democratisation. On the one hand, Islamic movements represent demands not covered in the ballot box and thus bring civil societies input into politics. In this, they contribute to democratisation. On the other hand, even if they have internal democracy, they may also pose a threat to democratisation because their finances and internal leadership selection, in their informality, remain outside the control of public accountability. Islamic political parties, nonetheless, have some level of transparency and an organisational commitment to play by the rules, but do not necessarily have to represent liberal democratic demands in their electoral quest for a moral role for the state. In short, Islamic movements and Islamic political parties adopt different means, pursue different goals, adjust various organisations, and thus have different political effects on democratisation.

Research Design and Methodology

Despite the importance of distinguishing between Islamic political parties and Islamic movements, most existing studies discuss differentiation within political Islam by comparing the political trajectories and transformations of Islamic parties across different contexts.[15] In this, they do not take Islamic movements which eschew party politics into their comparison and instead study them as single case studies.[16] As a result, by focusing on just one type of Islamic movement behaviour, they suffer from case selection bias. To avoid such a bias, this study uses a unique methodology and utilises *both* a comparative method of agreement and a comparative method of difference to study differentiation within Islamic movements. Foremost, this study uses a comparative method instead of a single case study because this allows for hypothesis testing in multiple case studies while also avoiding the surface-level comparisons of large-N statistical studies.[17] Nonetheless, its disadvantage is how to eliminate rival explanations with so few cases.[18] To avoid such a shortcoming, this study, firstly analyses the same behaviour, party formation and party non-formation, in three different contexts, following Skocpol's methodology in *States and Social Revolutions*.[19] Specifically, it studies three Islamic movements in three different contexts that have all chosen to participate (or not to participate) in party politics. By using such a comparative method, this study aims to pinpoint which independent variables have led to the same outcome; to the same dependent variable.

The problem with this type of comparison is nevertheless, as Geddes[20] has shown, that it may lead to a case selection bias in its lack of variance in the dependent variable. Thus, this book also uses a second type of comparative methodology in its use of 'within-case comparison', wherein it studies distinct political behaviour, party formation versus party non-formation, within the same context. In particular, it looks at why one Islamic movement has formed a political party while another Islamic movement has not when they both were facing the same regime. Hence, this study follows Kalyvas' research design in *The Rise of Christian Democracy in Europe* and focuses both on party formation and party non-formation.[21] In doing so, it analyses Islamic movements' parallel yet independent developments and directs its attention to how the internal dynamics of Islamic movements inform their differing political behaviour.

Through such a dual comparative methodology, this study differentiates itself from extant studies which have compared Islamic movements in different countries, thereby discussing the influence of socio-political institutions ('structures') on Islamic movements ('agents'). This study does this by comparing Islamic movements within the same country to each other, thereby focusing on the multiplicity of Islamic movements and their (agents') influence on their countries' socio-political transformations (on structures). By utilising such a dual comparative methodology, this study not only introduces variation in the dependent variable but is also able to closely examine the ways in which the independent variables under study in this book affect the dependent variable.

To explain empirically, this study foremost looks at Islamic movements' similar behaviour in three different regimes, in Morocco, Turkey, and Jordan, which vary in their (1) state–society relations, and in (2) the role of religion in the regime. Firstly, all three countries vary in their state–society relations. 'Repressive pragmatism', wherein the King of Morocco remains an absolute monarch and yet allows limited and controlled opposition to his rule, defines the Moroccan monarchy. Such an arrangement has emerged under the rule of late-King Hassan II, who ruled Morocco for 38 'lead years' (1961–1999). On the one hand, Hassan II consolidated his power by establishing a strong central government and by assuming the role of the 'Supreme Representative of the Nation'.[22] Within this role, the King outlawed criticism of the monarchy, enacted a state of emergency, and heavily repressed his opposition, specifically the left wing activists on university campuses and the military, which attempted a coup in 1971 and 1972.[23] On the other hand, in contrast to such political repressions, Hassan II's rule was also defined by pragmatic statesmanship. He introduced a multi-party system and co-opted 'political parties and civil society, providing them benefits and patronage in return for their acceptance of the legitimacy of the monarchy'.[24] Hence, Hassan II established the King's supremacy while also allowing for oppositional voices by pragmatically differentiating between 'loyal' and 'hard' opposition to his regime. Daadaoui has called this arrangement 'Hassanian democracy' to define the 'authoritarian pluralism' of the Moroccan regime.[25]

Different from state–society relations in Morocco, which were aimed at the preservation of the Moroccan monarchy, state–society relations in Turkey were redefined with the foundation of a Republic after the fall of the Ottoman Empire (1299–1922). After an Independence War (1919–1923) fought against European colonialists, the founders of the new Turkish Republic under Mustafa Kemal Atatürk, the *Kemalists*, aimed to transform the Turkish state and society into a modern and secular nation-state under their guidance. Hence, they introduced massive social reforms, such as the Hat Law enforcing Western attire and education reforms changing the alphabet to increase this 'civilising mission',[26] the Kemalists, diverging from King Hassan II's repressive pragmatism in Morocco, were believers in democracy. As such, Turkey held free and fair elections regularly, functioned as a multi-party democracy from the 1950s onwards, and allowed winning parties to form and to run the government. Moreover, even though Turkey witnessed military interventions in 1960 and 1980, they only lasted a few years with democracy quickly restored. Thus, unlike in Morocco, where the parliament functioned as the King's co-optation tool to differentiate between loyal and hard opposition, in Turkey, an active and independent party system came to life. The Kemalists' civilising mission, however, also limited the formation of a truly 'liberal' democracy in its aim to socially engineer society through the state. To this end, the Kemalists used the military and the judiciary when they believed their civilising mission was at risk: while the military intervened in party politics through military coups, the judiciary shaped party politics through political party closures. Consequently, the Kemalists, different from their Moroccan counterparts, had an ideological mission to transform society rather than a pragmatic mission to stay in power.

The Jordanian monarchy, meanwhile, was neither as repressive as that of Morocco nor aimed at societal transformation like in Turkey. Although Jordan was a monarchy like Morocco, its state–society relations differed from the latter in significant ways. Foremost amongst these was that, unlike Morocco's 'years of lead' wherein 'hard' opposition 'outside' the parliament was met with violent repression, the Jordanian monarchy was a relatively tolerant regime under the late King Hussein (who succeeded to the throne in 1952 and stayed there for 47 years until 1999). His regime drew on a 'broad and diverse spectrum of social forces'[27] moreover, allowing for an active civil society presence. He also constructed a relatively stable and moderate country through economic and industrial development and some level of political freedoms. In short, while King Hassan II of Morocco ruled with an iron fist, King Hussein of Jordan ruled with tolerance. Such tolerance, however, ironically did not translate into formal openness. While the Moroccan monarchy, despite its repressive nature, allowed for a multi-party system in order to co-opt its opposition, in Jordan, the parliament was closed down in response to the 1967 Arab–Israeli War and was 'on hold' for over 20 years until the 1984 by-elections and the 1989 general elections. Hence, while political parties with long histories in Morocco participated in parliamentary life, in Jordan the formal institutions for organised political opposition were mainly absent.

The Jordanian monarchy also differed from the Turkish Republic not only by virtue of it not being a democracy but also in its state–society relations. Unlike the founders of Turkey, the Jordanian monarchy had no interest in promoting a civilising mission and a total top-down transformation of the society. On the contrary, King Hussein aimed to preserve the status quo. To this end, he adapted a centrist and pragmatic political path combining Bedouin traditions with modernisation, and walking a balanced line between Westernisation and Arab Nationalism.[28] As a result, while the Kemalists in Turkey emphasised reform in their state–society relations, the Jordanian monarchy emphasised tradition.

In addition to such differences in their state–society relations, these three regimes have also varied in the respective role of religion within their regimes. Historically, the Moroccan King claimed religious legitimacy as the 'Commander of the Believers',[29] a self-appointed title from the 1970s in response to the rise of secular nationalists. Accordingly, the King and the monarchy were 'the only political institution[s] that were constitutionally allowed to combine both political and religious powers'.[30] Also, the King's 'sacredness' and 'inviolability' were constitutionally guaranteed.[31] Within this arrangement, the King was both the 'religious leader of a traditional patrimonial power' and the 'head of a modern state'.[32] While the former role consolidated the King's legitimacy, the latter role provided him with 'the modern institutional coercive mechanisms that constitute the contours of the monarchical power'.[33]

In opposition to such religio-political legitimacy, the Kemalists in Turkey followed laicism, a form of 'assertive secularism',[34] in which religious affairs were under the total monopoly of the Turkish state. In this, the Kemalists actively supervised religious activity throughout the country by bringing all mosques and religious education under the roof of the state. Different from secularism, where the state and religious institutions did not intervene with each other's spheres, under laicism, religious institutions did not intervene into state affairs while the state reserved its right to speak into the religious field if it believed secularism was at risk. As a result, unlike the Moroccan regime that took its legitimacy from the King's religious and political role as the 'Commander of the Believers', the Turkish regime protected its laic character and thus constitutionally guaranteed the non-involvement of religion in the state. In short, while religion gave legitimacy to the Moroccan regime, the state's precedence over the religious field gave legitimacy to the Turkish one.

Meanwhile, Jordan followed a path of non-involvement in the religious sphere. On the one hand, the Jordanian King grounded his power in his 'Hashemite' legacy, wherein the King argued for his prophetic descent and upheld *Sharia* [Islamic law] as part of the family code. On the other hand, the Jordanian King only used his religious status as a symbolic source for his political legitimacy. In particular, the Jordanian King only emphasised his religious titles ceremoniously, preferring to remain a relatively secular leader in politics. This was different to the Moroccan King, who proactively influenced the political sphere as the 'Commander of the Believers', by, for

Table 1.1 Comparative Method

	Morocco	Turkey	Jordan
State–Society Relations	Repressive pragmatism aimed to control and co-opt the opposition	Civilising mission aimed to transform society through the state	Tolerant authoritarianism aimed to preserve the status-quo
Role of Religion within the Regime	The political use of the King's title as the 'Commander of the Believers' and the repression of Islamic movements	Laicism and the repression of Islamic movements	The symbolic use of the King's Hashemite roots and tolerance for Islamic movements

instance, 'establishing a whole system of expression of "official Islam" through the promotion of non-political religious organisations, such as da^cwa associations – which he also used against the secular left – and the reactivation and control of the Council of "Ulama"'.[35] According to Krämer, in essence, the Jordanian King's legitimacy was based on 'function and services', wherein the monarchy functioned as a service-provider rather than a religious leader.[36] Hence, while the Moroccan King saw Islamic movements as a threat to his religio-political rule and thus sought to undermine them, the Jordanian King allowed the formation of Islamic movements and saw them as allies against secular Arab nationalism. Furthermore, distinct from the Turkish regime, which brought the religious field under its tight laic monopoly, the Jordanian regime allowed for religious pluralism in its laissez-faire treatment of Islamic movements.

Despite facing such vastly different state–society relations and roles for religion within the regimes of Morocco, Turkey, and Jordan (Table 1.1), some Islamic movements have pursued the path of participation in party politics, while their counterparts within the same regime have chosen to stay out of party politics in order to challenge the system as a social movement outside of institutional channels. To study such variation within the same context, this study looks also at two different Islamic movements in each country, one of which has formed a political party whilst the other has rejected party formation, and has instead chosen to stay as a movement (Table 1.2). In doing so, this study takes variation in the dependent variable into account.

In Morocco, this study looks at the different political behaviour of the

Table 1.2 Within-case Comparison

	Morocco		Turkey		Jordan	
Islamic Movement	*Movement for Unity and Reform*	*Justice and Spirituality Movement*	*National Outlook Movement*	*Gülen Movement*	*Muslim Brotherhood*	*Quietist Salafis*
Political Behaviour	*Formed the Party for Justice and Development (PJD)*	*Stays as a Movement*	*Forms multiple parties over the years*	*Stays as a Movement*	*Formed the Islamic Action Front Party (IAF)*	*Stays as a Movement*

Justice and Spirituality Movement, which rejects party politics, and the Movement for Unity and Reform, the mother movement of the governing Party for Justice and Development (2011–). While the former is the largest Islamic movement in Morocco today, has been politically active since the 1970s, and has no history of violence, the latter has a violent history in the Islamic Youth, which targeted the downfall of the Moroccan regime in the 1970s. Hence, it is puzzling today that this formerly radical movement is part of a regime it aimed to bring down, while the movement with the most potential to get votes, the Justice and Spirituality Movement, chooses to remain outside of party politics.

In Turkey, this study looks at the different political behaviours of the Gülen Movement and the National Outlook Movement. While the former has influenced Turkish politics through its socio-economic networks, the latter has formed various Islamic political parties and is the predecessor of the governing Justice and Development Party (2001–). After years of growing into the two most powerful Islamic movements in Turkey through different political paths, both actors are, as mentioned at the start of this chapter, clashing today.

In Jordan, this study looks at the differing political behaviours of the Quietist Salafis, a decentralised organisation that rejects party politics, and of the Muslim Brotherhood, which formed the Islamic Action Front Party. While the Muslim Brotherhood's socio-political strength diminished as a result of its marginalisation within party politics after years of friendly regime relations, Quietist Salafis have occasionally served as unlikely allies of the Jordanian regime despite their abstinence from institutional politics.

Besides the methodological importance of addressing such variation within political Islam in Morocco, Turkey and Jordan, it is also important politically, especially in the aftermath of the Arab Spring, as Islamic movements in these three contexts in question have followed similar paths in regards to party politics but with different results. In Morocco, while one of the Islamic movements under study, the Movement for Unity and Reform and its political party, Party for Justice and Development, has come to lead the Moroccan government (albeit under the close watch of the Moroccan monarchy), its counterpart, the Justice and Spirituality Movement, has grown into a powerful opposition outside the scope of institutional politics. Despite such Islamic political activism inside and outside of institutional channels, the Moroccan regime has nonetheless remained intact after the Arab Spring.

In contrast to such a status quo in Morocco, in Turkey, Islamic movements have become 'the' hegemonic powers countering the power of laicism and the civilising mission of the Kemalists. Both the National Outlook Movement (and later on its successor, the Justice and Development Party) and the Gülen Movement have achieved socio-political dominance despite the informal and formal limitations put on them by laic institutions. Over time, they have grown so much so that they have replaced the Kemalist hegemony with their own thereby redefining the socio-political fabric of Turkey today.

In contrast to the transfer of hegemonic power from Turkey's secular founders to today's Islamic movements, Islamic movements in Jordan have turned from loyal allies into marginalised actors. In the past, Jordan was considered to be unique in the Arab world for its friendly relations with Islamic movements. While the Jordanian Muslim Brotherhood and its charities were all registered as legal entities, thereby making the Jordanian Muslim Brotherhood the only legal Muslim Brotherhood branch in the Arab world at the time, the Quietist Salafis in Jordan were also relatively free to conduct their educational activities. In the last two decades, however, regime–Islamic movement relations have first embittered and then turned repressive. Today, the regime has confiscated all of the Brotherhood's financial assets and has raided its headquarters, and heavily monitors the Quietist Salafis and their socio-political activities. Hence, the once tolerant and religiously uninvolved regime of Jordan has today harshly established its monopoly over the religious field vis-à-vis its Islamic contenders.

Given such differences in the transformation of Islamic movements in three different contexts, the novelty of this study and thus the rationale behind choosing the cases of Morocco, Turkey, and Jordan lies not only in understanding variation in the behaviour of Islamic movements but also in assessing the consequences of this variation for Islamic political actors and the regimes today.

To study such variation and its consequences, this study will follow Castells' recommendation to see social movements through their 'own discourse', and look at each Islamic movement through 'their words' spoken by those who form the identity of these movements.[37] In this way, this study will aim to 'construct explanations of empirical events through analyses that respect the specifics of time and place but within a framework that both disciplines the detail and appropriates it for purposes that transcend the particular story'.[38] Hence, methodologically, this study is informed by in-depth qualitative fieldwork in Morocco, Turkey, and Jordan and thus by interviews in Arabic, Turkish, German, French, and English with leading party and movement leaders/ideologues, archival research on numerous party/movement documents, statements, and by archival materials from the countries' main Islamic and secular political outlets. Theoretically, this study is built on literature on party formation and change,[39] social movement theory,[40] political transitions from authoritarianism,[41] state power,[42] Islamic political thought,[43] and democratisation in the Middle East.[44] These literatures inform the three theoretical propositions of this study discussed in the next section.

Theoretical Framework

Participation in the party system is hardly a straightforward process: in some countries a party might be formed but not be allowed to run in elections, while in other nations a movement may run in elections without forming a party.[45] Thus, this study uses a minimum criterion for its dependent variable and defines 'participation' as running in elections and 'non-participation' as principally rejecting to do so through specific statements by its leadership. Here it should be noted that non-participation does not presume an apolitical stance. On the contrary, it refers to a political behaviour of consciously rejecting participation in electoral politics for political reasons. The decision of whether or not to participate is foremost shaped by the 'political opportunity and threat structures'[46] of the political context 'in which [Islamic movements] are embedded'.[47] Specifically, it is shaped by open political opportunity structures, such as by the 'openness of the system to new actors', and by political threat structures, such as by 'the extent to which the regime represses or facilitates collective claim making'.[48] Beyond formal/institutional opportunities and threats, the state and its institutions, or the regime, 'influence the meanings and methods of politics for all groups and classes in society'.[49] In this, they 'affect political culture, encourage some kinds of group formation and collective political actions (but not others), and make possible the raising of certain political issues (but not others)'.[50] Consequently, as Sewell suggests, whilst agents 'can instrumentally use ideas to delegitimate, context, and refashion existing institutions', structures 'give meaning to the material environment in which agents find themselves – and thus give content to what agents want in the first place'.[51] As a result, 'the political dynamics and historical context in which a given theology ascends, wins or loses salience'[52] defines a movement's political choices.

Nevertheless, Islamic party formation cannot solely be explained by political opportunity and threat structures, and thus as a function of political liberalisation or as a reaction to secularism. After all, Islamic movements have formed Islamic political parties in democracies (for example in Indonesia) and in authoritarian regimes (for example in Yemen), as well as in secular countries (for example in Turkey) and in countries using Islamic law (for example in Jordan). Moreover, Islamic movements have rejected forming a political party despite political liberalisations. For instance, in Senegal – a country that is widely considered to be one of the most democratic Muslim countries in the world – we have not seen Islamic party formation despite the strong presence and influence of Sufi Brotherhoods. Similarly, in Indonesia, another secular democracy, some smaller Islamic movements have formed the *Partai Keadilan Sejahtera* [Prosperous Justice Party], while the largest Islamic movement in the country, the *Nahdlatul Ulama* [Revival of the Religious Scholars], forbade its members to participate in party politics after years of political activism.[53] Hence, new political opportunities in the form of political liberalisations are by themselves not enough to explain Islamic party formation.

New societal constituencies, such as the rise of a new middle class, also shape the political options available to Islamic movements but by themselves these cannot explain Islamic movement behaviour either. Lipset and Rokkan[54] have famously hypothesised that fundamental transformations in societal cleavages are what led to party formation in Western Europe, wherein political parties emerged as the 'freezing' representations of societal cleavages created by macro-level socioeconomic transformations and were 'locked-in' into the party system decades ago. Lipset and Rokkan's analysis has found repercussions in studies of the Muslim World as well. According to Nasr,[55] the increasing weakness of state-led economies and the rise of an independent middle class, of the 'Muslim bourgeoisie', offered Islamic movements new opportunities to widen their societal appeal. In this, changing social conditions – such as changing demographics, urbanisation, increasing education and decreasing employment levels – 'created rising, but unfulfilled expectations, leading to the disenfranchisement of many individuals within Muslim societies undergoing rapid change'.[56] These alienated populations found political Islam appealing in answering their everyday concerns.

Nonetheless, as Mair points out, not every socio-political cleavage is translated into party politics; rather 'the primary agency at work is the party – or other organisation – that intervenes to politicise [necessary facilitating] conditions'.[57] In this way, political parties mobilise social cleavages rather than being mere expressions of them by 'sutur[ing] coherent blocs and cleavages from a disparate set of constituencies and individuals, who, even by virtue of sharing circumstances, may not necessarily share the same political identity'.[58] To give an example: the much talked about Muslim bourgeoisie in Turkey today only became visible in the 1990s, two decades after the establishment of the first Islamic political party, of the National Order Party, in 1969. Thus, party formation is not necessarily the consequence of societal demands, but rather (Islamic) political entrepreneurs politicise the masses by mobilising new social cleavages.[59] Thus, societal cleavages are not necessarily naturally 'locked-in' into party politics, but are mobilised into political parties and become salient through political organisations.[60]

Taking up such structural explanations, more recent studies have looked at how structural differences across the region produced different types of Islamic movement behaviour. Brown,[61] for instance, has compared the political trajectories of Muslim Brotherhood organisations in Egypt, Jordan, Kuwait, and the Palestinian Territories, and has discussed how they took advantage of political openings under these semi-authoritarian regimes and how these regimes took advantage of their participation. In another structural account of Muslim Brotherhood organisations, Hamid[62] has discussed how regime repression had a moderating effect on Islamic actors by forcing them to ally with secular forces and to accommodate the regime, while democratisation, by allowing Islamic actors to have a greater public space and control over public discourse, led to Islamisation. In another structural analysis, Mecham[63] has looked at the influence of macro-level institutions – the influence of state-religious elites relations, levels of Islamic common knowledge, and the presence of major changes in the state – on variation in Islamic mobilisation across 57 Muslim countries, where Muslims make up 25% or more of the population, between 1970 and 2010. In his socio-economic analysis, Yıldırım[64] has looked at the effects of economic liberalisation on the transformations of Islamic parties with fundamentalist aims into 'Muslim Democratic Parties' combining social conservatism, economic liberalism, and democratic commitment, and argued that whereas competitive economic liberalisation led to the rise of such Muslim Democratic Parties in its empowerment of a new Muslim middle class, crony economic liberalisation led to the rise of 'Islamist' parties in its marginalisation of lower income classes. In short, extant literature has addressed how macro-structures have shaped the political behaviour of Islamic movements.

These structural examinations of political Islam, however, have failed to understand Islamic movement differentiation at the sub-national level in their focus on macro-level structures. By focusing on how structures shape Islamic movements, they have failed to analyse why two Islamic movements facing the same socio-political and institutional structures make different political choices about party politics. As a result, these structural explanations have only partially explained Islamic movement differentiation.

To complete such structural explanations of Islamic movement differentiation, this study will echo Kalyvas' argument that structures do not 'automatically' lead to party formation but rather serve as 'constraints on what's possible'.[65] As Blyth states, 'structures do not come with an instruction sheet. There is still plenty of room for agents to make history apart from their structurally given interests'.[66] Thus, the first theoretical proposition of this study, which will be discussed further in chapter two, is:

P1: Political opportunity and threat structures define a 'menu of options' for Islamic movements to evaluate and to strategise about.

Although Islamic movements emerge and evolve within a framework delineated by structures, structures and the options they offer are also situational and thus perceived.[67] In this, an 'opportunity not recognised is no opportunity at all',[68] and thus opportunities are 'subjective' to the movement and thus can be seized as well as ignored.[69] Because the 'world' of political Islam is a multivocal field, wherein Islamic movements differ on how they interpret Islam and its texts, what strategies they see fit to realise Islam's call, and what that 'Islamic call' entails,[70] as Bayat states, 'individuals and groups with diverse interests and orientations may find their own, often conflicting truths in the very same scriptures'.[71] As a result, Islamic movements evaluate the structural menu of options available to them through widely different lenses.

Firstly, although Islamic movements are unified by their belief that 'Islam is the solution' to the contemporary problems of the Muslim community, they differ on the question of how to revive Islam[72] in a way that includes the introduction of 'more Islamic influences into the lives of Muslims'.[73] Whereas some foresee a bottom-up Islamic revival through grassroots activism at the local level, others expect a top-down Islamic revival starting with the control of the state apparatus under Islamic vanguards.[74] Furthermore, an Islamic movement's political identity 'is not a fixed set of characteristics; it is instead the product of historical processes and experiences through which individuals and groups come to see themselves, their place in the world, and their relationship with those around them'.[75] As a result, Islamic movements adapt varying 'ideological priorities', wherein they anticipate different future scenarios in regards to Islamic revival and thus choose diverse political behaviours for the realisation of this end.

Secondly, Islamic movements have differing organisational needs. As Sinno and Khanani show, a movement's existing organisation creates a path dependency in that the way a movement is organised influences its cost–benefit calculations.[76] For instance, the Egyptian Muslim Brotherhood as a movement with a mass following will have different priorities when evaluating the menu of options than the Prosperous Justice Party, which plays a niche role in Indonesian politics. Similarly, an umbrella movement with varying factions will have different priorities than a movement hierarchically organised around a charismatic personality. Hence, Islamic movements also take their 'organisational needs' into account while pursuing their ideological priorities pragmatically.

Such ideological priorities and organisational needs 'bind' an Islamic movement's rational calculations.[77] Hence, on the one hand, Islamic movements, à la rational choice theories, are rational actors behaving consistently and coherently, and engaging in strategic cost–benefit calculations.[78] On the other hand, à la constructivist theories, Islamic movements' rationality is not necessarily defined by an 'instrumental rationality', that operates by 'efficient pursuit of exogenously determined interests within the constraints of available information, the interests and strategies of other actors, and the distribution of power',[79] but by a 'practical rationality', by a rationality 'sensitive' to historical, social and normative contexts,[80] and thus they are driven by 'a logic of anticipated consequences'.[81] Hence, Islamic movements do rationally evaluate and strategise about the menu of options available to them, but they do so through the lenses of their strategic objectives which are constructed by this study's independent variables: their ideological priorities and organisational needs. As a result, the second proposition of this study, which will be taken up in chapter three, is:

P2: Islamic movements evaluate and strategise about the menu of options available to them in light of their strategic objectives, defined by their ideological priorities and organisational needs.

As Islamic movements evaluate the menu of options through the lenses of their strategic objectives while making a decision about party politics, they also enter onto a political path full of 'uncertainty' defined by the 'imprecision with which political actors are able to predict future interactions'.[82] They do not know whether the expected benefits of their chosen behaviour will materialise or whether projected costs will be higher than expected. After all, Islamic movements, like any other political actor, strategise about their next steps based on expectations informed by their strategic objectives. However, expectations do not always meet reality. For instance, participation might lead to political marginalisation within party politics as an ideological niche party instead of electoral success, or non-participation might result in massive repressions outside institutional politics instead of a powerful counter-hegemony. Furthermore, sometimes the costs of a chosen behaviour are heavier than expected, wherein the regime does not leave any breathing room for Islamic movements to engage in top-down or bottom-up influence. Thus, Islamic movements continuously strategise to minimise the costs and to maximise the benefits of their chosen political path.

While Islamic movements continue to make the most of their political options, they also face a changing regime. As Gramsci argues, a regime maintains its hegemony not just through repression and coercion but also through ideology.[83] In times of political transitions and thus uncertainty, a regime becomes especially proactive to preserve its hegemony vis-à-vis its contenders, its Islamic contenders in particular. Hence, the regime may learn to adapt its behaviour to counterbalance the Islamic challenge and thus to protect its hegemony. Within this quest for hegemony vis-à-vis Islamic movements, the regime may 'close in' on Islamic movements by increasing the regime's repressive capacity over the religious sphere. It can do so by, for instance, introducing tighter financial monitoring over grassroots activism, treating Islamic movements as enemies of the state and as illegal activists aiming at the destruction of the state, forcing them to open up their organisational structures to public scrutiny. Alternatively, the regime may 'close in' on Islamic movements by limiting the scope of political activism by, for instance, subjecting Islamic movements to various institutional checks and balances or changing the electoral system to prevent their electoral victories. The regime may also alter its behaviour, for instance, by emphasising its Islamic character more or by becoming more religiously intolerant, to counterbalance the Islamic challenge and thus to defend its hegemony.[84] In short, while Islamic movements may become more realistic in their political quest to minimise the costs and to maximise the benefits of their chosen political path, the regime may 'close in' on Islamic movements to preserve its ideological and political legitimacy over the society. In this 'cat-and-mouse game',[85] like a pendulum's swings becoming shorter as time passes, Islamic movements and the regime may redefine the political centre in the country. Hence, the third and last proposition of this study, which will be taken up in chapter four, is:

P3: While Islamic movements become more realistic about the menu of options available to them as a result of years of strategising in light of their strategic objectives, the regime closes in on them to preserve its ideological hegemony in the society, thereby redefining the political centre in the country.

The novelty of this three-part hypothesis (Figure 1.1) is that this study essentially makes an agential argument. As discussed above, the extant literature explains Islamic differentiation by attributing such multiplicity to the varying structural contexts. Instead, this study argues that it is the agent's (Islamic movement's) internal strategising that drives variation amongst Islamic movements

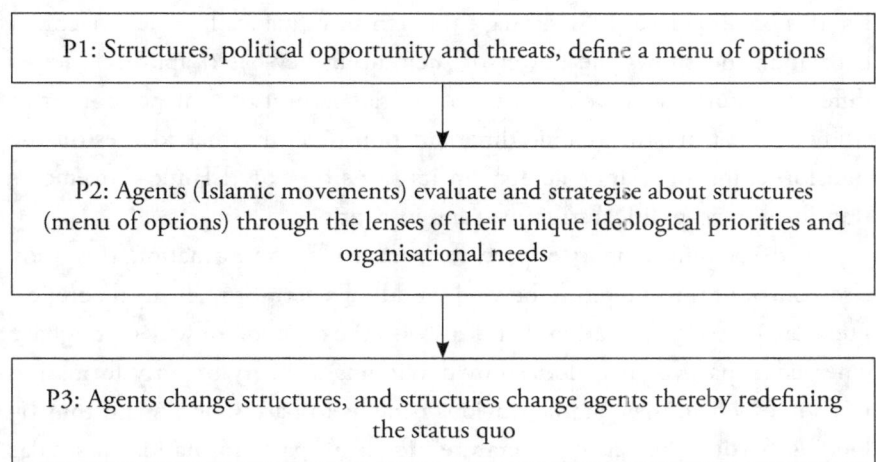

Figure 1.1 A Visual Representation of the Three Propositions

both across different cases and within the same case. Through this qualitative research, this study looks at the internal debates within Islamic movements and their ideological/organisational objectives and transformations. In doing so, it complements existing studies that focus on how structural variables, such as regime type or macro-economy, inform Islamic differentiation.

It also differentiates itself from existing agency-based accounts that categorise Islamic actors but do not discuss how these internal differences influence their interactions with socio-political and institutional structures, and thus how these internal differences inform the political trajectories of Islamic movements. Cofman-Wittes,[86] for instance, categorises Islamic movements into three groups: (i) *takfiri* (apostasy) Islamists, such as Al-Qaeda, that justify the use of violence ideologically against those who they believe are apostates, (ii) local/nationalist Islamists, such as Hezbollah in Lebanon and HAMAS in the Palestinian Territories, that offer Islamic solutions to local/national problems, and (iii) moderate Islamists, such as Islamist parties, that aim at bottom-up Islamic transformations. In another typology-driven study, Ozzano[87] also categorises religious parties into conservative, progressive, nationalist, fundamentalist, and camp parties based on their differences in ideology, attitudes towards pluralism, organisational models, relations with interest groups, social bases, and goals. Differing from such descriptive studies, this book looks at how strategic differences influence Islamic movement behaviour and shows the power of such an agency-based approach across different countries as well as within the same country. Furthermore, this study differs from the Islamic differentiation literature that focuses on the transformation of Islamic actors[88] in its focus on how Islamic movements transform socio-political structures and institutions.

By developing a theory of party formation and non-formation, this study also contributes to literature beyond Middle Eastern Studies, to theoretical literature on party formation that deals with the question of why parties have emerged in particular. It does so by developing a theory of party formation in regimes where there are no obvious benefits to party politics and thus by looking beyond the existing literature's focus on party formation in secular liberal democracies.[89]

Organisation

The rest of this book is organised into four chapters. The next (second) chapter will address the structures in which Islamic movements strategise about their political behaviour. In particular, it will examine the costs and benefits of political participation vis-à-vis non-participation in Morocco, Turkey, and Jordan, looking at both the unique and similar political opportunities and threats each option brings to the table. Chapter three will discuss the role of strategic objectives, of ideological priorities and organisational needs, and of strategising in Islamic movement behaviour in regards to party politics. It will largely look at variation in Islamic movement behaviour within the same national context by looking at two different Islamic movements, one of which forms a party whilst the other rejects party formation and chooses to stay as a movement. Through this within-case comparison, this study will also compare the various reasons for the same behaviour across the different structural contexts of Morocco, Turkey, and Jordan. After discussing Islamic movement behaviour in regards to political participation, chapter four will proceed with the consequences of these political choices. In this, it will debate the transformation of the political centre. Lastly, in chapter five, this study will conclude with a comparison of the political agendas and transformations of these six Islamic movements in three countries.

Notes

1. A form of secularism, in which the state strictly monitors and controls the religious field.
2. Doug McAdam, Sidney G. Tarrow, and Charles Tilly, *Dynamics of Contention* (Cambridge & New York: Cambridge University Press, 2001).
3. Nasr Abu Zayd, *Reformation of Islamic Thought: A Critical Historical Analysis* (Amsterdam: Amsterdam University Press, 2006).
4. This definition is borrowed from Tarrow's definition of social movements as 'collective challenges, based on common purposes and social solidarities, in sustained interaction with elites, opponents, and authorities'. In Sidney G. Tarrow, *Power in Movement: Social Movements and Contentious Politics* (Cambridge & New York: Cambridge University Press, 1998).
5. Alan Ware, *Political Parties and Party Systems* (Oxford & New York: Oxford University Press, 1996).
6. Wolfgang C. Müller and Kaare Strøm, *Policy, Office, or Votes?: How Political Parties in Western Europe Make Hard Decisions* (Cambridge & New York: Cambridge University Press, 1999).
7. Luca Ozzano and Francesco Cavatorta, 'Introduction: Religiously Oriented Parties and Democratization', *Democratization*, 20.5 (2013), 799–806.
8. Nathan J. Brown, *When Victory Is Not an Option: Islamist Movements in Arab Politics* (Ithaca, NY: Cornell University Press, 2012).
9. Ware, *Political Parties and Party Systems*.
10. Jillian Schwedler, 'Review Article: Can Islamists Become Moderates? Rethinking the Inclusion-Moderation Hypothesis', *World Politics*, 63.2 (2011), 347–76.
11. Schwedler, 'Review Article'.
12. Manfred Brocker and Mirjam Künkler, 'Religious Parties: Revisiting the Inclusion Moderation Hypothesis – Introduction', *Party Politics*, 19.2 (2013), 171–86.
13. See: Tarrow, *Power in Movement*; Charles Tilly and Sidney G. Tarrow, *Contentious Politics* (Boulder, CO: Paradigm Publishers, 2007); McAdam, Tarrow, and Tilly, *Dynamics of Contention*; Sidney G. Tarrow, *Democracy and Disorder: Protest and Politics in Italy, 1965-1975* (Oxford & New York: Oxford University Press, 1989); Donatella Della Porta and Mario Diani, *Social Movements: An Introduction* (Malden, MA: Blackwell, 2011); Charles Tilly, *Contention and Democracy in Europe, 1650-2000* (Cambridge & New York: Cambridge University Press, 2004); Arturo Escobar and Sonia E. Alvarez, *The*

Making of Social Movements in Latin America: Identity, Strategy, and Democracy (Boulder, CO: Westview Press, 1992).
14. Esen Kirdiş, 'Between Movement and Party: Islamic Movements in Morocco and the Decision to Enter Party Politics', *Politics, Religion & Ideology*, 16.1 (2015), 65–86.
15. See: Brown, *When Victory is Not an Option*; A. Kadir Yıldırım, *Muslim Democratic Parties in the Middle East: Economy and Politics of Islamist Moderation* (Bloomington, IN: Indiana University Press, 2017); Jillian Schwedler, *Faith in Moderation: Islamist Parties in Jordan and Yemen* (Cambridge & New York: Cambridge University Press, 2007); Quinn Mecham, *Institutional Origins of Islamist Political Mobilization* (Cambridge & New York: Cambridge University Press, 2017); Shadi Hamid, *Temptations of Power: Islamists and Illiberal Democracy in a New Middle East* (Oxford & New York: Oxford University Press, 2014).
16. See: Francesco Cavatorta, 'Salafism, Liberalism and Democratic Learning in Tunisia', *The Journal of North African Studies*, 20.5 (2015), 770–83; Monica Marks, 'Youth Politics and Tunisian Salafism: Understanding the Jihadi Current', *Mediterranean Politics*, 18.1 (2013), 104–11; Fabio Merone and Francesco Cavatorta, *Salafism After the Arab Awakening* (Oxford & New York: Oxford University Press, 2017); Joas Wagemakers, *Salafism in Jordan: Political Islam in a Quietist Community* (Cambridge & New York: Cambridge University Press, 2016); Hakan M. Yavuz, *Toward an Islamic Enlightenment: The Gülen Movement* (Oxford & New York: Oxford University Press, 2013); İştar B. Gözaydın, 'The Fethullah Gülen Movement and Politics in Turkey: A Chance for Democratization or a Trojan Horse?', *Democratization*, 16.6 (2009), 1214–36; Joshua D. Hendrick, *Gülen: The Ambiguous Politics of Market Islam in Turkey and the World* (New York: New York University Press, 2013); Francesco Cavatorta, 'Neither Participation nor Revolution: The Strategy of the Moroccan Jamiat Al Adl Wal Ihsan', *Mediterranean Politics*, 12.3 (2007), 381–97.
17. Arend Lijphart, 'Comparative Politics and the Comparative Method', *American Political Science Review*, 65.3 (1971), 682–93.
18. Lijphart, 'Comparative Politics and the Comparative Method'.
19. Theda Skocpol, *States and Social Revolutions: A Comparative Analysis of France, Russia and China* (Cambridge & New York: Cambridge University Press, 2015).
20. Barbara Geddes, 'How the Cases You Choose Affect the Answers You Get: Selection Bias in Comparative Politics', in James A. Stimson (ed.), *Political Analysis, Vol. 2* (Ann Arbor, MI: University of Michigan Press, 1990), pp. 131–50.

21. Stathis Kalyvas, *The Rise of Christian Democracy in Europe* (Ithaca, NY: Cornell University Press, 1996).
22. Shadi Hamid and James Liddell (n.d.), 'Hassan II of Morocco', *Oxford Islamic Studies Online* <http://www.oxfordislamicstudies.com/opr/t236/e1035> (last accessed 17 July 2018).
23. Hamid and Liddell, 'Hassan II of Morocco'.
24. Hamid and Liddell, 'Hassan II of Morocco'.
25. Mohamed Daadaoui, *Moroccan Monarchy and the Islamist Challenge: Maintaining Makhzen Power* (New York: Palgrave Macmillan, 2011).
26. Hootan Shambayati and Esen Kirdiş, 'In Pursuit of "Contemporary Civilization": Judicial Empowerment in Turkey', *Political Research Quarterly*, 62.4 (2009), 767–80.
27. Russell E. Lucas, *Institutions and the Politics of Survival in Jordan: Domestic Responses to External Challenges, 1988–2001* (Albany, NY: State University of New York Press, 2005).
28. Marion Boulby (n.d.), 'Hussein Ibn Talal of Jordan', *The Oxford Encyclopedia of the Islamic World, Oxford Islamic Studies Online* <http//www.oxfordislamicstudies.com/article/opr/t236/e1040> (last accessed 6 August 2018).
29. The royal house of Morocco, the Alawite dynasty, which has ruled the country since the late 1600s, claims succession from Prophet Mohammed.
30. Mohammed El Katiri, 'The Institutionalisation of Religious Affairs: Religious Reform in Morocco', *The Journal of North African Studies*, 18.1 (2013), 53–69.
31. Driss Maghraoui, 'The Strengths and Limits of Religious Reforms in Morocco', *Mediterranean Politics*, 14.2 (2009), 195–211.
32. Daadaoui, *Moroccan Monarchy and the Islamist Challenge*.
33. Daadaoui, *Moroccan Monarchy and the Islamist Challenge*.
34. Ahmet T. Kuru, 'Passive and Assertive Secularism: Historical Conditions, Ideological Struggles, and State Policies toward Religion', *World Politics*, 59.4 (2007), 568–94.
35. Azzedine Layachi, 'Islam and Politics in North Africa', in John L. Esposito and Emad El Din Shahin (eds), *The Oxford Handbook of Islam and Politics* (Oxford & New York: Oxford University Press, 2013), pp. 352–78.
36. Gudrun Krämer, 'The Integration of the Integrists: A Comparative Study of Egypt, Jordan, and Tunisia', in Ghassan Salamé (ed.), *Democracy without Democrats?: The Renewal of Politics in the Muslim World* (London: I. B. Tauris, 2001), pp. 200–26.
37. Manuel Castells, *The Power of Identity* (Malden, MA: Blackwell, 1997).

38. Kathleen Thelen, 'Historical Institutionalism in Comparative Politics', *Annual Review of Political Science*, 2 (1999), 369–404.
39. See: Robert Harmel, Uk Heo, Alexander Tan, and Kenneth Janda, 'Performance, Leadership, Factions and Party Change: An Empirical Analysis', *West European Politics*, 18.1 (1995), 1–33.
40. See: Tilly and Tarrow, *Contentious Politics*.
41. See: Juan J. Linz and Alfred C. Stepan, *Problems of Democratic Transition and Consolidation: Southern Europe, South America, and Post-Communist Europe* (Baltimore, MD: Johns Hopkins University Press, 1996).
42. See: Antonio Gramsci, *Selections from the Prison Notebooks of Antonio Gramsci* (New York: International Publishers, 1972).
43. See: Azzam Tamimi, *Rachid Ghannouchi: A Democrat within Islamism* (Oxford & New York: Oxford University Press, 2001); Abdelwahab El Affendi, *Turabi's Revolution: Islam and Power in Sudan* (London: Grey Seal Books, 1991).
44. See: Lisa Anderson, 'Searching Where the Light Shines: Studying Democratization in the Middle East', *Annual Review of Political Science*, 9 (2006), 189–214.
45. Brown, *When Victory Is Not an Option*.
46. For a detailed discussion of political opportunity and threat structures, see: McAdam, Tarrow, and Tilly, *Dynamics of Contention*; Tarrow, *Power in Movements*; Tilly and Tarrow, *Contentious Politics*; Herbert P. Kitschelt, 'Political Opportunity Structures and Political Protest: Anti-Nuclear Movements in Four Democracies', *British Journal of Political Science*, 16.1 (1986), 57–85; Hanspeter Kriesi, *New Social Movements in Western Europe: A Comparative Analysis* (Minneapolis, MN: University of Minnesota Press, 1995); Doug McAdam, *Political Process and the Development of Black Insurgency, 1930-1970* (Chicago: University of Chicago Press, 1999); Tarrow, *Democracy and Disorder*.
47. John D. McCarthy, Mayer N. Zald, and Doug McAdam, 'Introduction', in Doug McAdam, John D. McCarthy, and Mayer N. Zald (eds), *Comparative Perspectives on Social Movements: Political Opportunities, Mobilizing Structures, and Cultural Framings* (Cambridge & New York: Cambridge University Press, 1996), pp. 1–22.
48. Tilly and Tarrow, *Contentious Politics*.
49. Theda Skocpol, 'Bringing the State Back In: Strategies of Analysis in Current Research', in Peter B. Evans, Dietrich Rueschemeyer, and Theda Skocpol (eds), *Bringing the State Back In* (Cambridge & New York: Cambridge University Press, 1985), pp. 3–37.

50. Skocpol, 'Bringing the State Back In'.
51. Sewell William H., 'A Theory of Structure: Duality, Agency, and Transformation', *American Journal of Sociology*, 98.1 (1992), 1–29.
52. Irfan Ahmad, 'Genealogy of the Islamic State: Reflections on Maududi's Political Thought and Islamism', *The Journal of the Royal Anthropological Institute*, 15.1 (2009), 145–62.
53. The Jakarta Post (2011), 'NU Leaders Cannot Hold Political Posts', *The Jakarta Post*, 20 June, <https://web.archive.org/web/20110624120742/http://www.thejakartapost.com/news/2011/06/20/nation%E2%80%99s-largest-muslim-group-laments-%E2%80%98waning-influence%E2%80%99.html> (last accessed on 19 July 2018).
54. Seymour Martin Lipset and Stein Rokkan, *Party Systems and Voter Alignments: Cross-National Perspectives* (New York: Free Press, 1967).
55. Seyyed Vali Reza Nasr, *Forces of Fortune: The Rise of the New Muslim Middle Class and What It Will Mean for Our World* (New York: Free Press, 2009).
56. Thomas Butko, 'Unity Through Opposition: Islam as an Instrument of Radical Political Change', *Peace Research Abstracts*, 42.3 (2005), 33–48.
57. Peter Mair, 'Cleavages', in Richard S. Katz and William J. Crotty (eds), *Handbook of Party Politics* (London: SAGE, 2005), pp. 371–75.
58. Cedric de Leon, Manali Desai, and Cihan Tuğal, *Building Blocs: How Parties Organize Society* (Stanford, CA: Stanford University Press, 2015).
59. Kanchan Chandra, *Why Ethnic Parties Succeed: Patronage and Ethnic Head Counts in India* (Cambridge & New York: Cambridge University Press, 2004); Pradeep Chhibber and Mariano Torcal, 'Electoral Strategies, Social Cleavages, and Party Systems in a New Democracy: Spain', *Comparative Political Studies*, 30.1 (1997), 27–54.
60. Chandra, *Why Ethnic Parties Succeed*; Chhibber and Torcal, 'Electoral Strategies, Social Cleavages, and Party Systems in a New Democracy'.
61. Brown, *When Victory Is Not an Option*.
62. Hamid, *Temptations of Power*.
63. Mecham, *Institutional Origins of Islamist Political Mobilization*.
64. Yıldırım, *Muslim Democratic Parties in the Middle East*.
65. Kalyvas, *The Rise of Christian Democracy in Europe*.
66. Mark Blyth, 'Structures Do Not Come with an Instruction Sheet: Interests, Ideas, and Progress in Political Science', *Perspectives on Politics* 1.4 (2003), 695–706.

67. Tarrow, *Power in Movement*.
68. William A. Gamson and David S. Meyer, 'Framing Political Opportunity', in Doug McAdam, John D. McCarthy, and Mayer N. Zald (eds), *Comparative Perspectives on Social Movements: Political Opportunities, Mobilizing Structures, and Cultural Framings* (Cambridge & New York: Cambridge University Press, 1996), pp. 275–90.
69. McAdam, Tarrow, and Tilly, *Dynamics of Contention*.
70. Alfred C. Stepan, 'Religion, Democracy, and the "Twin Tolerations"', *Journal of Democracy*, 11.4 (2000), 37–57.
71. Asef Bayat, *Making Islam Democratic: Social Movements and the Post-Islamist Turn* (Stanford, CA: Stanford University Press, 2007).
72. I should note that I only look at nonviolent Islamic movements as the use of violence involves a different strategic thinking.
73. Kamran Bokhari (n.d.), 'Jamāat-I Islāmī', *The Oxford Encyclopedia of the Islamic World*, Oxford Islamic Studies Online <http://www.oxfordislamicstudies.com/opr/t236/e0408> (last accessed 10 April 2012).
74. Olivier Roy, *The Failure of Political Islam* (Cambridge, MA: Harvard University Press, 1994).
75. Jillian Schwedler, 'Islamic Identity: Myth, Menace, or Mobilizer?', *SAIS Review*, 21.2 (2001), 1–17.
76. Abdulkader H. Sinno and Ahmed Khanani, 'Of Opportunities and Organization: When Do Islamic Parties Choose to Compete Electorally?', in Mohamed Abdel Rahim M Salih (ed.), *Interpreting Islamic Political Parties* (New York: Palgrave Macmillan, 2009), pp. 29–49.
77. Kurt Gerhard Weyland, *Bounded Rationality and Policy Diffusion: Social Sector Reform in Latin America* (Princeton, NJ: Princeton University Press, 2006).
78. See: Asef Bayat, 'Islamism and Social Movement Theory', *Third World Quarterly*, 26.6 (2005), 891–908; Asef Bayat, 'Revolution without Movement, Movement without Revolution: Comparing Islamic Activism in Iran and Egypt', *Comparative Studies in Society and History*, 40.1 (1998), 136–69; François Burgat and William Dowell, *The Islamic Movement in North Africa* (Austin, TX: University of Texas Press, 1997); François Burgat, *Face to Face with Political Islam* (London & New York: I. B. Tauris, 2003); Cavatorta, 'Neither Participation nor Revolution'; Roy, *The Failure of Political Islam*; Eva Wegner (2004), 'The Contribution of Inclusivist Approaches towards the Islamist Opposition to Regime Stability in Arab States: The Case of the Moroccan Parti de La Justice et Du Développement', *EUI Working Paper RSCAS* <http://cadmus.

eui.eu/bitstream/handle/1814/2784/04_42.pdf?sequence=1> (last accessed on 17 July 2018); Michael J. Willis, 'Between Alternance and the Makhzen: At-Tawhid Wa Al Islah's Entry into Moroccan Politics' *Journal of North African Studies*, 4.3 (1999), 45–80; Michael J. Willis, *The Islamist Challenge in Algeria: A Political History* (New York: New York University Press, 1997); Quintan Wiktorowicz and Karl Kaltenthaler, 'The Rationality of Radical Islam', *Political Science Quarterly*, 121.2 (2006), 295–319; Roxanne L. Euben, 'Premodern, Antimodern or Postmodern? Islamic and Western Critiques of Modernity', *The Review of Politics*, 59.3 (1997), 429–59; Robert A. Pape, 'The Strategic Logic of Suicide Terrorism', *The American Political Science Review*, 97.3 (2003), 343–61; Mohammed M. Hafez, 'From Marginalization to Massacres: A Political Process Explanation of GIA Violence in Algeria', in Quintan Wiktorowicz (ed.), *Islamic Activism: A Social Movement Theory Approach* (Bloomington, IN: Indiana University Press, 2012), pp. 37–60.

79. Christian Reus-Smit, *The Moral Purpose of the State: Culture, Social Identity, and Institutional Rationality in International Relations* (Princeton, NJ: Princeton University Press, 1999).
80. Emanuel Adler, 'Constructivism in International Relations: Sources, Contributions, and Debates', in Walter Carlsnaes, Thomas Risse-Kappen, and Beth A. Simmons (eds), *Handbook of International Relations* (London: SAGE, 2013), pp. 112–44.
81. James G. March and Johan P. Olsen, 'The Institutional Dynamics of International Political Orders', *International Organization*, 52.4 (1998), 943–69.
82. Noam Lupu and Rachel Beatty Riedl, 'Political Parties and Uncertainty in Developing Democracies', *Comparative Political Studies*, 46.11 (2013), 1339–1365.
83. Gramsci, *Selections from the Prison Notebooks*.
84. Frédéric Volpi, *Political Islam Observed: Disciplinary Perspectives* (New York: Columbia University Press, 2010).
85. Brown, *When Victory Is Not an Option*.
86. Tamara Cofman Wittes, 'Three Kinds of Movements', *Journal of Democracy*, 19.3 (2008), 7–12.
87. Luca Ozzano, 'The Many Faces of the Political God: A Typology of Religiously Oriented Parties', *Democratization*, 20.5 (2013), 807–30.
88. See: Brocker and Künkler, 'Religious Parties'; Michael Buehler, 'Revisiting the Inclusion-Moderation Thesis in the Context of Decentralized Institutions: The Behavior of Indonesia's Prosperous Justice Party in National and Local

Politics', *Party Politics*, 19.2 (2013), 210–29; Schwedler, *Faith in Moderation*; Michael D. Driessen, 'Public Religion, Democracy, and Islam: Examining the Moderation Thesis in Algeria', *Comparative Politics*, 44.2 (2012), 171–89; Sarah Wilson Sokhey and A. Kadir Yıldırım, 'Economic Liberalization and Political Moderation: The Case of Anti-System Parties', *Party Politics*, 19.2 (2013), 230–55; Murat Somer, 'Moderation of Religious and Secular Politics, a Country's Centre and Democratization', *Democratization*, 21.2 (2014), 244–67; Sultan Tepe, 'Moderation of Religious Parties: Electoral Constraints, Ideological Commitments, and the Democratic Capacities of Religious Parties in Israel and Turkey', *Political Research Quarterly*, 65.3 (2012), 467–85; Güneş Murat Tezcür, *Muslim Reformers in Iran and Turkey: The Paradox of Moderation* (Austin, TX: University of Texas Press, 2011); Eva Wegner and Miquel Pellicer, 'Islamist Moderation Without Democratization: The Coming of Age of the Moroccan Party of Justice and Development?', *Democratization*, 16.1 (2009), 157–75; Carrie Rosefsky Wickham, 'The Path to Moderation: Strategy and Learning in the Formation of Egypt's Wasat Party', *Comparative Politics*, 36.2 (2004), 205–28.

89. See: Simon Hug, *Altering Party Systems: Strategic Behavior and the Emergence of New Political Parties in Western Democracies* (Ann Arbor, MI: University of Michigan Press, 2001); John H. Aldrich, *Why Parties?: The Origin and Transformation of Political Parties in America* (Chicago, IL: University of Chicago Press, 1995); Gary W. Cox, *The Efficient Secret: The Cabinet and the Development of Political Parties in Victorian England* (Cambridge & New York: Cambridge University Press, 1987); Maurice Duverger, *Political Parties, Their Organization and Activity in the Modern State* (London & New York: Wiley, 1954); Leon D. Epstein, *Political Parties in Western Democracies* (New Brunswick, NJ: Transaction Books, 1980); Richard Gunther, Jose R. Montero, and Juan J. Linz, *Political Parties: Old Concepts and New Challenges* (Oxford & New York: Oxford University Press, 2002); Robert Harmel and John D. Robertson, 'Formation and Success of New Parties: A Cross-National Analysis', *International Political Science Review*, 6.4 (1985), 501–23; Giovanni Sartori, *Parties and Party Systems: A Framework for Analysis* (Cambridge & New York: Cambridge University Press, 1976); Lipset and Rokkan, *Party Systems and Voter Alignments*; Kalyvas, *The Rise of Christian Democracy in Europe*.

2

FORM A PARTY OR STAY A MOVEMENT? STRUCTURES AND THE MENU OF OPTIONS

Rabat, the capital city of Morocco, is located on the African coast of the Atlantic Ocean. It drives its name from 'Ribat al-Fath' ['Fortress of Victory'] from when it served as a fortress for the Almohad Caliphate, a Berber Muslim empire that dominated twelfth century Maghreb and that fought against the Christian Kings of Spain.[1] When the Almohads lost control of their territory, Rabat came under the influence of Barbary pirates in the seventeenth century, who used the ports of the city to launch their attacks.[2] Around the same time, the Alaouite Dynasty, who claim to be descendants of Prophet Mohammed and who are still the ruling dynasty of Morocco today, was establishing its control around Fez and Marrakech south of Rabat. In 1912, when Morocco came under the French Protectorate, Rabat first regained its lost glory as the French moved the Protectorate's administrative capital there in order to escape the power dynamics in the imperial cities of the Alaouite Dynasty. Thereafter, the city continued to serve as a capital after Morocco became independent in 1956. As a result, today, the walled old city (the *medina*) with its small shops, historic mosques, and ancient gates sits next to the modern city with its National Library, Mohammed V University, and the Parliament. Like its capital Rabat, the Moroccan regime today is both traditional and modern in that the royal Alaouite family strongly associates its political legitimacy with its religious/Islamic roots dating back centuries while also portraying itself as a modern

Muslim nation-state resisting the religious and secular radicalisms of its neighbours.

Not unlike Rabat, the history of Ankara, the capital city of Turkey, is both ancient and modern. Its ancient history dates back to the Bronze Age when it was an important city at the 'northern edge of the central Anatolian steppe at the confluence of three small rivers'.[3] The city continued to be an important trade centre thereafter under the Roman and Byzantine Empires. Nonetheless, as modern-day Turkey came under the Ottoman Empire in the 13th century, the city lost its significance when the Ottomans shifted their focus to their newly conquered territories to the west and south of Ankara. When the new Turkish Republic was established after an independence war against European colonialism in 1923, the city became its capital. This move of capitals from Istanbul, which also was the symbolic seat of the Ottoman caliphate, to Ankara signalled a break of the new Republic with its Ottoman past. Here, the founders of the new Turkish Republic turned their vision of a modern nation-state into the city's unique architecture by constructing 'Republican' buildings to host the National Assembly, the Historical Society, the Ankara University, and multiple public parks and train stations. Like its capital, the Turkish regime today represents both a continuation of the past and a symbol of change. On the one hand, it continues the past as the heir apparent to the Ottoman Empire, and thus has a rather complicated relationship with Islam. On the other hand, the Turkish regime is also a symbol of change as a long-standing secular democratic nation-state in the Middle East/North Africa.

Similar to Rabat and Ankara, Amman, the capital city of Jordan, melts the old with the new. It sits on the ruins of an ancient site known as *Ain Ghazal* dating back to 7250 BC, discovered only in 1974. Although Amman served as a vital city both under the Roman and the Umayyad Empires as a result of its fertile and well-watered lands, an eighth-century earthquake along with the move of the Islamic caliphate from Syria to Iraq had sent the city into oblivion by the end of the thirteenth century.[4] The city would only be revived in 1921 when it became the capital to the Emirate of Transjordan, a protectorate 'created' by the British and led by the Hashemite family, who claimed to be descendants of Prophet Mohammed and who served as the *Sharif* (protector) of Mecca. Beating all the odds against their survival, the Hashemite royal family, the country of Jordan, and Amman as its capital have survived multiple wars, regional instability, and natural scarcities. Today, Amman's skyline features both skyscrapers of multinational corporations and banks as well as shantytowns. Like its capital city, the Jordanian regime today is both a 'construction' of colonial powers and yet also has managed to make this construction its own by offering a safe haven amidst turmoil not only for its citizens but also for refugees from the Palestinian Territories, Syria, and Iraq.

To understand how such dualities in the regimes of Morocco, Turkey, and Jordan influence Islamic movement behaviour, this chapter will discuss how a regime delineates a 'menu of options' for Islamic movements, first theoretically, and then empirically.

The Costs and Benefits of Participation vis-à-vis Non-participation

Political opportunity and threat structures define a 'menu of options' for Islamic movements to evaluate and to strategise about. On the one hand, participation in party politics in principle means increased public visibility, political influence over policy-making, and potential access to elite networks and state resources. Furthermore, participation enables Islamic movements to gain experience in real politics and thus to measure the popularity of their programmes and policies and to adjust them to popular demand. Participation also allows Islamic movements to use their voice within political institutions to counter elites. After all, as Roberts explains, 'it is only through an organisation that the many with few resources can leverage their weight in numbers as a countervailing power to the concentrated economic or institutional resources of elite groups'.[5] In short, participation, at least in theory, allows Islamic movements to gain political influence by working within the regime.

On the other hand, however, participation does not always bring such expected political influence in practice. In particular, participation in regimes with limited levels of political liberalisation, such as those found in the Middle East/North Africa, can be counterproductive, because in such systems elections are designed to consolidate the existing regime.[6] In what Linz and Stepan call 'authoritarian-democratic hybrid' regimes,

> Most major actors [within the regime] believe that they will lose legitimacy and their followers' support should they fail to embrace certain core features

of democracy (such as elections to produce the leaders of government), while believing at the same time that they must also retain (or at least allow) some authoritarian controls on key aspects of the emerging polity if they hope to further their goals and (again) retain their supporters.[7]

Such regimes 'on paper' introduce political openings, but 'in practice', they regulate the political field through a series of complicated bureaucratic procedures thereby bringing political openings under the control of the regime.[8] As a result, participation in party politics in such regimes means neither actual power in governance nor the ability to induce societal change.[9] On the contrary, it means the acceptance of the regime's legitimacy, and thus risks losing oppositional integrity,[10] especially in the eyes of those core supporters who champion Islamic movements for the challenge they pose to those regimes. Consequently, 'where party organisations drain human and financial resources [and] limit a leader's strategic autonomy', an Islamic movement 'may well decide that parties are not worth the effort'.[11] Within this logic, staying outside party politics and countering the hegemony of the regime/elites informally outside of institutional channels may give a movement popular credibility as a genuine political opposition. In the end, like any other movement aiming to challenge the status quo, Islamic movements 'owe their aura of autonomy and purity to their distance from established (party) politics, which are commonly seen as both corrupt and ineffectual'.[12]

Providing a real objection through non-participation, however, may not necessarily be the most pragmatic choice for an Islamic movement. In regimes, especially of an authoritarian/semi-authoritarian character, where political parties across the political spectrum preserve their societal base through patron–client networks,[13] and where 'the parliament is more a space for negotiation over resources and access to the circles of power',[14] participation in party politics may not only bring public visibility, but also access to state resources, and thus the chance to attract new supporters. Furthermore, an informal organisation with murky relations with the law/legality attracts fewer new supporters than a legal organisation with potential weight within formal institutions. Hence, participation in party politics may allow Islamic movements to reach new supporters.

That said, even if non-participation may scare off potential recruits, it may also help protect an Islamic movement's existing core base by bringing people together around a 'common purpose', and thus by consolidating a 'collective challenge' to the hegemonic order.[15] After all, relations within a movement are based on solidarity among members; they are informal and thus more personal. In a political party, however, relations become bureaucratised,[16] and as membership grows, the proximity between supporters decreases.[17] Exiting a movement, on the other hand, is harder because of peer pressure and personal relations, while in a party such pressures do not exist.[18] As a result, internal bonds are stronger between members and their leaders within a movement.

Building on such strong internal bonds, remaining outside party politics may also prevent the potential co-optation of the movement because once a movement participates within the system, it risks making *pragmatic* concessions to cast more votes from a wider constituency, which in the long run may force Islamic movements to abandon their *ideals*.[19] Furthermore, participation involves opening up a movement's internal finances and organisation to the public, creating a separate organisation with separate leadership, resources, and even constituencies[20] thereby risking fragmentation. It also involves working according to the electoral schedule[21] rather than an ideological programme, thus increasing the risk of co-optation.

While non-participation may avoid co-optation, nonetheless it also risks political repression by the regime as an illegal threat and thus being marginalised into assuming a passive 'wait-and-see' stance. Such a stance not only risks political stagnation but also potentially losing oppositional and organisational strength to contending Islamic movements that have chosen to participate in party politics, and thus have a legal presence and political influence within the regime.

Such a theoretical 'menu of options' (Table 2.1) is present for Islamic movements in Morocco, Turkey, and Jordan, albeit for different reasons.

Morocco

Morocco is a country of contradictions. It is an authoritarian regime, formally a constitutional monarchy, where the King reserves the last word in policymaking, yet where there is also a functioning party system with regular electoral schedules and for the most part free and fair elections. It is also a country deeply divided along economic class and yet somehow remains

Table 2.1 The Menu of Options

Reasons for Participation	Reasons for Non-participation
Participate to gain public visibility and political influence by working through institutions	Do Not Participate to remain a credible opposition outside corrupt institutions
Participate to reach new supporter bases	Do Not Participate to protect existing core base
Participate to avoid political stagnancy in the face of regime repressions	Do Not Participate to avoid co-optation by the regime

socio-politically stable even after the Arab Spring. Moreover, it is a country where the monarch claims religious legitimacy as a descendant of Prophet Mohammed while also seeking Western alliances. It is from within such a paradoxical context that regime–Islamic movement relations have evolved into their current state.

Historically, the Moroccan regime has used Islamic movements as a counterbalance to its secular contenders. In the 1970s, for instance, the King sidelined secular nationalists, who had fought alongside him for independence against the French, by establishing himself as the 'Commander of the Believers'. In this role, the King played 'the role of the "guardian" and "protector" of a particular form of [Moroccan] Islam that it deem[ed] necessary for the "balance" and "spiritual security" of the country and its citizens'.[22] Similarly, in the 1980s, the regime saw Islamic movements as a counter-balance to the Left, which the regime considered to be its main opposition at the time,[23] and thus allowed their growth in the society. Even though the Moroccan regime used Islamic movements against its secular opposition, it also saw Islamic movements as a fundamental threat to the King's role as the Commander of the Believers. In the early years of Morocco's independence (1950s/60s), for instance, the King, in alliance with the Nationalists, counterbalanced his main contender, Morocco's *Ulama* [religious clergy], through 'a policy of keeping a multitude of religious players to avoid the dominance of only one authority'.[24] In later years, in the 1990s in particular, the King proactively worked to divide-and-rule Islamic movements by offering them rewards and punishments in order to keep the Islamic opposition weak enough not to challenge his authority yet robust enough to outweigh his secular rivals.[25]

Participation in party politics in such an ambiguous context allowed Islamic movements 'to work from within' and thus to access state resources. Although the Moroccan monarchy was a limited parliamentary monarchy, where the King reserved the last word in policy-making, it was also a pragmatic monarchy differentiating between 'loyal opposition', opposition that does not question the regime's legitimacy, and 'illegal opposition', opposition that challenges the regime's legitimacy. The monarchy would do so by giving the former access to state resources and a seat in the parliament and repressing the latter.[26] As a result, participation in Moroccan party politics allowed Islamic movements to become part of the loyal opposition and thus to access its many advantages.

Although becoming a loyal opposition meant access to state resources, it also meant limited oppositional influence. In the end, this was a regime, where the King held his monopoly on crucial issues including national security, religion, and major strategic policy choices.[27] The King also got support in this from the *Makhzen*, the 'shadow government', a network of regime loyalists, who helped the King control political institutions, including the parliament, by serving as technocrats supervising legislation and the executive. In this, the King and the *Makhzen* formed 'a centralised political system with the Sultan (later king) at [the] centre of a structure comprising the army, bureaucracy, *ulema* [religious clergy] and the different Sufi lodges (*zawiya*)'.[28] Through such a centralised system, the King was able to exert his sovereignty both at the national and the local level, especially in rural areas, where a form of feudalism is still prevalent.[29] Within this elitist system, the parliament was a weak and ineffective institution unable to address societal demands. The state, which remained under the control of the *Makhzen*, for ordinary Moroccans, was an institution that affected their everyday lives, but they could not influence.[30] Thus, participation in an environment without trust or support for the parliamentary system was futile, while a non-participatory stance distanced an Islamic movement in the public eye from ineffective and fruitless policies. In particular, non-participation allowed an Islamic movement to mobilise on this alienation of the society from party politics by providing an alternative medium to voice their demands outside the control of the *Makhzen*. Although the Moroccan regime offered loyal opposition material and political rewards, it also expected the opposition

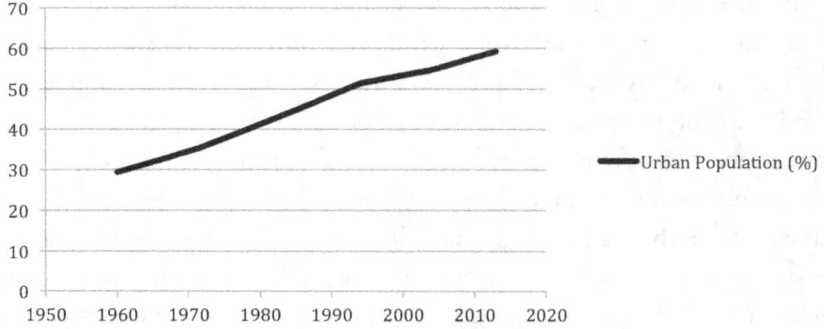

Source: World Bank (n.d.), 'World Bank Open Data', *World Bank*, <http://data.worldbank.org/> (last accessed 12 August 2018).

Figure 2.1 Urban Population (%), 1960–2013, results from Morocco

in return to scale back its opposition to the regime.[31] Thus, it was through non-participation that Islamic movements could pose a genuine challenge to the regime's hegemony.

Nonetheless, in a system where the King had by far the greatest political influence over socio-economic issues vis-à-vis non-state political actors, participation also provided a powerful medium to influence and to supervise public policy, and thereby break the monopoly of the *Makhzen*. Such political influence was especially significant considering that there were new constituents that remained unrepresented by the *Makhzen*. In this, participation allowed Islamic movements to represent urban (Figure 2.1) and educated (Figure 2.2) Moroccans, who had no access to *Makhzen* networks, and thus faced serious socio-economic problems. Hence, in a country where youth unemployment by 1991 was at 28.5% and unemployment with advanced education by 1995 was at 40.8%, and where, by 1984, the richest 20% of the country came to possess 46.2% of the country's wealth, while the lowest 20% only held 6.6%,[32] participation in party politics meant connecting with and representing the demands of these new constituents and thus expanding the movement's supporter base beyond an ideological core.

That said, establishing a small yet ideologically devoted supporter base through non-participation in an authoritarian context like Morocco was also crucial, where, in the face of increasing repressions from the regime, organisational solidarity could become a lifesaver for an Islamic movement. King

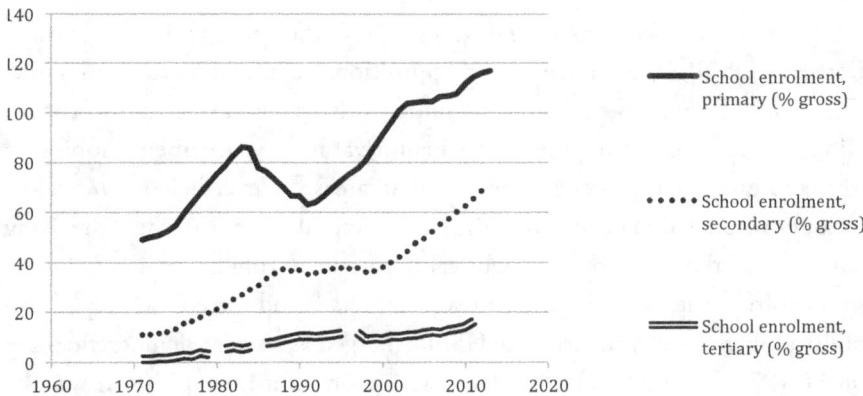

Source: World Bank (n.d.), 'World Bank Open Data', *World Bank*, <http://data.worldbank.org/> (last accessed 12 August 2018).

Figure 2.2 School Enrolment (%), 1970–2013, results from Morocco

Hassan II's long reign (1961–1999) was known for its maltreatment of political prisoners and its surveillance of all political activity.[33] King Mohamed VI's (1999–) current regime, although much more tolerant, has also been unpredictable because the Palace has vetoed certain journalists and political activists at its will. Such repression has been more prevalent for Islamic movements not only because they opposed the regime but also because they questioned the regime's religious, and thus political legitimacy.[34] Consequently, protecting organisational solidarity through non-participation was vital for the survival and longevity of an Islamic movement in Morocco.

Non-participation was also beneficial considering the co-optive forces of the Moroccan regime in party politics. The regime followed a policy of 'divide and rule' by proactively encouraging the formation of new political parties to counter-balance existing opposition parties. For instance, King Mohamed V (1957–1961) 'used the new rural-based MP [*Mouvement Populaire*] as a counter-force to the more urban-based *Istiqlal* [Independence]', and his son King Hassan II grouped 'technocrats and pro-palace independents' into a single political party[35] to divide-and-rule the opposition. Moroccan Kings also integrated oppositional forces into party politics at critical juncture points to secure their throne or to provide a smooth royal succession to supervise their oppositional activism and to counter-balance the military.[36] For instance, the two 'loyal opposition' parties today, the nationalist *Istiqlal* Party and the leftist *Union Socialiste des Forces Populaires* (Socialist Union of Popular Forces – USFP), were once major oppositional contenders to the regime. The *Istiqlal* Party, which fought for independence alongside the Moroccan King, was for a long time the King's main rival in the parliament mobilising 'the emerging younger generation' in urban areas.[37] Nevertheless, *Istiqlal* lost its oppositional dynamism and thus its electoral strength when the King 'encouraged the emergence of political parties favouring his policies',[38] drew support from the rural and tribal power-holders,[39] and forced the *Istiqlal* into political stagnancy. Similarly, the USFP emerged as a social-democratic party in the 1970s calling for further democratisation. Until the 1990s, it was the main opposition party in the country refusing to become a loyal opposition like *Istiqlal*. However, in the 1990s, the USFP was invited to form the new government as the winner of the elections and was promised fundamental democratic reforms if the Party would 'not contest the overarching powers of the monarch'.[40] However, such reforms were not forthcoming, and the USFP lost its oppositional credibility by accepting to become a loyal opposition party. In short, Moroccan party politics showed that co-optation was a significant risk for those who participated.

Notwithstanding such risks of participation, given the regime's treatment of 'unrecognised' opposition, Moroccan political history also showed that non-participation could be very costly. In the end, Moroccan politics took place in the shadows of the civil war (1991–2002) in Algeria, which started when the Islamic Salvation Front won the 1991 elections, but was ousted out of power by an internationally backed military coup. As a result, non-participation risked domestic and international marginalisation, while participation had the benefit of signalling to the Moroccan regime as well as to the international community a moderate stance and a desire to avoid the Algerian experience.

Unlike such 'frenemy' relations between the Moroccan regime and Islamic movements, Islamic movements in Turkey faced a democratic yet hostile regime.

Turkey

The Turkish Republic was built not only upon 'the ashes of the Ottoman Empire'[41] but also in opposition to it. Hence, the founders of the Turkish

Republic, the *Kemalists*, have engaged in massive political transformations and social engineering projects to leave the Ottoman past behind, a past which they believed to be defined by religious fundamentalism and regression. In this, the Turkish regime saw Islamic movements as 'backward forces' aiming at the revival of the Ottoman past and religious fundamentalism, and thus as an ideological/hegemonic threat to its own mission towards secular modernisation.

The Kemalist regime, to avoid such hegemonic threats, under the banner of 'laicism', strictly controlled the religious field, through the Ministry of Education, which was responsible for religious education in schools, and through the Directorate of Religious Affairs (*Diyanet*), which was in charge of appointing all clerical personnel in the country through a centralised system.[42] Within this arrangement, religious activism outside the state's supervision was banned. Despite such formal hostility, informally Islamic movements also occupied a central role in Turkish politics. Firstly, Islamic movements were informally allowed by the Turkish regime to exist as long as they remained loyal to the Republic and accepted operating as apolitical religious foundations under the state's surveillance. Secondly, Islamic movements remained popular with the masses, because the regime's civilising mission and its top-down approach to rapid social transformation 'left the "day-to-day" in limbo. Even in the most stringently secular times of the Republic, Islam filled the void'.[43] Thus, Islamic movements offered an 'alternative atmosphere of socialization within the secular Republican context'.[44]

In the face of such hostile regime–Islamic movement relations, unlike in Morocco, where participation provided access to state resources, participation in Turkey provided an ideological influence over society. Specifically, working within the Turkish state provided access to the Directorate of Religious Affairs and to religious education, and thus allowed Islamic movements to influence society through the state. Furthermore, participation, unlike in Morocco or Jordan, allowed Islamic movements to acquire a substantial political influence within the parliament given the presence of a democratic electoral system.

Despite the presence of a democratic electoral system, however, the Turkish regime was not a consolidated liberal democracy either. While in Morocco participation was futile in a party system under the authoritarian

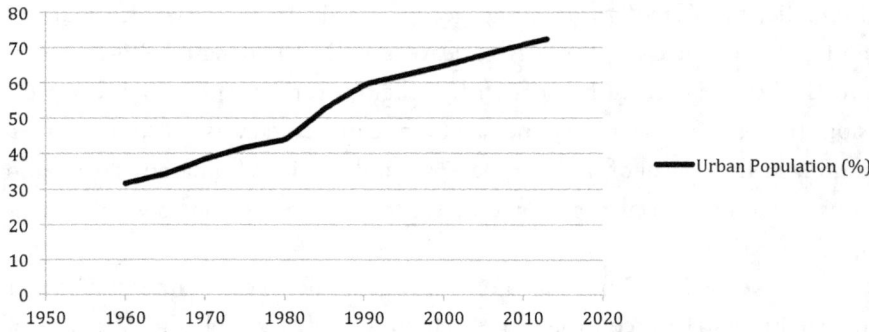

Source: World Bank, (n.d.), 'World Bank Open Data', *World Bank*, <http://data.worldbank.org/> (last accessed 12 August 2018).

Figure 2.3 Urban Population (%), 1960–2013, results from Turkey

thumb of the Moroccan King, party politics in Turkey was ineffective in its fragmentation and volatility. Multiple political parties both on the right and the left of the political spectrum had emerged, but none of them was able to govern by itself. Thus, coalition governments became the norm from the 1960s onwards. Furthermore, as voters identified less and less with particular political parties, the party system had become more volatile, and voters were switching from one party to the next in successive elections. As a result, the party system was insufficient to introduce change. Instead, non-participation was offering an alternative space for political activism outside the limiting scopes of laicism and fragmented ineffectiveness of the party system.

Nevertheless, participation also meant mobilising new constituents. Like in Morocco, an educated (Figure 2.3) and urban (Figure 2.4) constituency with new demands had emerged, and their problems were unaddressed by existing political parties. According to the earliest available data, in 1991 youth unemployment was about 15.3% while by 1987 the richest 20% of the country came to possess 49.9% of the country's wealth, with the lowest 20% only holding 5.9%.[45] Within this context, party politics offered Islamic movements the chance to mobilise the dissatisfaction of these new constituents that were the products of the Republic's modernisation but had not benefitted from it. Moreover, participation brought more *public* appeal and

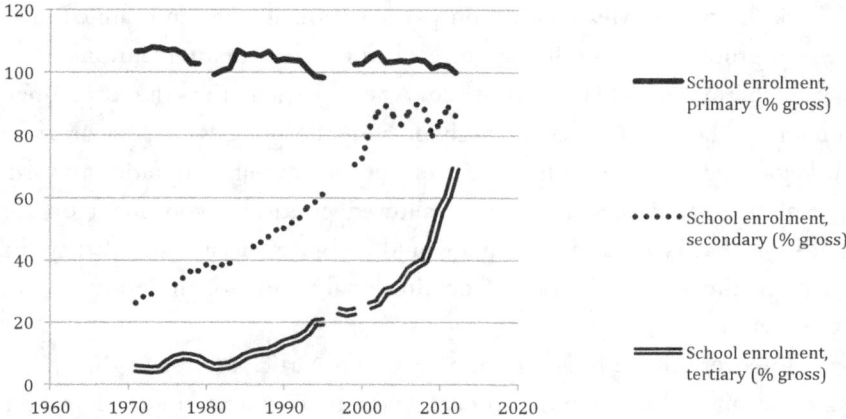

Source: World Bank, (n.d.), 'World Bank Open Data', *World Bank*, <http://data.worldbank.org/> (last accessed 12 August 2018).

Figure 2.4 School Enrolment (%), 1970–2013, results from Turkey

thus allowed an Islamic movement to reach a wider constituency in a system where Islamic movements were outlawed and forced to operate underground. In short, participation allowed Islamic movements to represent the voice of the unrepresented within the legal framework of party politics.

Representing the unrepresented was nevertheless a difficult task for Islamic movements. For decades, Turkish party politics was based on a duality between 'the centre' and 'the periphery'.[46] While the latter, composed mostly of rural citizenry, provided support for centre-right political parties, the former, consisting of the military, the judiciary, and the bureaucracy, guarded the Turkish state and its institutions against the latter in case they engaged in activities outside the scope of designated areas of politicisation. As a result, these 'guardians of the state' intervened into Turkish politics at different times and for various reasons. For instance, the military intervened and suspended democratic life twice in 1960 and 1980 to 'save' democracy from politicians and political polarisations.[47] Similarly, the Turkish Constitutional Court banned multiple political parties for their opposition to laicism and for promoting Kurdish nationalism and thus undermining national unity. In such a context, although participation allowed political access, such influence also remained limited given the control of the 'centre' in Turkish politics. Meanwhile, non-participation allowed an Islamic movement to protect itself and its supporters from such state interventions.

Furthermore, unlike in Morocco, where participation risked co-optation in the face of the regime's divide-and-rule policies, participation in Turkey risked co-optation because it meant ideological co-optation towards an embrace of laicism. The regime allowed political involvement on the condition that Islamic movements would embrace laicism, and if they did not, tried them at the Turkish Constitutional Court for undermining the Constitution.

Moreover, unlike in Morocco, where non-participation and thus refusing to become a loyal opposition outside the party system risked repression, in Turkey, participation risked repression. Specifically, the Turkish state informally tolerated Islamic movements as long as they remained outside of formal politics as apolitical organisations engaged in religious services. Thus, in this particular arrangement between the Turkish state and Islamic movements, where Islamic movements protected themselves from potential state repressions by allying themselves with the state,[48] the best form of protection was to remain an *apolitical* Islamic movement and thus outside of the party system. Hence, non-participation allowed Islamic movements to protect their supporter base from state repression but came at the cost of political stagnancy, where venues for political mobilisation outside the party system remained limited. They also were treated with suspicion for Islamism and for having a hidden agenda to replace the current order thereby politically forcing Islamic movements into political stagnancy.

Ironically, in contrast to such hostile regime–Islamic movement relations within the democratic framework of Turkey, friendlier relations have defined regime–Islamic movement relations within the authoritarian context of Jordan.

Jordan

In contrast to Morocco's contradictory policies and Turkey's hostility towards Islamic movements, relations between the Jordanian regime and Islamic movements in the country were defined by a mutual respect. Islamic movements in Jordan respected the Jordanian regime and the King because they provided stability in the midst of regional turmoil. Historically, the monarchy

Survived the acquisition of the West Bank as a result of the 1948 war with Israel; the first King Abdullah's assassination; his son Talal's deposition in 1952; the turbulence surrounding Arab nationalism in the 1950s; the loss of the West Bank to Israel during the Six-Day War of June 1967; and bloody domestic clashes between royal troops and Palestinian nationalists during the 'Black September' of 1970.[49]

Jordan had also survived despite the absence of natural resources. Thus, Jordanians saw the King as a leader who made a miracle happen in keeping Jordan stable despite all the odds.[50]

Within this socio-political context, unlike the Moroccan regime that saw Islamic movements as a potential threat to its religious and thus political legitimacy, and unlike the Turkish regime that saw them as backward forces aiming at the fall of the secular Republic, the Jordanian regime saw Islamic movements as strategic allies. In particular, the King and Islamic movements were allies of convenience against the rise of Arab nationalism and left-wing politics that swept through the region throughout the 1950s and 1960s.[51] Within this understanding, the Jordanian regime saw Islamic movements as a tool to control the street and thus to provide political stability.[52] In all of this what differentiated relations between the Jordanian regime and Islamic movements from their counterparts in Morocco and Turkey was that they did not see each other as ideological/hegemonic threats but as intentional partners based on mutual respect aiming at the preservation of stability in Jordan. This relationship was not a friendship, however, but rather a 'wary and guarded'[53] relationship wherein if Islamic movements 'ventured too far into the political field or seemed to edge into overt opposition, the regime responded by pressuring leaders or suspending movement publications'.[54] Although the Jordanian King, as a Hashemite and thus a proclaimed descendant of Prophet Mohammad, enjoyed religious legitimacy, he also was cautious in empowering Islamic movements too much in order to avoid Islamic movements from becoming a real challenge.

In such a regime, participation allowed an Islamic movement to utilise on tolerant regime relations and to make demands without threatening instability and without questioning the domestic legitimacy of the King. Thus, while participation in Morocco and Turkey allowed Islamic movements to

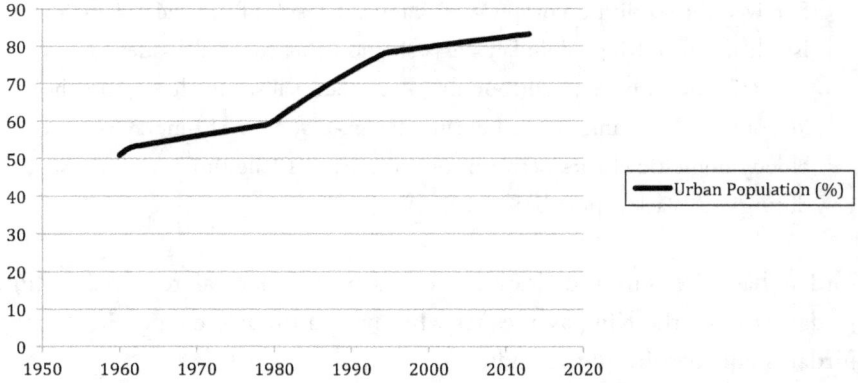

Source: World Bank, (n.d.), 'World Bank Open Data', *World Bank*, <http://data.worldbank.org/> (last accessed 12 August 2018).

Figure 2.5 Urban Population (%), 1960–2013, results from Jordan

challenge the regime from within, participation in Jordan endowed an Islamic movement with a unique quality of working as a partner of the regime.

Within a context defined by survival, however, party politics had a limited sphere of influence. Firstly, for decades, the parliament was suspended, effectively eliminating its role in decision-making. Secondly, after the reopening of the parliament in 1988/1989, unlike functioning parliamentary monarchies, such as those in Britain, where the monarchy plays a symbolic role, it was the parliament that played a symbolic role in Jordan because political parties remained ineffective and because the King of Jordan remained the real decision-maker. In this, different from Morocco or Turkey, both of which hosted an active party system, Jordan's party system remained ineffective and inconsequential in its electoral rules designed to prevent any party from winning a majority. Thus, participating in such a party system risked political irrelevance.

In this arrangement, the middle classes, according to a Jordanian journalist, were the real victims because they were stuck between the regime and fulfilling their desires: they were educated but had no economic power, they had high-status jobs as professors and doctors but had no political power.[55] As a result, participation connected Islamic movements with educated (Figure 2.5) and urban (Figure 2.6) constituents. At the end, Jordan was no different from Morocco or Turkey: youth unemployment, by 1990,

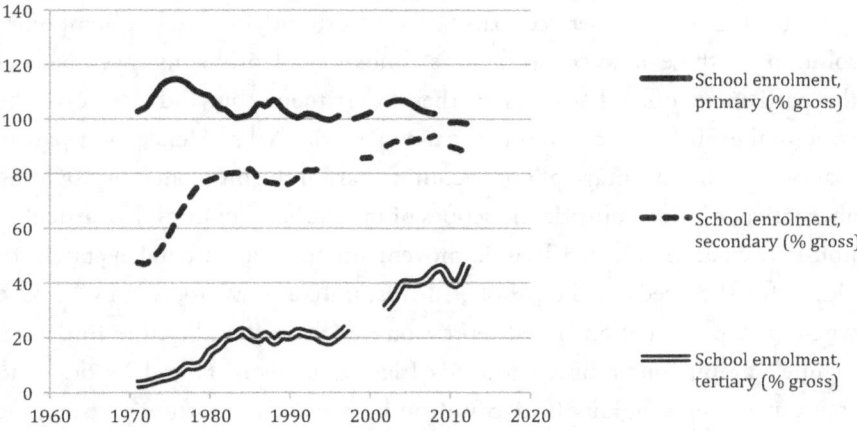

Source: World Bank, (n.d.), 'World Bank Open Data', *World Bank*, <http://data.worldbank.org/> (last accessed 12 August 2018).

Figure 2.6 School Enrolment (%), 1970–2013, results from Jordan

was at 41.6%. Likewise, by 1986, the richest 20% of the country possessed 43.8% of the country's wealth, while the lowest 20% only held 7.3%.[56] So participation allowed an Islamic movement to represent the demands of these new constituents by allowing Islamic movements to serve as these constituents' 'service providers' in the parliament. Lust-Okar and Hourani explain:

> Many Jordanians refer to their legislative representatives as 'service MPs'. It is a label which reflects the widespread notion that helping constituents to gain access to health, education, and other services, to get jobs, or to navigate (and if need be, to bypass) the sprawling state bureaucracy is what being an MP is all about. This last function – call it 'MP as fixer' – is particularly important in Jordan, where a weak rule of law and a chronic lack of official transparency can make it hard for ordinary citizens to obtain even the most seemingly routine public goods and services. As one young Jordanian attending a campaign event put it, 'Everyone in [Jordan] needs a VIP to solve his problems'.[57]

As a result, forming a political party would allow an Islamic movement to access such state resources, to provide extensive services for its supporters, and thus to widen its constituency.

Turning into a 'service party', however, only offered a temporary solution to these new constituency's fundamental problems. Members of the parliament offered services to their constituents but did not solve the structural problems necessitating the use of 'service MPs'. Hence, non-participation had the advantage of not becoming part of the problem but providing alternative solutions outside the scopes of institutional politics. In particular, non-participation allowed Islamic movements to create a parallel state providing for the needs of the people. In this, unlike in Morocco and Turkey, where non-participation risked repression due to its illegality, the Jordanian regime's ambiguous attitude towards Islamic movements and its desire to stay out of the religious field could be used as an opportunity to engage in political activism freely. Furthermore, forming a political party required Islamic movements to open their membership records to the regime. Such an opening risked regime interference into their internal affairs and thus risked vulnerability and disturbing internal cohesion. As a result, non-participation allowed Islamic movements to create their own networks outside the regime and thus the ability to offer long-term solutions, such as free education and healthcare services, to their followers.

More so, participation, like in Morocco and Turkey, risked co-optation in Jordan because political openings in Jordan were tactical and served for regime survival. Specifically, the 1989 political opening was a survival tactic to deal with an impending political and economic crisis and popular uprising. Thus, according to a Jordanian scholar, political openings in Jordan were about keeping the core of the dictatorship.[58] Hence, this was a limited political opening wherein the Jordanian regime 'undertook sufficient reform to assure its political longevity, but without altering the core structures of power in Jordan'.[59] In this way, elections were held not for the sake of an actual transfer of power, but to renew the regime's legitimacy. Consequently, participating under such circumstances risked co-optation.

However, non-participation was equally costly in Jordan. Unlike in Morocco and Turkey, where the regime was distrustful of Islamic movements outside institutional channels, in Jordan, the regime welcomed Islamic movements – if they remained apolitical. Consequently, non-participation risked political stagnancy in its apoliticisation.

Summary

'Regimes often have the opponents they deserve. Frequently, their successors are the political forces that they, themselves, have largely helped to create'.[60] As such, the three regimes in question in this study – Morocco, Turkey, and Jordan – created political opponents that are their products. Hence, although the three regimes in question varied widely in their state–society relations and the role of religion in the state, they also left Islamic movements with three similar strategic trade-offs. The first strategic trade-off Islamic movements faced in Morocco, Turkey, and Jordan, albeit for different reasons, was what kind of a challenge they aimed to pose to the regime. Particularly whether they wanted to reform the system from within the ranks of institutional politics to represent those marginalised by existing political parties, or whether they wanted to form an Islamic counter-hegemony outside the limiting scopes of institutional politics to voice the demands of the very same societal constituencies. The second strategic trade-off was whether Islamic movements wanted to seek new supporters by becoming part of party politics and thus widening their mass appeal or whether they wanted to preserve their existing supporter base by staying out of the disruptive forces of party politics to engage in an ideological rather than electoral quest for socio-political power. The third strategic trade-off was whether Islamic movements could afford to risk co-optation as a result of participation or political stagnancy as a result of non-participation. Despite facing such similar strategic trade-offs, different Islamic movements pursued opposing political paths in their respective countries – the subject of the next chapter.

Notes

1. Jonathan M. Bloom and Sheila S. Blair (n.d.), 'Rabat', *The Grove Encyclopedia of Islamic Art and Architecture*, Oxford Islamic Studies Online <http://www.oxfordislamicstudies.com/article/opr/t276/e771> (last accessed on 19 July 2018).
2. Yves Levant and Leila Maziane, 'The Republic of Sale (1627–1641/1666); An Alternative Pirate Organisation Model?', *Management & Organisational History*, 12.1 (2017), 1–29.
3. Jonathan M. Bloom and Sheila S. Blair (n.d.), 'Ankara', *The Grove Encyclopedia*

of Islamic Art and Architecture, Oxford Islamic Studies Online <http://www.oxfordislamicstudies.com/article/opr/t276/e79> (last accessed on 19 July 2018).
4. Jonathan M. Bloom and Sheila S. Blair (n.d.), 'Amman', *The Grove Encyclopedia of Islamic Art and Architecture, Oxford Islamic Studies Online* <http://www.oxfordislamicstudies.com/article/opr/t276/e76> (last accessed on 19 July 2018).
5. Kenneth M. Roberts, 'Populism, Political Conflict, and Grass-Roots Organization in Latin America', *Comparative Politics*, 38.2 (2006), 127–48.
6. Malika Zeghal, 'Participation without Power', *Journal of Democracy*, 19.3 (2008), 31–6.
7. Alfred Stepan and Juan J. Linz, 'Democratization Theory and the Arab Spring', *Journal of Democracy*, 24.2 (2013), 15–30.
8. Quintan Wiktorowicz, 'Civil Society as Social Control: State Power in Jordan', *Comparative Politics*, 33.1 (2000), 43–61.
9. Zeghal, 'Participation without Power'.
10. Eva Wegner, 'The Contribution of Inclusivist Approaches towards the Islamist Opposition to Regime Stability in Arab States: The Case of the Moroccan Parti de La Justice et Du Développement', *EUI Working Paper RSCAS*, 2004 <http://cadmus.eui.eu/bitstream/handle/1814/2784/04_42.pdf?sequence=1> (last accessed on 17 July 2018).
11. Roberts, 'Populism, Political Conflict, and Grass-Roots Organization in Latin America'.
12. Gudrun Krämer, 'Cross-Links and Double Talk? Islamist Movements in the Political Process', in Laura Guazzone (ed.), *The Islamist Dilemma: The Political Role of Islamist Movements in the Contemporary Arab World* (Reading: Ithaca Press, 1995), pp. 39–67.
13. Ellen Lust-Okar, *Structuring Conflict in the Arab World: Incumbents, Opponents, and Institutions* (Cambridge & New York: Cambridge University Press, 2006).
14. Zerhouni, Saloua, 'The Moroccan Parliament', in Ellen Lust-Okar and Saloua Zerhouni (eds), *Political Participation in the Middle East* (Boulder, CO: Lynne Rienner Publishers, 2008), pp. 217–38.
15. Sidney G. Tarrow, *Power in Movement: Social Movements and Contentious Politics* (Cambridge & New York: Cambridge University Press, 1998).
16. Angelo Panebianco, *Political Parties: Organization and Power* (Cambridge & New York: Cambridge University Press, 1988).

17. Manfred Brocker and Mirjam Künkler, 'Religious Parties: Revisiting the Inclusion-Moderation Hypothesis – Introduction', *Party Politics*, 19.2 (2013), 171–86.
18. Panebianco, *Political Parties*.
19. Robert Michels, *Political Parties: A Sociological Study of the Oligarchical Tendencies of Modern Democracy* ([S.l.]: General Books, 2009).
20. Nathan J. Brown, *When Victory Is Not an Option: Islamist Movements in Arab Politics* (Ithaca, NY: Cornell University Press, 2012).
21. Brown, *When Victory Is Not an Option*.
22. Driss Maghraoui, 'The Strengths and Limits of Religious Reforms in Morocco', *Mediterranean Politics*, 14.2 (2009), 195–211.
23. Marvine Howe, *Morocco: The Islamist Awakening and Other Challenges* (New York: Oxford University Press, 2005).
24. Mohammed El Katiri, 'The Institutionalisation of Religious Affairs: Religious Reform in Morocco', *The Journal of North African Studies*, 18.1 (2013), 53–69.
25. Malika Zeghal, *Islamism in Morocco: Religion, Authoritarianism, and Electoral Politics* (Princeton, NJ: Markus Wiener Publishing, 2009).
26. Zeghal, *Islamism in Morocco*.
27. Mohammed Masbah (2014), 'Morocco's Slow Motion Reform Process', *Stiftung Wissenschaft und Politik*, <http://www.swp-berlin.org/en/publications/swp-comments-en/swp-aktuelle-details/article/moroccos_slow_motion_reform_process.html> (last accessed 19 July 2018).
28. Mohamed Daadaoui, *Moroccan Monarchy and the Islamist Challenge: Maintaining Makhzen Power* (New York: Palgrave Macmillan, 2011).
29. Daadaoui, *Moroccan Monarchy and the Islamist Challenge*.
30. Henry Munson, *Religion and Power in Morocco* (New Haven, CT: Yale University Press, 1993).
31. Zeghal, *Islamism in Morocco*.
32. World Bank (n.d.), 'World Bank Open Data', World Bank, <http://data.worldbank.org/> (last accessed 12 August 2018).
33. Munson, *Religion and Power in Morocco*.
34. Stephen O. Hughes, *Morocco under King Hassan* (Reading: Ithaca Press, 2006).
35. Farid Boussaid, 'The Rise of the PAM in Morocco: Trampling the Political Scene or Stumbling into It?', *Mediterranean Politics*, 14.3 (2009), 413–19.
36. Emad Eldin Shahin, *Political Ascent: Contemporary Islamic Movements in North Africa* (Boulder, CO: Westview Press, 1997).

37. Edmund Burke III (n.d.), 'Istiqlal', *The Oxford Encyclopedia of the Islamic World, Oxford Islamic Studies Online* <http://www.oxfordislamicstudies.com/article/opr/t236/e0399> (last accessed 19 July 2018).
38. Burke, 'Istiqlal'.
39. James N. Sater, 'Parliamentary Elections and Authoritarian Rule in Morocco', *The Middle East Journal*, 63.3 (2009), 381–400.
40. Sater, 'Parliamentary Elections and Authoritarian Rule in Morocco'.
41. Stanford Jay Shaw and Ezel Kural Shaw, *History of the Ottoman Empire and Modern Turkey: Volume 2, Reform, Revolution, and Republic: The Rise of Modern Turkey 1808-1975* (Cambridge & New York: Cambridge University Press, 1977).
42. Sencer Ayata, 'Patronage, Party, and State: The Politicization of Islam in Turkey', *Middle East Journal*, 50.1 (1996), 40–56.
43. Şerif Mardin, 'The Nakshibendi Order of Turkey', in Martin Marty and R. Scott Appleby (eds), *Fundamentalisms and the State: Remaking Polities, Economies, and Militance* (Chicago, IL: University of Chicago Press, 1993), pp. 204–32.
44. Halil Inalcık, 'Tarihsel Bağlamda Sivil Toplum ve Tarikatlar' ['Civil Society and Religious Orders in Historical Perspective'], in Emin Fuat Keyman and Ali Yaşar Sarıbay (eds), *Global Yerel Eksende Türkiye* [*Turkey within the Global-Local Axis*] (Istanbul: Alfa Yayınları, 2000), pp. 593–616.
45. World Bank (n.d.), 'World Bank Open Data', World Bank, <http://data.worldbank.org/> (last accessed 12 August 2018). Because there is no data prior to 1987 available from this source, we will assume that there is a backward trend and that income inequalities had started to rise prior to 1987.
46. Şerif Mardin, *Religion, Society, and Modernity in Turkey* (Syracuse, NY: Syracuse University Press, 2006).
47. Hootan Shambayati and Esen Kirdiş, 'In Pursuit of "Contemporary Civilization": Judicial Empowerment in Turkey', *Political Research Quarterly*, 62.4 (2009), 767–80.
48. Emin Yaşar, 'Dergâh'tan Parti'ye, Vakıftan Şirkete Bir Kimliğin Oluşumu ve Dönüşümü: Iskenderpaşa Cemaati' ['Identity Formation and Transformation from Lodge to Party, from Foundation to Company: Iskenderpaşa Congregation'], in Yasin Aktay (ed.), *Modern Türkiye'de Siyasi Düşünce, Cilt 6: Islamcılık* [*Political Thought in Modern Turkey, volume 6: Islamism*] (Istanbul: Iletişim Yayınları, 2004), pp. 321–40.
49. Russell E. Lucas, 'Deliberalization in Jordan', *Journal of Democracy*, 14.1 (2003), 137–44.

50. It should also be noted here that the King also has a very positive international image as a pro-Western monarch. This international image is a crucial asset for a country like Jordan that is dependent on foreign aid.
51. Hamed El Said and James E. Rauch, 'Education, Political Participation, and Islamist Parties: The Case of Jordan's Islamic Action Front', *The Middle East Journal*, 69.1 (2015), 51–73.
52. Mohammad S. Abu Rumman and Hassan Abu Hanieh, *The "Islamic Solution" in Jordan: Islamists, the State, and the Ventures of Democracy and Security* (Amman: Friedrich-Ebert-Stiftung, 2013).
53. Nathan J. Brown (2006), 'Jordan and Its Islamic Movement: The Limits of Inclusion?', *Carnegie Papers 74* , <https://carnegieendowment.org/files/cp_74_brown_final.pdf> (last accessed 19 July 2018).
54. Brown, *When Victory Is Not an Option*.
55. Anonymous interview with a Jordanian journalist by the author, 11 February 2010, Amman, Jordan.
56. World Bank (n.d.), 'World Bank Open Data', World Bank, <http://data.worldbank.org/> (last accessed 12 August 2018).
57. Ellen Lust-Okar and Sami Hourani, 'Jordan Votes: Election or Selection?', *Journal of Democracy*, 22.2 (2011), 119–29.
58. Anonymous interview with a Jordanian scholar by the author, 10 February 2010, Amman, Jordan.
59. Glenn E. Robinson, 'Defensive Democratization in Jordan', *International Journal of Middle East Studies*, 30.3 (1998), 387–410.
60. François Burgat and William Dowell, *The Islamic Movement in North Africa* (Austin, TX: University of Texas Press, 1997).

3

ISLAMIC MOVEMENTS TAKE AGENCY: THE DECISION OVER PARTICIPATION

In the mid-1960s, the Islamic Youth in Morocco, the predecessor to the Movement for Unity and Reform and the incumbent Party for Justice and Development, was a violent Islamic movement targeting the fall of the Moroccan regime, whereas Abdessalam Yassine, the founder of the Justice and Spirituality Movement, was a school inspector questioning his Sufi mentor's teachings. Today, while the Movement for Unity and Reform is legitimising the same Moroccan regime it once aimed to bring down by participating in the party system through the Party for Justice and Development, the Justice and Spirituality Movement is challenging the Moroccan regime's religio-political legitimacy by rejecting to do so.

In the mid-1960s, whilst Islamic circles in Turkey, under the leadership of the *Nakşibendi* Order and Islamic parliamentarians, who later on would form the National Outlook Movement, were searching for an alternative to existing right-wing political parties, Fethullah Gülen, the founder of the Gülen Movement, was a state preacher attracting an increasing number of followers with his passionate speeches. Today, the 'descendants' of the National Outlook Movement under the Justice and Development Party are the sole governing party of Turkey since 2002. Meanwhile, the Gülen Movement, the country's largest Islamic movement, is under investigation for allegedly infiltrating state institutions including the military, judiciary, and bureaucracy, and for conspiring to attempt a military coup against the governing Justice and Development Party.

In the mid-1960s, as the Jordanian Muslim Brotherhood was a strategic ally to the Jordanian monarchy and the only socio-political force in Jordan competing with the charities of the royal Hashemite family,[1] indeed Salafism in Jordan was still pretty much a foreign concept before the settlement of Muhammad Nasir al-Din Albani, a famous Salafi Sheikh, from Syria into Jordan. Today, the Brotherhood is marginalised and fragmented after the Jordanian regime's seizure of its assets and closure of its charities, while Quietist Salafis are suffering from internal disunity despite their apathy towards the fragmenting climate of party politics.

This chapter, aiming to analyse how these six different Islamic movements in three different socio-political contexts ended up where they are today, will look at how they all made (1) similar political choices in diverse socio-political contexts, and (2) different political choices within the same socio-political context.

Islamic Movements and the Decision to Participate in Party Politics

Islamic movements evaluate and strategise about the menu of options available to them in light of their strategic objectives, defined by their ideological priorities and organisational needs. Islamic movements vary in their strategic objectives because, although they are unified by their belief that 'Islam is the solution' to the contemporary problems of the Muslim community, they differ regarding how to start an Islamic revival. The main theoretical barrier to achieving this revival is the dilemma of sequencing: that there can be no Islamic state without an Islamic society, but also that there can be no Islamic society without an Islamic state.[2] Thus, whereas some Islamic movements anticipate a bottom-up Islamic revival starting at the societal level through a grassroots organisation with a mass following (grassroots movements), others anticipate a top-down Islamic revival starting at the state-level under a small vanguard organisation led by a few Islamic leaders (vanguard movements).

Vanguard movements believe that Islamic revival will 'not result from mobilising the masses to topple the existing order, but from taking political power and affecting broad reforms from the *top down*' (emphasis added).[3] In this line of thought, the state occupies a central role because it can decide 'what you are to wear or what not to wear; whom you are to marry and at what age; what you are to teach your kids and what mode of life you are to choose; [...] what language and script you are to adopt', not leaving 'even the most peripheral issues of life independent of its ultimate right to intervene'.[4] Hence, capturing the state and reviving Islam through the state forms the backbone to these Islamic movements' ideological priorities. However, this does not necessarily mean organising a revolution 'in the sense of seeking to overturn the existing social order'.[5] Rather, it involves 'a program of training a vanguard "Islamic elite", who oversee the revival of Islam on a national level and mobilise the masses using religious symbols and ideals'.[6] The expectation is that such a vanguard organisation will 'bring awareness from the top' to larger segments of society and lead the way to re-engineer state and society.[7]

Unlike vanguard movements, grassroots movements do not see the underdevelopment of the Muslim world in the failure of state institutions but in the decline of the Islamic civilisation as a whole. Hence, Islamic revival goes beyond the reformation of the state and instead encompasses all aspects of life. In forming their ideological priorities, grassroots movements look at the first Muslims in Medina and argue that the *ummah* [the Muslim community] came before the establishment of an Islamic state.[8] Thus, they believe that 'an Islamic state should result from the re-Islamisation of the *ummah*',[9] from a bottom-up transformation starting with the spiritual education of the individual. To accomplish such a transformation, 'instead of leading to a sudden revolutionary transformation, these movements often both coexist and compete with the dominant social arrangement'.[10] In this, they do not simply aim 'at capturing state power [...] but focus on the gradual capture and possession of the society by exerting moral and intellectual leadership over civil institutions and processes'.[11] The belief is that once such a transformation takes place, the new Islamic state will form itself naturally. As Muhammad Abduh, the influential Islamic political thinker of the nineteenth century, explains with an analogy to the French Revolution:

> The shift of the government of France, for example, from an absolute monarchy [...] to a free republic, did not occur by the will of those in authority alone. Rather, the strongest contributing factors were the conditions of the people, the increase in their level of thought, and their new awareness.[12]

Hence, for grassroots movements 'a true revolution [...] is not just winning state power but winning society by institutional, intellectual, and moral hegemony'.¹³ According to Wickham, this resembles a Gramscian understanding of change wherein 'cultural and ideological change can pave the way for change in relations of power by undermining the legitimacy of ruling institutions and elites and justifying collective resistance to them'.¹⁴ To start this transformation these movements adapt an organisation, prioritising mass recruitment at the local level. Such a mass organisation, however, does not necessarily indicate a loose organisation. On the contrary, most grassroots organisations are structured to carry out their mass recruitment and grassroots mobilisation efforts.

As a result of such varying perspectives to Islamic revival, grassroots and vanguard movements evaluate the costs and benefits of participation vis-à-vis non-participation differently. Foremost, this study expects vanguard movements to value the benefits of participation in party politics over its costs in light of their strategic aim to revive Islam top-down under the leadership of their vanguards. Why? Because, ideologically, participation allows vanguard movements to socially engineer society through the state top-down by using the state's resources and institutions. Moreover, because in the long run vanguard movements count on governing the country, they believe that participation is a good medium to gain experience in actual (as opposed to idealistic) politics and to test the adaptability and popularity of their policies. Thus, participation creates a win-win situation for vanguard movements allowing them short- and long-term benefits to turn their top-down vision into reality.

Organisationally, because vanguard movements' organisations start from a small group of Islamic vanguards, they do not need to worry about preserving strong internal ties, as there is no significant supporter base to begin with. Hence, their calculations revolve around winning new supporters. Thus participation is a strong medium to connect these Islamic vanguards with the masses and to thereby create a new societal base, by allowing vanguard movements to increase their public visibility, platform, and access to state resources. It is also important to note here that in political parties the leadership (the vanguard) controls the party platform. Hence, a political party not only offers vanguard movements the chance to win new supporters but also the opportunity to do so while preserving the party itself for the Islamic vanguard, who trains and guides the masses.¹⁵ Lastly, vanguard movements also do not see co-optation of their ideals, the major risk of participation, as a possibility because they believe their vanguards, composed of a small and exclusive organisation, are impenetrable and thus immune to co-optation.

In contrast to vanguard movements, this study expects grassroots movements to value the benefits of non-participation in party politics over its costs in light of their strategic aim to gradually transform the society through grassroots activities. Ideologically, grassroots movements aim at the bottom-up creation of a counter-hegemonic Islamic community. Nonetheless, such an Islamic counter-hegemony by definition is hard to create by being involved with the state where the rules are set by the state, by 'the hegemon'. Thus, staying outside the formal realm of politics enables grassroots movements to challenge the hegemon independently. Moreover, grassroots movements are not interested in gaining political experience in office in the short-run, because they already are in constant interaction with the people through their grassroots activism, and thus believe that they already have a sense of how people will receive their politics.

Organisationally, grassroots movements prioritise preserving strong internal ties because their aim is the creation of a powerful Muslim community that stands in solidarity against external challengers. Nonetheless, forming a party is a danger to the internal cohesion of a movement because party politics often creates internal fragmentations in its temptations for power. It also bureaucratises relations within the movement leading to departures. Meanwhile, staying as a movement and eschewing party politics allows a movement to preserve its organisational solidarity outside the fragmenting forces of party politics and instead allows the movement to concentrate on building personal and thus stronger relations between its leaders and followers. It also allows grassroots Islamic movements to socialise their followers from an early age into their worldview thereby solidifying internal relations of the organisation to withstand external pressures.

Lastly, grassroots movements, given their political experiences as a result of 'working day and night organising grassroots activities, integrating new members, preparing for the future'[16] and as a result of constant regime repression, do not believe they will assume a 'wait-and-see stance' since non-participation involves the continuation of their ongoing efforts and suppression is not a new cost. Rather, co-optation is a greater risk in their view since

Table 3.1 Independent Variables and Expectations

	Vanguard Movements	**Grassroots Movements**
Ideological Priorities	Social engineering under the vanguards	Gradual transformation of the society through grassroots activism starting at the individual level
Organisational Needs	Small leadership cadre, the 'vanguards', in need of connecting with the masses	Mass movement seeking to consolidate internal ties
Expected Political Behaviour	Participation in party politics	Non-participation in party politics

party politics involves pragmatism and moderation towards an embrace of the status quo, and in this, risks alienating ideologically motivated supporters, who form the core base of the movement.

To address these expectations (Table 3.1) empirically, the remainder of this chapter will look at the similarities and variations in Islamic movement behaviour in regards to party politics in Morocco, Turkey, and Jordan.

Morocco

In the late 1990s, when the Moroccan monarchy was preparing for a smooth royal succession, the regime approached two Islamic movements in the country inviting them to participate in electoral politics. By doing so, the regime aimed to bring Islamic opposition into its institutional framework and thus under its supervision. While the Movement for Unity and Reform embraced this offer, the Justice and Spirituality Movement rejected it.

Movement for Unity and Reform

The leaders of the incumbent Party for Justice and Development (PJD) (*Parti de la Justice et du Développement* or *Hizb al-Adala wa Tanmia*) today were once part of a small, exclusive, and violent organisation called the 'Islamic Youth' that terrorised the Moroccan Left in the late 1960s. This movement was an 'illegal political movement' under the leadership of Abdulkarim Muti[17] aiming to fight atheism and leftist groups[18] by mobilising university students.[19] Influential Egyptian political thinker Sayyid Qutb, who advocated fighting those in a state of ignorance, inspired the Islamic Youth.[20] As such, the leaders of the Islamic Youth believed that the Moroccan regime, in a state of ignorance, was oppressing the people, and thus that it needed to be taken down under their vanguards.[21] Unlike Qutb, however, the Islamic Youth believed that the nation as a whole was *not* in a state of ignorance and therefore that the nation could not be accused of apostasy. Rather, they believed that the nation was largely composed of those who were oppressed by a corrupt power. To counter the state's 'ignorance', they proposed to lead a battle against those who governed[22] where the use of violence was a legitimate tool.[23] In this, they believed that the masses would eventually follow them once they took control of the state apparatus.

Organisationally, the Islamic Youth attempted a top-down revolution under its vanguards. The Supreme Guide controlled decision-making, recruitment, and training.[24] In this organisational structure, one could not join the Movement unless the Supreme Guide confirmed your membership.[25] Under the Supreme Guide, the Movement also had a dual structure: (1) a militant wing composed of paramilitaries trained in martial arts and weapons handling, and (2) a preaching wing consisting of professors, teachers, students, workers, and artisans, who were not involved in violent activities.[26] The militant wing was composed of activists organised into cells.[27] Each cell was headed by a 'board' that was chaired by one 'inspector' who was in turn subject to the authority of the 'group leader'.[28] Each team leader was subject to the power of the movement leader – the Supreme Guide.[29] Today's core PJD leaders were part of the latter preaching wing responsible for spreading the message of the movement: Abdelilah Benkirane, the current head of the PJD and former Prime Minister, was a major recruiter, Saadeddine Othmani, former chairman of the PJD and current Prime Minister, was an ideologue, and Mustafa Ramid, a long-time member of the PJD and the current Minister of Justice, was a university activist for the Islamic Youth.[30]

Within this framework, the Islamic Youth took a violent path and got involved in the assassination of a known leftist trade unionist, Omar Benjolloun, in 1975. In 1976, the Movement was banned, and its key leadership was imprisoned, resulting in the Movement's disintegration. According to a former member of the Islamic Youth's preaching wing and current PJD leader, they split from the Islamic Youth because (1) there was no internal democracy under Muti's strict control, and because (2) the Movement had radicalised.³¹ Some of these splinters under the direction of Abdelilah Benkirane (the current head of the PJD and the former Prime Minister of Morocco), Mohammed Yatim (member of the Parliament and the PJD General Secretariat), Abdellah Baha (late Minister of State from the PJD), and Saadeddine Othmani (former head of the PJD and current Prime Minister of Morocco), formed a new movement under the name 'Islamic Society' in 1981–1982.³² In this new Movement, in contrast to the Islamic Youth, they advocated collective action instead of a single leader and denounced violence.³³ Later, they changed their name to the 'Movement for Reform and Renewal' to get rid of all Islamic associations.³⁴

Ideologically, the Movement did 'not follow a uniform line of thought',³⁵ and instead has been composed of various political trajectories and pragmatic decisions.³⁶ At the core of this general discourse has been a 'culturally, socially and religiously conservative organisation focusing much of its energy on social justice and on combating corruption as well as on highly symbolic issues within the socio-cultural domain (combating alcohol, prostitution, homosexuality)'.³⁷ Hence, the Movement focused on law, behaviour,³⁸ and issues of social justice, development, and institutional reform.³⁹ In this, the group, unlike its predecessors in the Islamic Youth, did not want to establish an Islamic state but instead, according to Ahmed Raissouni,⁴⁰ one of the ideologues of the Movement, aimed at societal reform. In their 1989 charter, the Movement announced its key ideological objectives as:

(1) to renew the understanding of religion,
(2) to call for respect of individual rights and public freedoms,
(3) to advocate the implementation of *Sharia*,
(4) to improve Muslims' material and living conditions,
(5) to perform charitable work,
(6) to achieve a comprehensive cultural resistance,
(7) to work on accomplishing the unity of Muslims,
(8) to confront ideologies and ideas that are subversive to Islam, and
(9) to raise the Moroccan people's educational and moral levels.⁴¹

With these ideological objectives, the Movement aimed to take the lead in reviving Islam.

Organisationally, this newly reformed movement 'never had one clear leading voice. Rather, the Movement was constituted of a rather large group of prominent individuals and organisations, which came together in a hybrid organisation over time'.[42] In 1994, other smaller Islamic movements joined the Movement for Reform and Renewal: (1) the Islamic Preaching Movement, a movement active since 1976 in Fez under the leadership of Abdeslam Al Harass, (2) the Islamic Association of Ksar El Kebir, a movement active since 1976 under the leadership of Ahmed Raissouni, and (3) the Islamic Dawn Association, a former splinter of the Islamic Youth Movement.[43] As a result, this was 'a network of at least two hundred Islamic associations',[44] which aimed to cut ties with their violent past in the Islamic Youth. In 1996, this 'umbrella' movement altered its name to the Movement for Unity and Reform (MUR)[45] (*Mouvement de L'Unicité et de la Réforme* or *Harakat al-Tawhid Wal Islah*) to signal 'unity' amongst these various groups.[46] Furthermore, by shedding direct Islamic references in their name, according to a Moroccan scholar of Islamic movements, they also wanted to disassociate themselves from the violent civil war in neighbouring Algeria and the Islamic party (Islamic Salvation Front) there and thus to avoid potential regime repressions.[47]

Coming from such a background, the MUR sought to participate in electoral politics. Participation was an ideological fit for the MUR's top-down vision of change, because for the MUR the real problem in Morocco was its Western-trained elite at the top of the regime. Thus, the Movement, in the words of a Minister from the PJD, believed that their job was 'to give priority to the *country's elite*' by 'hold[ing] Morocco's Westernized elites accountable to Islam'.[48] This in turn would 'allow society to have a new elite that could resolve and contribute in (sic) the resolving of economic and social crises'.[49] Within this understanding, MUR's first step was to gain experience in political office. Ahmed Raissouni, who was one of the first leaders within the Islamic Youth to advocate legalisation and non-violence, explained: '[Islamic movements] produced masses of supporters, fighters, and resisters but they produced little knowledge, experience, and efficiency for exercising politics and rule'.[50] Hence, participation would allow the MUR to correct this historical mistake. Moreover, participation, according to another Minister from the PJD, would give the MUR the opportunity to gain such experience by getting involved in top-down influence and by having influence over legislation, policy formulation, and the executive.[51] As a result, the Movement, according to a PJD leader, believed societal reform could only be achieved under their guidance by influencing policy, by sitting in the parliament, by holding higher posts of power, and by forming the new elites of Morocco.[52]

Through such access and influence, the MUR would also accomplish its organisational aim of connecting its vanguards with new societal constituents. Specifically, by becoming publicly visible through party politics, the MUR would be able to introduce its vanguards to the Moroccan public. In this, the leaders of the MUR believed that they could come out of the 'underground' and become a *public* opposition by forming a political party.[53] In 1992, the rejected party application of the Movement for Reform and Renewal for the 'National Revival Party' may give a further indication of the popular base of the MUR at the time. This proposed party's central committee had thirty-four members, twenty-four of whom were teachers and seven university professors.[54] These founders were engaged in sixteen different cities, where Casablanca and Rabat comprised a third of the workforce.[55] Moreover, twenty-five of the thirty-four were born after independence, so this was a younger movement.[56] Given such an urban, young, and educated supporter base, the MUR needed public visibility to reach beyond Casablanca and Rabat into the rural areas of the country, where illiteracy and tribalism were the defining characteristics.

Participation would also allow the Movement to reform the state from within without risking political instability or political marginalisation because participation would re-establish the Movement as a 'loyal opposition' that would not repeat the mistakes of its Algerian counterpart and that would not carry Morocco into political uncertainty. Mistrust was at the root of the problem in Algeria: state elites did not trust the Islamists because the Islamists had not guaranteed them the preservation of their privileges. Hence, the MUR needed to avoid such relationships of mistrust. In this, according to a Minister from the PJD, they had realised that the political elites of Morocco did not trust the MUR while party formation was a way to overcome this mistrust.[57] In this reasoning, it is important to note the radical and violent history of the MUR going back to the Islamic Youth that raised serious questions about the Movement's intentions and reliability as a moderated group. Thus, participation offered the MUR the opportunity to become an opposition that did not threaten the stability of the country yet that also aimed to break the monopoly of the *Makhzen* and its elitism. In other words, participation offered the MUR the opportunity to engage in politics without risking repression or stagnancy.

Evaluating the costs of participation further, the Movement assessed the experiences of the Moroccan Left, of the National Union of Popular Forces (*Union Nationale des Forces Populaires* – UNFP), a leftist group aiming at radical and revolutionary change in Morocco in the 1960s. In the 1970s, this group had split into two. While one group had continued to advocate for radical/revolutionary change, the other group had formed a centre-left party under the banner of the 'Socialist Union of Popular Forces' (*Union Socialiste des Forces Populaires* – USFP). By the 1980s, while the radical group was heavily repressed and driven underground, the USFP had won a firm oppositional stance for itself within the Moroccan parliament. Because those segments of the Left which did not participate ended up being politically marginalised and because those that did form a party 'succeeded in widening [their supporter base], developing positions in the society and reflecting what the Moroccan society is looking for',[58] the Movement, per a PJD leader, concluded that non-participation risked political stagnancy. A member of the Parliament from the PJD explains:

> To participate is the only way to improve things. If you choose not to participate, you cannot have an influence on the regime. People who decide not to participate are the ones who are waiting for something to change. However, if you stand by, nothing will change.[59]

The Movement also dismissed the risk of co-optation. Farid al-Ansari, a prominent member of the MUR at the time and a religious scholar, criticised the decision to participate by stating that politics would spoil the religious mission of the Movement.[60] Ignoring such voices, the Movement, according to a high-ranking leader of the MUR, decided that it was time to become 'more realistic' and to 'stop dreaming of how Morocco should be'.[61] All in all, the strategic benefits of participation, such as widening the Movement's mass base and reforming the state from within, outweighed the cost of participation, namely the risk of co-optation.

In 1992, the MUR first proposed to form the 'National Revival Party'.

However, the regime rejected this proposal.[62] In 1996, a new opportunity emerged for the MUR as the regime, in a quest to secure a smooth royal succession, approached the Movement. The regime wanted to integrate the MUR into the party system as part of a minor, somewhat defunct, but loyal political party, the Popular Democratic Constitutional Movement Party (*Mouvement Populaire Démocratique et Constitutionnel*). The MUR accepted this proposal, and in 1998, MUR leaders renamed the Party the 'Party for Justice and Development (PJD) (*Parti de la Justice et du Développement or Hizb al-Adala wa Tanmia*) taking full control of it. The MUR's counterpart, the Justice and Spirituality Movement, however, disagreed with MUR's political calculations despite facing the same potential risks and benefits of party politics and despite receiving a better offer from the Moroccan regime to form a political party.

Justice and Spirituality Movement

Unlike the MUR, which is a fusion of various ideologues and leaders, the Justice and Spirituality Movement is the brainchild of Abdessalam Yassine, who synthesised Maghrebi Sufism and political activism[63] under a new ideology called 'the prophetic way'.[64] Formerly, Yassine was a school inspector and a student of Hajj al-Abbas at the *Boutchichiyya* Sufi Brotherhood. However, to walk his 'prophetic way', Yassine first left the *Boutchichiyya* Brotherhood (not Sufism),[65] where his political actions were limited.[66] Later on, in 1974, he came to public light when he sent the late King of Morocco, Hassan II, a 120-page public letter stating that deviation from Islam had led to decay in the Muslim World and that once the rightful Caliph would come back, he would restore equality in the society. Moreover, Yassine accused the King of leading an un-Islamic regime and refused to accept the King's role as the 'Commander of the Believers', for which he was put into an insane asylum for three and a half years (1974–1977).[67] In this, unlike MUR's predecessor, the Islamic Youth, Yassine never called for the use of violence in his critique of the Moroccan monarchy.

After his release, Yassine started publishing his first magazine, *Al-Jamaa* [The Society],[68] which would be banned in 1983. In 1981, he started an Islamic movement, and in 1982, he requested legal status for this Movement. This application was rejected because the movement 'mixe[d] religion with politics'⁶⁹ – a role that only the King could play as the Commander of the Believers. 'In December 1983, Yassine tried to publish another newspaper entitled *Al-Subḥ* [The Dawn], but this, too, was immediately banned, and he was sentenced to two years in prison. He was released in January 1986'.⁷⁰ After that, the Moroccan regime banned Yassine from preaching in mosques. Regardless, Yassine continued to build up his movement, and in 1987, the movement acquired its current name, the Justice and Spirituality Movement (JSM) (*Al-Adl wal-Ihsane*). The name summarised Yassine's dual goals of spiritual education and political activism.⁷¹ In response, in 1989, the regime put Yassine under house arrest and banned visitations to his house.

Through these engagements, Yassine, unlike the leaders of the MUR, who heavily borrowed their ideology from Qutb and Algerian Islamists, formulated a *new* Islamic discourse synthesising various schools of thought. Foremost, Yassine's ideology had roots in Maghrebi Sufism wherein 'popular forms of practices (*maraboutism*) and religious brotherhoods known as *zawaya* ... played important social and political roles for much of Moroccan history'.⁷² Historically, Sufi Brotherhoods at times challenged and on other occasions cooperated with the ruling elites. They also garnered widespread popularity by organising 'individual lives and rituals' and by 'offer[ing] social services'.⁷³ Thus, Yassine's ideology had roots in this particular brand of Maghrebi Sufism wherein Yassine often used Sufi terminology,⁷⁴ and he was considered by his followers to be a 'living saint'.⁷⁵

Going beyond Maghrebi Sufism, Yassine, inspired by the Muslim Brotherhood and its founder Hassan al-Banna, also encouraged political activism and resistance.⁷⁶ Hence, Yassine differed from the leaders of the MUR in going back to al-Banna rather than adapting Qutb, whose ideas were very popular across the Arab world at the time. As a result, according to Lauzière, Yassine was neither a Sufi nor a Salafi but a leader 'who strive[d] to merge two religious styles in an attempt to walk the surest path between the mystical and the legal dimensions of Islam'.⁷⁷ Yassine called this middle way the 'prophetic method' because he believed, like 'Muhammad [who] interpreted and applied God's laws [and] simultaneously cultivated his people's spirituality' that 'one must combine Sufi spirituality and Salafi legalism to revive Islam and to respond to the problems of the contemporary *umma*'.⁷⁸

Within this formulation, Yassine believed that 'contemporary Muslim societies have been de-Islamicised by imported ideologies and values as well as the monarchy, which he view[ed] as enabling social and moral disorder'.[79] In this, he believed that 'the contemporary *umma* suffer[ed] from a disease [through which] its body was ailing because its spirit [was] sick',[80] and proposed a four stage transformation to remedy this ailment. In this way, Yassine believed that the Muslim community's 'rising out of its political, economic and cultural backwardness and subjugation' would start with the 'spiritual education' of the individual.[81] Thus, per Yassine, 'education' was their 'profession and [...] means for changing people'.[82] This first stage was followed by an 'organisation' stage, wherein the Movement organised grassroots activities across the country to widen its mass appeal. For Yassine, community and community building were of utmost importance as 'a man without [community], without companionship and without a guide, [was] a lost man'.[83] This approach stood in contrast to the MUR, which focused on overtly political issues rather than the spiritual transformation of the individual.

The third stage, the 'propagation' stage, involved a constant engagement with the community to 'liberate and educate the Muslim Mind'.[84] In this stage, JSM followers taught JSM's vision to others.[85] The JSM also engaged in civil disobedience to propagate societal awareness in this stage. For instance, Abdessalam Yassine's daughter Nadia Yassine gave an interview in which she criticised hereditary monarchy and called for a republican form of government. Even though she was never imprisoned for these words, she risked imprisonment with this interview given that criticising the monarchy was (is) punishable by law. Hence, while the MUR was trying to appease the Moroccan regime to prove that it has cut all its ties to the radical Islamic Youth, the JSM, through these propagation activities, was challenging the Moroccan regime by raising mass awareness about the corrupt nature of the Moroccan regime. The Movement believed that once Moroccan society gains awareness, a bottom-up mass 'uprising', the last stage in the JSM's vision, wherein Moroccans would demand the non-violent reconstitution of the regime, would be inevitable.[86]

Organisationally, various committees carried out this grassroots plan. The Executive Committee provided the political and organisational direction of the Movement, whereas the Guidance Committee provided spiritual guidance.[87] In this, according to a veteran Moroccan scholar of Political Islam, having a charismatic leader like Yassine unified the political vision of the Movement and gave the Movement its organisational strength to efficiently execute its ideology.[88] Under Yassine's leadership, decisions within the Movement were taken by vote. The Movement first discussed the issues at hand and then voted on them. This process of debating and voting was called *Shura* [consultation]. According to a JSM youth leader, *Shura* was better than democracy because while democracy was based on conflict Shura was based on building strong bonds of brotherhoods between members.[89] Furthermore, the JSM did not claim that it had the 'right' Islam interpretation. According to a high-ranking JSM leader they did 'not claim that [they were] representing Islam. No interpretation [was] absolute. We should debate, and the majority decides. Imposing ideas does not work. We have seen this in the USSR experience'.[90] Such an internally democratic organisation stood in contrast to the MUR, which to this day remains under the control of a few leaders.

Meanwhile, the financing of the Movement was self-sufficient and did not involve foreign financing. Every member either contributed according to their material capabilities or served in an intellectual capacity. For instance, teachers who have no significant material resources contributed to the Movement by educating new members.[91] In this, the Movement engaged in community building and relied on seventy provincial branches all over Morocco to elect almost all of the members of the General Secretary. Furthermore, the 'political circle' under the General Secretary, 'train[ed] potential political activists, conduct[ed] research and prepare[d] programmes that propose viable alternatives'.[92] As a result, according to an expert on Moroccan Islamic movements, the real strength of the JSM was its organisation: the group was so well organised everywhere that Yassine's ideology was efficiently executed through grassroots activities throughout the country.[93] In this, JSM was a coherent group organised through grassroots activism and around Yassine, while the MUR remained an umbrella organisation bringing various smaller actors together.

Given such political activism, in 1990, the Movement was officially outlawed. After that, movement–regime relations followed a particular trend. The regime first showed its 'tolerance' by releasing JSM members. However, when socio-economic crises hit, the regime, to protect itself from the popularisation of Yassine's criticism, imprisoned members, who were released a few years later, restarting the whole process.[94] Members of the Movement were imprisoned despite the public rhetoric of democratisation.

Meanwhile, according to Abdelkébir Alaoui M'Daghri, the Minister of Religious Affairs between 1985 and 2002, the Moroccan regime, to ensure a smooth royal succession, approached Yassine:

> In 1990, I asked Hassan II authorization to begin negotiations with them. As you know, 'the board of guidance' was entirely in prison. Abdessalam Yassine was under house arrest. The King gave me the green light. A committee was established for this purpose; we took the committee with Yassine and us went to Salé prison. The negotiations began after mid-afternoon and ended after dawn, during several days. [95]

The regime proposed to give the Movement many privileges, such as ministry positions, financial help, and legal status if the Movement would accept the King's religious and political legitimacy as the Commander of the Believers.[96] Similarly, one of the members of the JSM's board of guidance who was in prison at the time, recalls that there were two meetings with the regime: the first one took place with people from the *Makhzen* and the second one took place with people from the Interior and Religious Ministries.[97] Yassine refused to negotiate stating that he would first need to talk to his Board of Guidance, all of whom were in prison at the time.[98] After their consultation, the JSM, in contrast to the MUR, rejected this proposal and has continued to do so to this day.

The JSM, like the MUR, looked at the same potential costs and benefits of party politics, but, unlike the MUR, found party politics to be counterproductive to its four-stage grassroots transformation plan. The Movement, as a grassroots organisation dedicated to the promotion of a 'Sharia-abiding type of mysticism that is also concerned with the welfare of hearts and souls',[99] believed that 'the socio-political projects of Qutb and al-Mawdudi [had] failed to become mass movements because they neglected [spiritual guidance]'.[100] Thus, while the MUR saw opportunities to gain political influence and experience in party politics, for the JSM party formation risked minimising the Movement's dedication to spiritual education by diverting the Movement's efforts into party politics. Instead, they wanted to focus on a more wholesale transformation. In Nadia Yassine's words, Islam's original message was to bring 'universal spirituality and social equity with multiple applications'.[101]

Furthermore, the JSM believed that Muslim societies were in decadence both at the individual and at the government levels.[102] In this, after the death of Prophet Mohamed, Islam was 'taken as a hostage by political power and was made to serve the cause of tyrants with the complicity, conscious or unconscious, of a particular jurisprudence'.[103] Starting with the Umayyad dynasty, the situation had led to 'a legal and political system legitimising autocracy, depriving them of any political culture and excluding them from any voluntarist initiative'.[104] Within this understanding, the existing political system including the party system with its elitism under the King and the *Makhzen*, was insufficient to offer a solution to this political decay. Hence, while the MUR aimed to make this elitist system more inclusive by forming a new elite for Morocco, the JSM aimed to fundamentally alter this elitist system by demanding a new constitution where the King was not above but under the law and was accountable to the people.[105]

Yassine also believed that the ballot box on its own was insufficient to solve this contemporary crisis because what Morocco needed was not exclusive parliamentary discussions behind closed doors but open public debates informing the public.[106] Hence, Yassine argued that 'the work of education and changing outlooks and attitudes [was] not a matter for improvising', and 'inventing the future and the form of power require[d] not some simple election platform or elaborate government programme, but long-distance vision and a plan for a society that meets permanent needs'.[107] Consequently, party politics, according to Yassine, did not offer a genuine change/reform in Morocco but working outside the system through hard work and dedication did.[108]

The JSM also found party politics to be a danger to its grassroots organisational needs, because party politics endangered the internal cohesion the Movement had built over the years. The JSM was engaged in various grassroots activities, such as in 'assisting the sick, the widowed and the unemployed [...] run[ning] blood banks and help[ing] people organise funerals'.[109] In this, according to a JSM leader, the Movement was following a strategy of mass recruitment through (1) direct action on the ground, (2) its affiliated branches at the local level, and through (3) its youth, women, and worker sub-branches.[110] As a result of their spiritual education and grassroots activism, according to Nadia Yassine, the Movement, unlike the MUR, had already built a mass following over the years, and was appealing to the middle classes[111] with higher levels of education.[112] Therefore, the Movement was already appealing to new constituents as a social movement outside the system. This organisational strength was the reason why the Moroccan regime wanted to integrate the JSM into the system, but also why the Movement found party politics to be strategically futile. Party politics not only threatened to subject the Movement's mass base to the fragmenting political climate of the Moroccan party system but also risked losing oppositional integrity. In this, unlike the MUR and its aim to establish relations of trust as a former radical movement by becoming a loyal opposition within the party system, the JSM aimed to protect the trust between the Movement's leadership and its followers by staying out of the fragmenting context of Moroccan party politics. As a result, party formation was not only unnecessary for the Movement's dedication to promoting spirituality but also counterproductive to it. After all, it was the JSM's 'outsider' stance that attracted old and new supporters, as Nadia Yassine explains:

> However, what constitutes our force is the fact that we have decided to remain outside the system ... if our discourse continues to be credible for the Moroccan youth it is because it is clear that the real opposition is the one that operates outside this locked system.[113]

As a result, participation offered the JSM neither the ability to preserve its internal solidarity nor the opportunity to draw new supporters.

On top of all, the cost of non-participation, namely political stagnancy as a result of political marginalisation, was not a vital threat for the JSM. Foremost, repression was not a new cost because repression was the Movement's status quo. According to a JSM leader, 200 organisations linked to the JSM were closed down, and JSM newspapers and meetings were banned.[114] Furthermore, gaining political experience was not limited to the electoral sphere for the JSM, as members were actively involved in grassroots politics nationwide and thus were gaining political experience first-hand. Instead, the real danger for the JSM was co-optation. According to a youth leader of the JSM, the regime for decades had used political participation to weaken the opposition.[115] In this, the regime would first oppress the opposition by denying them every constitutional right. Then the regime would propose conditional political participation to the opposition, asking them to accept the King's legitimacy as the Commander of the Believers – a condition that would mean putting any actual 'opposition' to the regime aside. Within this understanding, JSM's differing interpretation of the Moroccan Left's experience compared to the MUR's interpretation is very telling. For the JSM, the Left, before participation, represented a robust and genuine opposition. However, after participation, according to Nadia Yassine, they transformed from 'warrior knights into doormats'.[116] Hence, the JSM feared the same fate awaited them if they were to participate. In the words of a JSM leader:

> The idea of participating and changing the system from within is good in the abstract. However, in practice, it does not work. We have seen this in the experience of the Left, which used the same approach of working from within. Do you expect the same from us? Instead, they have lost credibility and trust of the people.[117]

In the JSM's perception, royal succession had not changed this process either. Their motto was 'a person died, but the system is still the same'.[118] Rather, 'elections [were not] important events in Morocco, being, in fact, a staging'.[119] Therefore, they believed participation would not diminish repression but only co-opt the Movement and divert it from its dedication to religious education and grassroots political activism. Nadia Yassine explains:

> Co-opting is a classic in politics. As soon as a political force that has a popular base emerges, and I believe that [the JSM] is the only real political entity in Morocco that has a genuine popular base, the power does everything to neutralize it. The *Makhzen* tries to involve its opponents by including them in a system that is locked, and where the rules are imposed by a system of laws but also by a *Makhzenian* ritual. For me there are no parties and royal prerogative, both are sides of the same coin; just as there are no executive and legislative powers. Parties see us as rivals to the extent that we interfere with the role that is officially assigned to them. The recent elections showed

how great their debacle is. We surely do not want to resume their roadmap, which was proven to be a deadlock.[120]

Therefore, the JSM, unlike the MUR, believed that remaining outside the system, engaging in spiritual education, and challenging the regime's hegemony externally through grassroots activism would eventually lead to a new era.

Like the JSM, the Gülen Movement in Turkey pursued a similar political path of non-participation despite facing a democratic multi-party system, while the Gülen Movement's counterpart in Turkey, the National Outlook Movement, pursued party politics.

Turkey

As with the mid-1990s in Morocco, Turkish politics in the mid-1960s was at a crossroads. Although secular establishments were losing their strength in party politics to new centre-right parties, they also were not taking a backseat, intervening both through the military and the judiciary in party politics. Meanwhile, new calls for religious expressions, such as the right to wear the veil at universities, were becoming more visible. It is in such a socio-political context that two Islamic movements, the National Outlook Movement and the Gülen Movement, both of which would define Turkish politics for the last four decades, emerged and pursued different political paths.

National Outlook Movement

The National Outlook Movement (*Milli Görüş Hareketi*) brought together the *Nakşibendi* Order, a religious organisation 'hierarchically organised around a *sheikh* [teacher] and submission to him [... with ...] centuries-long existence and broad geographic presence in Turkey',[121] and Islamic parliamentarians working from within existing centre-right parties, all of whom were disappointed with governing centre-right parties of the time (mid-1960s) to represent their Islamic demands. At the time, the *Nakşibendi* Order, especially its *İskenderpaşa* Lodge in Istanbul, was economically the most powerful religious order in Turkey but lacked political power.[122] It had been active in Turkey since the fifteenth century, but different from its historical clientele, it had started attracting urban elites alienated by Westernisation offering them spiritual guidance.[123] In 1952, Mehmed Zahid Kotku had become the leader of the *Iskenderpaşa* Lodge and was aiming to turn the Order from 'a mosque-based community into a semi-political movement'.[124] Thus, in his collected sermons 'Jihad' and 'Qualities of the Believer', he expressed his belief that 'Muslims should try to capture the higher summits of social and political institutions in their country and to establish control over the society',[125] and encouraged his supporters to permeate state institutions to do so. Hence, unlike the leader of the Islamic Youth, Muti, who was aiming to take over the Moroccan state by violence at around the same time, Kotku was advising infiltration of the state through non-violent means.

To this end, Kotku had first sought out the support of right-wing parties. This would also help in the protection of the Order from Turkey's militantly secular laws outlawing religious activities. This arrangement had worked perfectly under the Democrat Party (*Demokrat Parti*), which was the major right-wing party of the 1950s.[126] As a result, by the 1960s, Kotku's supporters were active in all levels of the State Planning Organisation, a key organisation advising the executive on matters of economic and social development policies and staffing municipalities.[127] Within the State Planning Organisation, according to a high-ranking National Outlook Movement leader, they were referred to as the '*Takunyalılar*',[128] literally 'those wearing wooden clogs', because men, like women wearing the veil to show their piousness, were wearing wooden clogs both while entering a mosque and their office in order to carry their political views into the public space and thereby to make a public statement. However, under the Justice Party (*Adalet Partisi*), a new right-wing party influential in the 1960s and 1970s that adapted a liberal pro-Western agenda, Islamic demands were neglected and marginalised at higher institutional levels. Hence, the *Nakşibendi* Order had to start searching for an alternative to the Justice Party to bolster the Order's goal of permeating state institutions.

In the meantime, Islamic parliamentarians working from within existing centre-right parties, such as Hasan Aksay, Arif Hikmet Güner, Süleyman Arif Emre, Fehmi Cumalıoğlu, and Ekrem Ocaklı, were also increasingly marginalised by the same Justice Party, according to one of the founders of the National Outlook Movement, and thus were also searching for an alternative to it.[129] In particular, in 1968, Hatice Babacan, a student of Theology, had been suspended from Ankara University because she was taking her classes with a veil.

This event had triggered many Islamic groups in Turkey to claim that the Justice Party's government was repressing Muslim beliefs.[130] Although mass protests took place in major cities, the Justice Party government had done nothing to ease these Islamic tensions. Furthermore, there were rumours at the time that Süleyman Demirel, the leader of the Justice Party, was a freemason, and that he was recruiting other Freemasons in places of power at the expense of Islamist and nationalist wings within the Justice Party.[131] Watching these developments closely, these Islamic parliamentarians, like their Moroccan counterparts within the MUR, believed that they, as a vanguard group, had a duty to stop such Westernisation and demoralisation of the Turkish state under the Justice Party.[132]

First, these Islamic parliamentarians attempted to form an alternative coalition to the Justice Party within the parliament. They estimated they could gather close to 100 deputies supporting their Islamic agenda[133] and believed they could even take over the administration of the Justice Party with this many deputies.[134] However, Demirel, the leader of the Justice Party, fearing his position within the Party, blocked this initiative by marginalising and banishing the Islamic parliamentarians from the Justice Party, buying off some individuals by offering them political favours, and by appointing his own supporters to posts of power within the Party. After witnessing such roadblocks from centre-right parties, in the words of a veteran parliamentarian from the NOM, Islamic parliamentarians were realising that '[their] split and decentralised stance had no benefit for [their] cause at all'.[135]

Throughout these developments, in 1969, a new political figure, Necmettin Erbakan, a young mechanical engineer and a pupil of Kotku,[136] was on his way to becoming a public figure, when he, with the support of small town merchants, was first elected the head of the Union of Chambers and Commodity Exchanges (*Türkiye Odalar ve Borsalar Birliği*), the highest legal entity in Turkey representing the private sector, and then ousted from this elected position by the governing Justice Party.[137] This new public presence would result in Erbakan's leadership of a new movement, the National Outlook Movement (NOM) (*Milli Görüş Hareketi*).[138] The idea behind the formation of the NOM was that Erbakan would be the young, charismatic leader and the public face of this new Islamic movement along with the Islamic parliamentarians. This way, the NOM would be able to overcome the legal (laic) barriers to the *Nakşibendi*

Order's politicisation.[139] In the late 1980s, the then-leader of the Iskenderpaşa Lodge, Esad Coşan, in response to being marginalised by Erbakan within the NOM, in a now notorious statement, would recount this hidden and untold story[140] of NOM's early years stating that the NOM had 'started as an action of [the *Nakşibendi*] Order', and that they had 'supported them [the NOM] from head to toe' giving them 'people for their central administration, presidencies, vice-presidencies, [and] youth branches'.[141]

This new Movement, the NOM, was ideologically built around a moral critique of laicism. In this, like the MUR and its opposition to the *Makhzen*, the NOM claimed that Westernisation and thus an alienation from Turkey's traditional Islamic culture was leading to its moral decay. Furthermore, there was an inborn social engineering project at play, in which NOM leaders saw themselves not just as the representatives of the people but rather as vanguards with a mission to awaken an Islamic 'truth' in the people.[142] According to a veteran Turkish journalist, the NOM was adapting an engineering mentality where the strategy was not to bring order to the society, as other political forces in Turkey have historically aimed to do, but to reconstruct/redesign/re-engineer society.[143] Hence, the NOM's aim was not to gradually Islamise society, but to 'make' society Islamic top-down.[144]

In this, the NOM took inspiration from Ottomanism, an ideology that has roots in the late nineteenth century Ottoman Empire. According to Erbakan, the leader of the NOM, 'National Outlook meant the views of our nation. It was the same belief as what was in Mehmed the Conqueror's heart when he conquered Istanbul. Our nation dominated the world for a thousand years with the National Outlook'[145] – a thousand years referring to the Ottoman heritage. In this line of thought, when the Ottoman Empire was in decline in the nineteenth century, Islamic thinkers of the time had concluded that resurrecting Islam could save the Ottoman state, because, in their view, Islam was the only binding glue of the Ottoman state to its subjects. They came to believe that societal change was only possible through the state and thus aimed to take over it, because 'capturing the state would necessarily involve securing control over the society and institutions [...] facilitat[ing] the realisation of social reforms'.[146] Within this understanding, the aim was never to reform the society directly through grassroots activities, but rather to reform the Ottoman state, which in turn would transform the society.[147]

Taking up this Ottomanist ideological framework, the aim, per Erbakan, was to 'bring awareness from the top' to larger segments of the society.[148] For Erbakan, to prevent people from going into wrong directions, to direct them into the NOM, was equivalent to 'compassion', which was a key duty of all practising Muslims.[149] Thus, in Erbakan's view, politics was about people who found their true callings in Islam, prepossessing the society to accept what was right and beneficial in an institutional format.[150] Their mission was not to represent the society but to convince people to come to their ranks.[151] In this, NOM leaders believed their vanguards had 'potential' support in the society, because almost everyone in Turkey was a potential NOM supporter as practising Muslims.[152] Hence, like the MUR, which aimed to get out of the underground and to come into the public light through a political party, the NOM hoped to 'organise' the pious masses through a political party under its vanguards.

To this ideological end, the NOM adapted a vanguard organisation under a small group of close-knit individuals. According to one of the founders of the NOM, this was a movement of 'a few idealists who had decided to start from scratch instead of acting like an orphan looking for shelter' with the mission to stop moral decay in the country.[153] Like the MUR in Morocco, which was formed by smaller Islamic movements joining forces after the radicalisation and fragmentation of the Islamic Youth, the NOM also aimed to bring Islamic leaders together under the NOM umbrella. For this purpose, Erbakan, the leader of the NOM, started visiting the houses of leading Islamic figures, introducing their new Movement to these Islamic elites, according to a NOM founder.[154] He even visited Fethullah Gülen, the leader of the Gülen Movement, to win him over to their cause, but Gülen rejected this offer because he was not interested in party politics. Erbakan, in these meetings, talked about the militant laicism in Turkey and how this was undermining religious freedoms.[155] He explained to these Islamic elites why they needed to voice their demands louder,[156] and suggested to form a new organisation under a political party to unify Islamic elites under the same roof.[157]

For such a vanguard organisation aiming at top-down influence, party formation was an ideological fit because participation, foremost, offered the NOM the chance to affect the state. In this, like the MUR that aimed to become part of Morocco's new elite, the NOM aimed to become part of the Turkish state. Capturing 'the state' in a political context like Turkey was of uttermost importance for Islamists because, as mentioned in earlier chapters, the founders of the Turkish Republic, the Kemalists, had throughout the Republican history used 'the state' to 'civilise' the society. Similarly, the NOM's Ottomanist Islamism also put a high value on 'the state' as a medium of reform. Hence, the common belief in Turkish politics was that whoever controlled the state, also controlled societal transformation, and thus could establish their own ideological hegemony over the society. Consequently, the NOM saw a political party as a direct claim to capturing 'the state'.

Party formation was also an organisational necessity for this vanguard movement. Like the MUR and its limited appeal as a former radical movement, the NOM, as an amalgam of religious orders, had limited societal appeal. Although religious orders, such as the *Nakşibendi* Order, were established centuries ago and were supported by a loyal base, their societal influence remained minimal. Even in their heyday, religious orders had at most a million members, and their numbers were decreasing under the strict laic laws of the country, which banned their legal existence.[158] Hence, a political party was expected to introduce them to a wider audience while preserving the Party itself for the Islamic vanguards. In this, NOM leaders also believed that they would swipe elections immediately through a political party. In almost all of my interviews with the leaders of the NOM, a common theory for why the NOM never attained great power in its early years was that elections were fixed by Western forces who were afraid of the rise of an Islamic party to political authority in a geostrategic country like Turkey. The accuracy of these claims about Western powers is less important than the fact that the leaders of the NOM genuinely believed that they could win elections and thus come into power immediately if they were not 'stopped' by foreign forces.

The biggest cost of participation, co-optation, was not seen as a risk either because the NOM leaders believed the NOM, as a small and tight vanguard movement, would not be co-opted, and that those who were susceptible to co-optation already had bailed out and joined other governing political parties.[159] After all, this was a movement of those that stayed idealistic and rejected the temptations of joining other political forces with actual political power. Consequently, these remaining vanguards, according to a veteran parliamentarian from the NOM, would be able to overcome the limitations of the laic system together in solidarity.[160] In this, like the Moroccan MUR, which feared political marginalisation if it chose not to participate in party politics, the NOM saw party politics as a way to escape the ongoing marginalisation of Islamic leaders and orders within centre-right parties.

As a result of all these ideological and organisational considerations, in 1970, Kotku supported the formation of the National Order Party (*Milli Nizam Partisi*) stating that 'for the government to fall into the hands of its true representatives [...], forming a political party [was] an inevitable historical duty' for them.[161] In accordance, this new Party under Erbakan was formed, according to its first programme, 'to uncover the existing high ethical standards and virtues in the society at the ideational level and make them into reality'.[162] Since then, NOM parties have become a staple in Turkish party politics. The Gülen Movement also became a staple in Turkish politics in the meantime, albeit by following a different political path.

The Gülen Movement

The Gülen Movement (GM), like the NOM, started its activities in the mid-1960s facing the same socio-political opportunity and threat structures of the laic Turkish regime which the NOM met. Like its Moroccan counterpart, the JSM, and its leader Abdessalam Yassine, the GM was established by Fethullah Gülen, a religious scholar who worked for more than twenty years as a state preacher under the Directorate of Religious Affairs (he retired in 1981). Gülen started this Movement by lecturing in the provinces and in the villages of Izmir, the third biggest urban setting in Turkey, where he was appointed as a state preacher (1966–1971). He also arranged meetings in coffee houses, organised summer camps for students, and set up student study and boarding halls in the region with the financial help of the locals.[163] Gülen's speeches were also recorded on tape and video, published as anthologies, and distributed nationwide.[164] According to his biography, 'it is at this point that a particular group of about one hundred people began to be visible' around Gülen.[165] Hence, unlike the NOM, which started as an 'Islamic vanguard's' initiation, the GM started out by attracting everyday people around Fethullah Gülen.

In its early years, the Movement started growing through its educational activities. 'Lighthouses', flats rented or purchased by the GM where students, usually from poor rural families, were allowed to stay during their studies in the city under the guidance of an older brother or sister, formed the cornerstone of the GM's education efforts.[166] Later on, students of these lighthouses would become activists themselves, returning to their hometowns and visiting surrounding towns to spread the Movement in rural areas. Fethullah Gülen in later years would refer to the 'graduates' of these lighthouses as the 'Golden Generation' to adhere to the 'Golden Era' of Islamic civilisation.[167] In the GM's view, this new generation of practising Muslims would form 'a new Turkish-affiliated Muslim elite, well-versed in science and technology, successful in a global free-market economy, yet extremely devout'.[168] In addition to these lighthouses, the Movement, in later years, would expand its educational activities by opening primary and secondary schools and university exam preparatory schools (*dershane*). Hence, like the MUR in Morocco, the GM started its strategy with education.

The graduates of these schools and houses were also subject to suspicion because these students would often end up taking high-level jobs, including high-ranking government jobs.[169] While the GM argued that such a strong presence at various state institutions was a natural result of an altruistic investing in education for decades by the Movement,[170] there were suspicions that such a strong presence within the state was a coordinated effort by the GM to infiltrate public institutions.[171] In the mid-1980s, for instance, the Turkish military dispelled and/or disciplined students at military academies for having ties to the GM because the military suspected that these students were hand-selected and groomed for the military academy by the GM in an attempt to infiltrate the military's highest levels in the long-run.[172] Such relations of distrust and suspicion would follow the GM throughout its evolution.

In addition to its educational activities, what differentiated the GM from other Islamic movements in Turkey and even in the Muslim world was that the Movement diverged from the Islamic norm that pious Muslims should not be invested in worldly matters and not work towards wealth accumulation. Instead, Fethullah Gülen, similar to the logic of the Protestant Ethic, argued for economic development. Within this logic, the GM was in favour of better relations with the West and thus of economic globalisation.[173] As a result, small town businesspeople coming from pious backgrounds, who benefited from economic globalisation, found a natural draw to the GM.[174] These businessmen came from smaller Anatolian cities without connections to state elites and they were similar to Protestant missionaries in their:

> Belief in the individual study of holy scriptures; the urge to live a life of piety and self-sacrifice; the enthusiasm for knowledge in general and knowledge of the natural sciences in particular; the urge to carry this knowledge to others through various educational projects; an enterprising spirit; the urge to do good deeds (activism); and a strong impulse to break open the borders of one's own national milieu to reach out to other countries and places around the globe.[175]

In consequence, unlike the JSM in Morocco, which appealed to the middle classes, the GM came to appeal to pious capitalists, which in return gave the Movement financial independence and backing to support its grassroots activities all across Turkey and beyond.

While Fethullah Gülen's fame and his Movement were growing, his ideological aims remained rather ambiguous over the years. On the one hand, even though Fethullah Gülen himself never was a student of Said Nursi (1878–1960), a prominent Islamic theologian, and Nursi's followers rejected Gülen and his Movement as one of their own, Fethullah Gülen drew inspiration from Said Nursi, who aimed to form 'an Islam that brought all Muslims under the umbrella of a common faith',[176] and who believed in the 'inherent harmony between Islam and modern science, together with an emphatic plea for Muslims to become educated in modern knowledge, albeit with a grounding in Islamic morality'.[177] Within this framework, Gülen, different to the NOM's focus on laicism, envisioned that 'knowledge via education, public consensus via the media and economic power through building competitive companies and financial institutions'[178] would be essential to their mission. In this, Gülen, like Yassine in Morocco and his focus on individual and societal transformation, argued that the 'three greatest enemies' on this path were 'ignorance, poverty, and an internal schism', wherein 'ignorance [could] be defeated through education, poverty through work and the possession of capital, and internal schism and separatism through unity'.[179] On the other hand, however, observers were also questioning the sincerity of these claims and were wondering whether Fethullah Gülen's stated aims of education, economy, and national unity were indeed his ultimate ideological goals or whether they were the means to achieve a long-term systemic change. According to Yavuz, for instance, the 'the strategies and tactics of the Gülen Movement were continuously revised and refined towards the longer-term objective of thorough control'.[180] Furthermore, observers argued that Gülen, in a tape released in the 1990s, which Gülen himself claims to have been fabricated, gave away the Movement's 'unofficial' political agenda:

> You must move in the arteries of the system without anyone noticing your existence until you reach all the power centres [...] until the conditions are ripe, they [the followers] must continue like this. If they do something prematurely, the world will crush our heads, and Muslims will suffer everywhere, like in the tragedies in Algeria, like in 1982 [in] Syria ... like in the yearly disasters and tragedies in Egypt. The time is not yet right. You must wait for the time when you are complete, and conditions are ripe until we can shoulder the entire world and carry it. You must wait until you have gotten all the state power until you have brought to your side all the power of the constitutional institutions in Turkey.[181]

Consequently, the GM's public relations with the Turkish state, political parties, and non-state actors have remained rather ambivalent over the years as political actors across the political spectrum, both at the state and non-state levels, at times saw the GM as a benign movement invested in creating a 'Turkish Islam' in peace with democracy and the West,[182] and at other times, saw the GM as having a hidden agenda to take control of Turkey's sociopolitical institutions.[183] As a result, unlike the NOM leadership, Fethullah Gülen went above and beyond to accommodate the secular regime. To do so, Fethullah Gülen stood by the laic regime and against other Islamic movements on vital debates. For instance, Fethullah Gülen rejected joining the boycott of the Islamic Institute in 1977 saying 'there's no such thing as boycott in Islam', and did not support protests over the veil ban in universities.[184]

The GM's ideological ambiguity carried over to its organisation. On the one hand, the GM argued that there was no 'formal membership' to the GM. According to a high-ranking leader of the Gülen-linked Journalists and Writers Foundation (*Gazeteciler ve Yazarlar Vakfı*), their organisation was based on shared common principles and beliefs.[185] Such an organisation, according to a researcher at the same Foundation, resembled the concept of a car, which in essence is a vehicle for transportation with four wheels and an engine yet with thousands of models ranging from luxurious sports cars to family station wagons.[186] As such, the GM had established a generic car model that was modified according to local circumstances.[187] Hence, according to another official at the same Foundation, a centralised organisation was impossible, and thus rather, there was consensus on principles and values.[188]

On the other hand, the GM nonetheless also had an organisational structure in place.[189] Specifically, GM's organisation, similar to the Moroccan JSM's layered structure, consisted of three 'circles' coordinating and carrying out the grassroots activities of the Movement. The 'Core' close to Fethullah Gülen led movement activities.[190] They were often made up of university students brought up at lighthouses under the leadership of 'Elder Brothers'.[191] The 'Affiliates' acted as leaders in the Movement's local foundations and engaged in grassroots activism.[192] They were mainly small town merchants and businesspeople.[193] Lastly, there were the 'Sympathisers', who did not 'share Gülen's goals but [...] participate[d] in their realisation'[194] through their participation in GM's grassroots activities. In addition, how decisions were made, whether they were discussed at all, and how they were implemented all remained outside the scopes of external observers as well as of the state. Ruşen Çakır, a veteran journalist following Islamic movements in Turkey, for instance, has theorised that the GM had a 'civilian' wing visible to the public and engaged in education and media efforts, and a 'clandestine' wing operating behind the curtains and engaged in the infiltration of the state.[195] As a result, the GM's organisation in its ambiguity stood in stark contrast to the NOM's vanguard organisation under a few but publicly visible and well-known leadership cadre. According to Hendrick, the GM adapted such an ambiguous organisation for strategic reasons in order to protect itself from secular persecution and leave enough room for deniability.[196] All in all, in the words of Turkey's most well-known scholar of political Islam, Şerif Mardin, who has spent some time in a Gülen-run student housing, outsiders 'could never figure out [the GM's] internal organisation'.[197]

Facing the same potential costs and benefits of participation vis-à-vis non-participation, the GM chose a different path from the NOM. In this, instead of equating participation with increased top-down political influence, the GM, like the Moroccan JSM, saw significant risks in getting involved in party politics in a political context like Turkey, where politics is not fully institutionalised and based on patronage networks.[198] According to Kara, the GM was adapting a more pragmatic and cautious strategy than the NOM because it was aiming to escape the prosecutions of laic establishments by staying out of institutional politics and thus out of the reach of the regime.[199] Fethullah Gülen, early in his career in the 1960s, for instance, had criticised the New Asia Movement, another Islamic movement inspired by Said Nursi, for its open support for the centre-right Justice Party and claimed that this misdirected believers from true faith.[200] Instead, Fethullah Gülen expected to consolidate and grow his Movement outside party politics[201] by filling in the vacuum left by laic establishments in the society. This stood in contrast to the NOM that saw participation as a way to overcome the laic barriers to religious politics.

Furthermore, because the Movement positioned itself 'above politics' by staying out of everyday politics, occasionally supporting governing parties, and by accommodating laic establishments, it also portrayed the Movement as an alternative to the NOM. Thus, while the NOM was limited by the rules of the party system, the GM, in Turam's words, by 'not resisting the Turkish regime, was growing stronger'.[202] Thus, many costs associated with non-participation, such as repression, were not applicable to the GM. In this respect, the GM's non-participation was less costly than that of the JSM in Morocco. While the latter risked regime repression through its non-participation in Morocco, the former overcame such risks by positioning itself 'above politics'.

Non-participation was also an organisational fit as it allowed the GM to stay out of the disruptive forces of party politics. In this, the GM, like the JSM in Morocco, prioritised its organisational cohesion over the potential organisational benefits of participation. To illustrate this, during the initial steps of party formation, Erbakan, the leader of the NOM, had asked Fethullah Gülen to join forces with him under the NOM umbrella saying that Gülen should stop bothering with educating children and instead enter party politics with him to change Turkish politics. Gülen rejected such an offer saying that he wanted to protect his new Movement from the distracting forces of a polarised party system.[203] Furthermore, Nursi, the Movement's ideological forefather, had advised his pupils never to enter politics as he, as a former politician, had observed firsthand how the community of believers ended up in factions after entering formal politics. He saw politics as power games, expedience, and hierarchical mobilisation – things he advised his pupils to avoid to protect their organisational integrity.[204] In a now famous quote, Nursi, in stark contrast to Kotku, the leader of the *Nakşibendi* Order, who advocated increased involvement in political activism for his pupils, stated: 'I take shelter only in God from the devil and politics'.[205] Instead, Nursi believed that society could be transformed using alternative mediums, which would preserve organisational solidarity.[206] According to this line of thought, for Gülen, formal politics presented only one aspect of their mission.[207] Hence, for the GM, like for the Moroccan JSM, party politics was only one venue for change while non-participation would offer a more wholesale transformation.

Moreover, the GM, unlike the JSM in Morocco, by avoiding the direct challenge of the Turkish regime, did not politically stagnate. On the contrary, the GM freely engaged and widened its engagements in education and media without having to open up its internal organisation to public oversight and by working outside formal institutions. As a matter of fact, it could be argued that the NOM has faced more political stagnancies along the way than the GM as a result of its participation in party politics and the institutional repressions the NOM has faced in consequence, such as party closures. The GM, instead, remained outside the regime's institutional control and thus avoided political repressions.

Given these ideological and organisational considerations, the GM, despite looking at the same menu of options as the NOM, has not valued direct political participation in the party system as a strategic option and instead opted for mobilisation outside institutional channels in its early years while retaining friendly relations with both the Turkish regime and incumbent political parties.

Such sentiments for non-participation were echoed by some of the leaders of the Muslim Brotherhood and by the Quietist Salafis in Jordan.

Jordan

Like the mid-1990s in Morocco and the mid-1960s in Turkey, the mid-1980s was a political turning point for Islamic movements in Jordan because the King of Jordan, in response to a deepening economic crisis and deteriorating political stability, started a process of political liberalisation wherein he reopened the Jordanian Parliament. While some members of the Jordanian Muslim Brotherhood saw this as an opportunity to be part of decision-making, others within the Brotherhood were more cautious. The Quietist Salafis, on the other hand, did not even consider this political liberalisation process as a new political opportunity.

The Jordanian Muslim Brotherhood

The Jordanian Muslim Brotherhood (JMB) (*Jama'at al-Ikhwan al-Muslimin fi al-Urdun*) was founded in 1945 with the permission of the Jordanian King Abdullah I, who welcomed the Brotherhood as long as the movement had 'no other aim but utter devotion to God, to His work for His sake and the benefit of the Muslim Brothers'.[208] Similarly, in an interview in 1947, the then-prime minister Samir al-Rifai both welcomed the Brotherhood stating 'it would be a mistake to show signs of disapproval as long as the Movement was religious', but also warned the Brotherhood saying the regime 'would intervene if the local branch showed signs of political activities'.[209] In effect, the Brotherhood's formation was welcomed by the Jordanian regime as long as the Movement remained loyal and avoided oppositional politics. Hence, unlike the early politicisation of Islamic movements in Morocco and Turkey, the Brotherhood in its early years focused its energies on apolitical grassroots activism, and engaged in education and charity, thereby building its loyal core supporter base.

Nonetheless, in the 1951 and 1954 elections, some Brotherhood members ran in elections as individual candidates. In 1956, the Brotherhood also ran as a group.[210] The then-JMB general secretary was against such political participation as he believed that 'time was not yet ripe for a strong performance'.[211] However, his colleagues disagreed because they believed participation would serve as a medium to 'spread the group's ideas and introduce its activists to the public'.[212] Notwithstanding such debates, this experimentation with party politics soon came to an end when the Jordanian Parliament was suspended in 1967 in response to the Arab–Israeli War.

From 1967 to 1989, when the Jordanian parliamentary life was on hold, the Brotherhood engaged in grassroots activism. During these years, what differentiated the Jordanian Brotherhood from its counterparts in Morocco and Turkey was that the Jordanian regime allowed for the Brotherhood's legal existence. Hence, while Islamic movements in Morocco and Turkey were all trying to be recognised by the state, the JMB was enjoying the perils of its legal existence. During these years, although the regime and the Brotherhood disagreed over a series of regional policies, the JMB also never directly challenged the regime. Even in the Black September events of 1970, when conflict broke out between the Palestinian Liberation Organisation and the Jordanian regime, the Brotherhood took a neutral stance thereby tacitly standing by the regime.[213] According to a veteran Brotherhood member who served in multiple leadership positions, there was a 'gentlemen's agreement' with the regime wherein the Brotherhood understood early on that they 'do not have to have clashes with the government'.[214]

With the help of such tolerant regime relations, the Brotherhood, like the JSM in Morocco and the GM in Turkey, formed an Islamic counter-hegemony, parallel to and independent of the Jordanian regime. During this period, the JMB's charitable work became so extensive that the need to bring all these Brotherhood activities under a single umbrella emerged. To do so, in 1963, the Brotherhood formed the Islamic Centre Charity Society 'to organise, manage, and oversee the social activities of the movement in various sectors, including health, education, sport, accommodation, and renovation of housing units for the poor'.[215] It was estimated that 'the Centre sponsor[ed] more than 20,000 orphans, operate[d] 55 schools and ha[d] more than 3,500 employees' and that [it] had more than $1.5 billion in assets.[216] These Brotherhood centres also served as venues for recruitment and outreach programmes, such as sports competitions and scouts activities.[217] In all these endeavours, the JMB widened its counter-hegemonic Islamic bloc by becoming the only rival to the charities organised by the Royal Hashemite family.[218] Furthermore, the Brotherhood became active on university campuses.[219] JMB members started to take over student councils,[220] and many professional associations[221] – which were important alternative power bases to the regime given the absence of the party system in Jordan during this period.²²² The guiding ideology behind these engagements, according to a former Executive Committee Member of the JMB was to gradually build 'an Islamic home, Islamic society, Islamic government, and Islamic world'.²²³

In addition to its grassroots recruitment activities, the Brotherhood, like its counterparts in Turkey, also recruited through its connections within the state and benefited from the perks that came with it. Specifically, the Brotherhood came to control political activism on university campuses when in the early 1970s Ishaq Farhan, a high-ranking Brotherhood member, took over the Ministry of Education.²²⁴ However, Farhan's acceptance of a ministerial position also caused an uproar within Brotherhood. The Brotherhood leadership at the time wanted to stay away from the Jordanian regime and instead build their own independent counter-hegemony. Thus, they protested Farhan's move and asked for his resignation, leading Farhan to freeze his membership during his ministerial post.²²⁵

Besides his Ministry, Farhan also served in other positions of power. He was the Director of the Royal Scientific Society from 1975 to 1978, the president of the University of Jordan from 1976 to 1978, and a member of the Consultative National Council from 1978 onwards.²²⁶ In all these engagements, Farhan not only managed to create better relations with the Jordanian regime but was also able to use his position to expand the Brotherhood's call further. Other Brotherhood leaders followed his example: Abdullatif Arabiyat and Mohammed Aweidah worked for the Ministry of Education, Abdulrahim Akour served several leading positions within the Ministry of Religious Affairs, and Majid Khalifeh served as the acting Dean of the Law College at the University of Jordan.²²⁷ Through these high-ranking connections, the Movement provided 'members who cannot find jobs in the government opportunities to work in its institutions, where they were given priority in employment'.²²⁸ Furthermore, mosques were also used by the Brotherhood for recruitment, specifically through the Brotherhood's influence within the Ministry of Religious Affairs, which appoints mosque preachers and orators.²²⁹ Such high-level connections, in turn, increased the Brotherhood's societal appeal and widened its constituency. Thus, over the years, the Brotherhood, similar to the GM in Turkey with its own schools and media networks, established a 'parallel state'[230] to that of the Jordanian regime. Specifically, the JMB 'owned two large hospitals, 15 clinics, one university, one female community college, 28 primary and secondary schools, and 23 kindergartens' and financially supported thousands of poor families and students.[231.]

The 1984 by-elections and the 1989 general elections, both of which took place after an almost twenty-year hiatus in party politics, brought new political opportunities for the Brotherhood. Within this new climate of political openings, the Brotherhood, for the next few years, debated whether, in what capacity, and in what form to participate in party politics. The initial reaction of the Brotherhood, unlike its counterparts in Morocco or Turkey, was to participate without much fanfare. Thus, in the 1984 by-elections, Brotherhood candidates ran and won three of the eight vacant parliamentary seats.[232] Quickly after that, the Brotherhood also participated in the 1989 general elections and ran with the slogan 'Islam is the solution', 'promised to place ethics and morality at the core of every human activity, and proposed a strong fight against corruption and corrupt officials',[233] and won twenty-two seats out of eighty. Furthermore, JMB leaders participated in the Royal Committee for new reforms and focused on taking Islam 'from being a source of legislation to *the* source of legislation'.[234]

Taking participation further, in 1991 the Brotherhood joined the cabinet of Prime Minister Mudar Badran on the condition that 'all members of the Brotherhood who have been terminated from their [public sector] jobs'[235] get their jobs back. This decision to participate in the government, however, was not as easy as the decision to run in elections. It was preceded by heated debates between those who saw participation in the government as equivalent to 'participation in a *jahili* [pre-Islamic ignorant] regime',[236] and those who saw participation in the government as a once in a lifetime chance to advance their Islamic agenda.[237] At the end of these debates, the Brotherhood participated in the Badran government and held the Ministries of Education, Health, Justice, Social Development and Islamic Affairs.[238] Hence, the Brotherhood became an integral part of the new coalition government under Badran wherein Abdellatif Arabiyat, from the JMB, was elected Speaker of the Parliament.[239]

However, participating in both the elections and the coalition government also had its shortcomings. Foremost amongst these was that participation 'included taking part in the implementation of policies that were not [the Brotherhood's] own and accepting joint responsibility because of [the Brotherhood's] very participation'.[240] As a result, the failure of the Badran government to introduce fundamental reforms and its failure in the eyes of the public were also associated with the failure of the Brotherhood. Furthermore, JMB's electoral victory had led to a change in its relations with the regime in that the administration was starting to see the Brotherhood as its main contender, as a result of the Brotherhood's unexpected electoral success, rather than as its strategic partner to counter-balance the regime's secular opposition. In light of such results of participation, when the Jordanian regime approved a new Political Parties Law in 1992 that legalised political parties for the first time since 1957, the JMB started discussing whether they should remain as a social movement or continue to participate in electoral politics by forming a political party. As a result, the Brotherhood debated the merits and costs of participation in party politics vis-à-vis non-participation after its rather unproductive experience in party politics.

This new debate over participation was mainly between the hardliners and the reformists.[241] These two trends within the Brotherhood were the results of the Brotherhood's ideological evolution throughout the decades. From the 1960s onwards, a new generation of Brotherhood activists educated in the Gulf and in Egypt[242] had taken over the JMB. Different from previous generations, who were politically accommodationist, this new generation had a more critical stance towards the Jordanian regime[243] because, according to a former Executive Committee Member of the JMB, (1) they were politicised by regional developments, specifically by the Israel–Palestine conflict,[244] rapid socio-economic changes within and around Jordan, and by the rise of global Islamism after the Iranian Revolution,[245] and because (2) they, like the Islamic Youth in Morocco, were heavily influenced by the writings of Sayyid Qutb (1906–1966). A radical and outspoken thinker, Qutb advocated abstinence from the state because in his view the current political system, in which 'men are in servitude to other men' and not to the Divine, represented a state of ignorance (*jahiliyyah*).[246] Instead, Qutb proposed to form 'saved' communities that would cut themselves from the rest of the 'ignorant' society and turn to Islam. These saved communities would also not compromise their convictions at any cost: 'We will not change our values and concepts either more or less to make a bargain with this *jahili* (ignorant) society. Never!'²⁴⁷ By forming such a tightly bound Islamic counter-hegemony, the Islamic movement would expand: it would grow from 'three individuals ... to ten, the ten to a hundred, the hundred to a thousand, and the thousand ... to twelve thousand'.²⁴⁸ Influenced by Qutb, the new leadership of the JMB renewed the curriculum of the Brotherhood.²⁴⁹ However, unlike the Islamic Youth in Morocco that radicalised with Qutb's ideas, they chose to form their Islamic counter-hegemony outside the scopes of the Jordanian regime through non-violent grassroots activism. Thus, in their quest for social transformation outside the limiting scopes of institutional politics, the JMB followed a similar path to that of the Moroccan JSM and the Turkish GM.

The rise of these Qutb-inspired 'hardliners' was met with the emergence of a more pragmatic group of leaders, who recognised that it was more efficient to recruit new members through the public school system. In particular, like the NOM and the GM in Turkey, Brotherhood members started infiltrating the Ministry of Education to influence the development of curricula and the appointment of teachers.²⁵⁰ With the turn of the 1980s, this new 'reformist' trend found a legitimising discourse for their strategy in the ideas of Hassan al-Turabi, the leader of Sudanese Islamists.²⁵¹ In al-Turabi's vision, the old ways of educating the masses through tightly knit groups were too slow and inefficient to allow the movements to gain political authority.²⁵² In particular, he argued that 'political activism did not need to be preceded by indoctrination or education, since service to the people in politics, trade unions, was itself the best education' and encouraged the opening up of Islamic movements by having less restrictive membership requirements.²⁵³ For al-Turabi, the failure of the modern Islamic movements was that they were idealists without a particular programme bridging the gap between reality and their ideals. Because of this, when these movements would fail to bring about an Islamic revolution from below, they would blame the society and withdraw from it.²⁵⁴ However, exiting from political life was not the solution, per Turabi, and instead he believed that Islamic movements should become more realistic about the state and recognise the power of the state over the society.²⁵⁵ Firstly, like the NOM and the GM in Turkey, Turabi argued that Islamic movements should work from within the system to use the state's power over the society.²⁵⁶ Secondly, he argued that Islamism should be led by educated elites (vanguards).²⁵⁷

These two trends within the Brotherhood, the hardliners and the reformists, co-existed under a centralised organisation. Hence, unlike Islamic movements in Morocco and Turkey, what differentiated the JMB was the public existence of different factions with different ideological leanings under the same organisational umbrella. At the core of the organisation was the *usra* [family] unit: small groups under the guidance of a mentor who followed a curriculum; engaged in group activities; met other groups; attended conferences, lectures, and discussions; and analysed political events in order to familiarise new members with the teachings of the Brotherhood.²⁵⁸ Through these 'family' units, the Brotherhood also aimed to solidify its relations by strengthening family ties. In particular, the Movement arranged 'dates and marriages among group members, thus becoming more coherent and immune to schisms'.²⁵⁹ One step up the *usra* unit were the local branches clustered around urban cities. Each of these local branches also had their own representative, who was appointed directly by the central leadership.²⁶⁰ It was estimated that there were 'about 15,000 people distributed among 35 divisions scattered across all Jordanian governorates' and that 'more than 100,000 individuals who benefited socially and economically from the services provided by the group'.²⁶¹ Each local representative also participated in the election of the 'Consultative Council' every four years.²⁶² The Consultative (*Shura*) Council functioned as the central administration. The Council also elected the Executive Bureau and the Rights Committee every four years. Whereas the Executive Bureau was the highest decision-making body of the JMB and was headed by the Chairman of the JMB,²⁶³ the Rights Committee was responsible for the settlement of disputes concerning the interpretation of Islamic laws and the establishment of any political direction decision of the organisation.²⁶⁴ Decisions at these top bodies were made by majority vote. However, since there were only a few members of the *Shura* Council, the decisions it made did not necessarily represent the majority of the organisation.²⁶⁵

Under such a centralised organisation, the hardliners and the reformists disagreed on the futility of party politics towards the achievement of their strategic objectives to revive Islam. Ideologically, for the reformists, participation in party politics as a political party offered the possibility to use state institutions for the Islamic cause. Like the Turkish NOM and the Moroccan MUR, they believed that sitting in the parliament meant being part of the legislature and demanding Islamic changes to the law. In the words of a former deputy from the Brotherhood:

> We want to participate because we want to take part in legislation, in enacting laws [...] to address people's problems and issues, to be there, to make sure the government is not suppressing, practicing tyranny over the people.[266]

After all, according to a former deputy from the Brotherhood, 'even if we cannot make the laws Islamic, at least it will not be against Islam'.[267] Sitting in the parliament also meant 'supervising the government, particularly regarding corruption',[268] according to another former deputy from the Brotherhood. It also meant access to state elites. A high-ranking leader of the JMB explains:

> When a personality in the society says I want to meet the minister of education, he says all right I do not have time today, you can come after in two days. However, if I was a parliamentary member or a former minister like myself I can go any time, any hour, and they will open the doors.[269]

The hardliners, however, according to a former Executive Committee member of the Brotherhood, were uncertain whether participation would benefit the objectives of the Brotherhood.[270] In this, the hardliners were uncomfortable with participating in a regime based on a Constitution that is not entirely based on *Sharia*, according to one of the most prominent hardliners, Mohammad Abu Faris.[271]

In addition to such ideological differences amongst the two groups, the organisational benefits versus costs of participation were another issue of disagreement. For the reformists, party formation offered the possibility to reach more people through attaining higher posts. Although the JMB, unlike the Turkish NOM or the Moroccan MUR, was not a small movement trying to connect its vanguards to the masses, it still lacked visibility and influence in rural areas since the JMB was an urban movement. Thus, being part of the parliament, according to a former Deputy from the Brotherhood, meant greater visibility across Jordan including the countryside – not only in the cities:

> We need to be visible because the parliament is the window ... the media emphasis on the parliament is great, and you have to be there. Through being in the parliament, you can talk about your convictions like foreign affairs.[272]

And, increased visibility meant a growing constituency, according to another former Deputy from the Brotherhood:

> Either we win or not, the parliament period is an excellent opportunity for us to promote our ideas and our programmes. So, we can enter the houses; we can go to villages. People will understand our programme [...] Parliament is superb to promote our ideas loudly.[273]

In the words of another high-ranking leader of the JMB:

> Those who did not hear from the Islamic movement or those who did not have any gains from it socially or economically [...] they have [...] the parliamentary member stays and says Islam, Islam, Islam and broadcasts his speech and he will be present in every home.[274]

Moreover, the reformists expected that forming a new party would bring new alliances, especially with independent Islamists.[275] To be a member of the JMB one had to follow strict guidelines for life, such as abiding by certain dress codes, working under an organisational hierarchy, and showing religious commitment. According to a leading member of the JMB, a new party would not only be more open to other views but also have less restrictive membership criteria.[276] Hence, the assumption was that party formation would eliminate these strict internal rulings of the JMB and create a 'large umbrella to enable anyone who wants to work on political issues'.[277] This change would open up the Brotherhood to everyone who believed in the role of Islam in politics but who were not necessarily JMB members, according to a former deputy from the Brotherhood.[278] As a result, like the NOM in Turkey and the MUR in Morocco both of which aimed to cut themselves off from the limitations of their past organisations, the reformists in the JMB believed that a new political party would serve to break ties with the Brotherhood's institutional norms and give the Movement organisational flexibility. This break in return would attract new members.

The hardliners, according to a former Executive Committee Member of the Brotherhood, on the other hand, worried a separate political party would create factions within the Movement in the long run[279] – a possibility that was a direct threat to strong internal ties. In particular, according to a former member of the JMB, they worried that participating within the rules the regime had set – rules they could not control – would harm the Brotherhood's unity.[280] Furthermore, they believed,

> participation in state institutions would weaken the focus of the Brotherhood from its broader objective of Islamic reform by distracting members with issues such as coalition building, campaigning, and the need to negotiate with government and opposition groups.[281]

Hence, they worried, like Yassine and Gülen, that 'worldly' matters, such as electoral campaigns, would turn the JMB into an un-spiritual/un-Islamic political force where members would come together as professionals under a party and not as part of a larger Islamic community.[282]

Both sides also disagreed over what cost was riskier. For the reformists, non-participation was riskier, because they feared that if the JMB did not establish a new political party now, other Islamists would and they would take away their constituency by setting up a party, according to a Jordanian scholar[283] and they could not afford to 'wait and see'. In this, the reformists echoed the NOM and the MUR both of which equated non-participation with political stagnancy. For the hardliners, participation was riskier, because they feared the uncertainty of this new situation and thus treated participation with caution. In the end, a vital potential cost of non-participation did not exist in the Jordanian context: the JMB was a 'legal' entity that had escaped repression throughout the years. Hence, participation, unlike for the MUR in Morocco, was not a move that would bring the JMB out of the underground. They were also concerned that by becoming a political party, they would be dependent on government rulings over them.[284] One of the harshest proponents of this view, Bassam Umoush, stated 'we cannot accept everything. We have strong constant principles which we cannot change or amend'.[285] Hence, the hardliners took the same cautious steps of Yassine and Gülen in their opposition to party formation. Moreover, according to the new Political Parties Law, a political party could not have administrative or financial links with any foreign power or political group. However, the JMB was an offshoot of the International Muslim Brotherhood Movement.[286] Lastly, transforming into a political party meant losing 'the right to work inside mosques, professional associations, unions, and charitable and *da ͑wa* [missionary] work', but not doing so by remaining as a movement also meant becoming apolitical.[287]

At the end of these debates between the hardliners and the reformists, a concession was reached when they decided to continue the JMB as a social movement while establishing a separate political party, the Islamic Action Front Party (IAF) (*Jabhat al-ʿAmal al-Islami*). This new Party was established following a long Consultative Council meeting with a majority vote of 85% with the following public statement:

> The Muslim Brotherhood views parliamentary action and involvement in parliamentary elections as a means to address the masses, communicate with them, adopt their issues and stands, explain facts, ward off doubts, defend stands, and to present programmes and plans with the objective of contributing to the homeland's progress and development. Based on this, although we have strict reservations about the law amending the current Election Law, and despite the fact that this law was issued to reduce the Islamic Movement's representation in the coming parliament, the Muslim Brotherhood, proceeding from its sense of responsibility toward its call, homeland, and citizens, and out of its awareness of our nation's delicate circumstances, has decided to take part in the coming parliamentary elections through its members who are affiliated with the IAF Party with the objective of unifying and rationalising Islamic action in the service of the issues of the nation and the homeland.[288]

The first edition of the *Islamic Action* magazine, a publication of the IAF, reaffirmed the Brotherhood's reasons for establishing the IAF:

> Theories are no longer useful in the midst of the conflict between the combative world forces, policies, and ideas. Therefore, the Islamic movement is duty-bound to enter the arena of political struggle through a legal institution so that it may convey its message to the various sectors of the state, prove the practical and fruitful model of Islamic action, and confirm the

ability and suitability, of the Islamic approach to the successful resolution of all aspects of social problems.[289]

As a result, while the IAF functioned as the political wing of the Brotherhood, the JMB itself continued along its road as a social movement. Having two parallel organisations gave the Brotherhood the benefit to eschew party regulations imposed by the regime, such as the disclosure of their budgets and lists of members, and to avoid a potential future ban on political parties thereby preserving the networks the JMB had built over decades.[290] While the Brotherhood was following a third way to party politics, the 1989 openings were insignificant for the Quietist Salafis in Jordan.

Quietist Salafism

In contrast to the Brotherhood's highly structured organisation, there is no Salafi 'Movement' in Jordan in the sense that Salafism is not an organised movement with a centralised decision-making body engaged in systematic policies. Rather, Salafism is composed of individuals, who are connected to each other informally through their shared Islam interpretations and personal relationships.[291] Hence, different from the Jordanian Muslim Brotherhood, which is more than the accumulation of its leaders and which has a consistent organisation going beyond individual personalities, Salafism in Jordan has emerged and developed around individuals. As a result, unlike the JMB's 'origin story' wherein particular individuals started a new movement with the permission of the regime, there is no such origin story for Salafism in Jordan. Rather, Salafism is thought to have been 'started' by Jordanian expatriates exposed to Salafism during their studies or work abroad. One particular turning point in the rise of the Quietist Salafism in Jordan was the relocation of Muhammad Nasir al-Din Albani, a famous Salafi Sheikh from Syria, who resettled in Jordan in 1979 to escape the increasing repressions of the Syrian regime.[292] The resettlement of Albani in Jordan 'precipitated an explosion in Salafi activism', such as engagements in 'study groups, lessons in private homes, and other religious activities'.[293]

With the return of Afghan War fighters, a more militant form of Salafism has also been brought into Jordan. Because these individuals had military training and were radicalised by fighting, they had a more critical view of the

Jordanian regime.[294] In particular, this 'Jihadi' trend 'formed militant underground organisations designed to challenge the state through violence'.[295] In the 1990s, this group radicalised even further with the First Gulf War and the subsequent deployment of US troops in Saudi Arabia. As a result, this Jihadi trend engaged in violent activities in Jordan, such as the bombings of cinemas and liquor stores.[296]

This Jihadist group remained marginal, however, in that most Salafis in Jordan have followed the 'Quietist' trend,[297] which rejected violent means. In contrast to the Jihadi Salafis' radical aims, the Quietists' strategy was to purify and to re-educate the individual. Although Quietists Salafis were similar to the Moroccan JSM and the Turkish GM in their quest for the religious re-education of the individual, they also differed from them significantly. In particular, the Quietists Salafis aimed to follow the example set by the early companions of Prophet Mohamed, the *Salaf*, through a purified understanding of religion, rather than to formulate a new Islam interpretation like their counterparts in Morocco and Turkey.[298] Furthermore, like the JMB, Quietist Salafis believed Islam to be a comprehensive religion encompassing all aspects of life and thus that Islam 'should regulate and guide behaviour and action in all aspects of social existence'.[299] However, different than the JMB, which aimed to influence the regime through its counter-hegemony, Quietist Salafis believed that 'circumstances [were] not right for a direct challenge and that they must bide their time before acting'.[300] In this, they viewed themselves 'not as revolutionaries, but as guardians of the true faith'.[301] Hence, Quietist Salafis did not actively engage in politics. Rather, they believed in 'grassroots change that begins at the level of the individual and personal transformation, without directly challenging the system of power'.[302] Consequently, Quietist Salafis, like the Moroccan JSM and the Turkish GM, believed that the education of the individual would lead to the re-education of the society, and eventually to that of an Islamic state.[303] But, unlike their Moroccan and Turkish counterparts and their public visibility, Quietist Salafis chose to remain under the regime's radar in this quest.

Despite their rejection to engage in active politics, Quietist Salafis in Jordan could not be defined as apolitical either. As Olidort states, despite his slogan later in life that 'the best policy is to stay out of politics', Albani himself took vocal, if not often controversial, stances on some political issues. For example, Albani condemned armed resistance against Israel, and supported the ideological cause of the jihad in Afghanistan.[304]

Hence, on the one hand, Quietist Salafis were subservient to the Jordanian regime, but on the other hand, they were also not participating in the Jordanian regime for a political reason, namely that this was an un-Islamic regime.[305]

There was no central leadership cadre in Quietist Salafism, unlike the JMB and its centralised and hierarchical organisation. Hence, Quietist Salafis in Jordan were distinct from the Moroccan JSM and the Turkish GM, both of which engaged in grassroots activism, yet were also built on a strongly institutionalised organisation around charismatic leaders. Instead, there were multiple teachers, hence various charismatic figures, with their student following within Quietist Salafism.[306] In general, these students and followers of Quietist Salafism came:

> from the working classes and the more impoverished and economically, politically and socially marginalised communities in the country. The majority of them [were] also of Palestinian origin, as the spread of Salafism, was concentrated in the more wretched Palestinian refugee camps, slums and outskirts of cities – particularly the city of al-Zarqa, which, to this day, remains the main hub of Salafism in Jordan.[307]

In this, because Quietist Salafis aimed to 'facilitate the movement's goal of transforming society through religious education',[308] relations within this trend were also based on teacher-student relations. As a result, Quietist Salafism had an amorphous and informal organisation based on a hierarchy of scholarship. According to Wiktorowicz, Quietist Salafis also strategically chose to have an informal organisation so that they could escape the limitations of the Jordanian regime.[309] Particularly, Albani, as a victim of state repression himself in Syria, wanted to prevent a formal organisation so that his followers in Jordan would never be targeted.[310] Nonetheless, because membership in Quietist Salafism was fluid and volatile,[311] unlike the united stance of the JSM in Morocco and the GM in Turkey, Quietist Salafism also witnessed many rifts, specifically disagreements over leadership successions[312] and over 'the question of the scholarly and social functions'.[313]

In 1989, when the political system was opening up, Quietist Salafis, unlike the JMB, did not even consider party politics to be a viable option. Ideologically, according to the Quietist Salafi leader Albani, political participation at any capacity in the modern nation-state was unacceptable as it contradicted the example set by the *Salaf*.[314] Participation was also not an ideological fit because Quietist Salafi, like the JSM in Morocco and the GM in Turkey, believed that purification and the re-education of the individual, and thus the re-Islamisation of society and eventually of the state, could not be achieved through party politics while party politics was based on 'fabrications and innovations that were imposed on the way and approach – or the *manhaj* [path] – advocated by the Prophet (May Peace Be upon Him)'.[315] Hence, different from the JMB, which evaluated the prospects and risks of party politics vis-à-vis its usefulness to the Brotherhood's ideological cause, Albani rejected such debates saying that 'the ends do not justify the means'.[316] Instead, their ideological priority was to prevent sacrificing Quietist Salafi teachings to attain political ends.[317] According to Albani, 'the umma [was] not in need of revolutions, assassinations, and strife, but [was] in need of faith education and intellectual cleansing. This [was] among the most successful means of returning the umma to its might and glory'.[318] In this, they believed that governance should be left to the government and instead attention should be paid to the education and *daʿwa* activities in society to prepare the society for an Islamic state.[319] Consequently, their focus, like their Moroccan and Turkish counterparts, was on 'cleansing and education', cleansing from non-Islamic teachings and educating a new generation of believers, in particular.[320] Albani's secretary Isam Hadi summarised their alternative path as:

> We want to go to the top of the pyramid, the caliphate, but the pyramid has a base, and you have to build the base before you can reach the top. That is why the Shaykh Nasir used to believe that the best thing to do for us as Salafis is not to work in politics, not just because there are rulers who oppress us and watch us, but because the Muslim group is not prepared for political action because they have not been raised or educated well about the correct Islam.[321]

In addition to its ideological incompatibility, participation in party politics was also organisationally useless for Quietist Salafis. Unlike the Brotherhood, which aimed to win new supporters by accessing state resources and thereby providing services to its followers, the reason why individuals joined Quietist Salafism was that Salafis distanced themselves from the Jordanian regime. According to Abu Rumman and Abu Hanieh:

> Many of them [were] depressed and frustrated with the political situation, which they [felt] they [were] unable to change or affect in any way, and in which they [felt] the futility of their involvement.[322]

Thus, studying Islam, instead of expending efforts on politics, was more attractive to new recruits.[323] In this, like the Moroccan JSM, the Quietist Salafis' attraction to their followers was their outsider stance and, like the Turkish GM, that the Quietist Salafis aimed to protect their supporters from the fragmenting forces of party politics. Hence, they believed that 'partisanship and divided affiliations [were] nothing more than a regression and diversion from the path of Islam'.[324]

Lastly, participation also was a costly path for Quietist Salafis. Firstly, Quietist Salafis were critical of the Brotherhood's political participation and pragmatism, believing that such actions opened the Brotherhood up to co-optation and alienation from true belief.[325] In this, Quietist Salafis, similarly to the JSM in Morocco and the GM in Turkey, believed that forming a political party would 'create a sense of loyalty and allegiance towards the party and its leadership, rather than to Islam, God and Muslims alone', and that 'this naturally [would] lead to disunity and division'.[326] Secondly, they believed that 'premature action that challenges the regime in any direct or open way before circumstances were right would jeopardise the movement'.[327] Therefore, participation rather than non-participation risked political stagnancy for Quietist Salafis. As a result, to this day, Quietist Salafis in Jordan have eschewed party politics.

Summary

Why do some Islamic movements in contexts as diverse as Morocco, Turkey, and Jordan all pursue participation in party politics by forming Islamic political parties, while their counterparts within the same country reject doing so? This chapter looked at this question and argued that strategic objectives, defined by a movement's ideological priorities and organisational needs, influence the way in which Islamic movements strategise and evaluate the menu of options available to them. In particular, it examined how Islamic movements aiming at top-down changes under their vanguards formed political parties because they valued the benefits of party politics, such as the chance to broaden their mass appeal beyond a vanguard through their access to state resources as a member of the parliament, over its potential costs, such as co-optation. This chapter also examined how Islamic movements aiming at bottom-up changes through grassroots mobilisation eschewed party politics because they saw the prospect of shifting to party politics as too costly given that the same benefits of party politics, such as widening the movement's mass appeal, had no additional incentive for a movement focused on creating a counter-hegemony with an already established mass base and given that the cost of party politics, co-optation, threatened to erode the movement's ideological integrity.

Perplexing, however, is how the reality has become more complex in the face of shifting regime–Islamic movement relations – the subject of the next chapter.

Notes

1. Curtis R. Ryan, 'Islamist Political Activism in Jordan: Moderation, Militancy, and Democracy', *The Middle East Review of International Affairs*, 12.2 (2008), 1–13.
2. Olivier Roy, *The Failure of Political Islam* (Cambridge, MA: Harvard University Press, 1994).
3. Seyyed Valid Reza Nasr (n.d.), 'Mawdudi, Sayyid Abu al-Ala', *The Oxford Encyclopedia of the Islamic World*, <http://www.oxfordislamicstudies.com/opr/t236/e0517> (last accessed 12 April 2012).
4. Irfan Ahmad, 'Genealogy of the Islamic State: Reflections on Maududi's Political Thought and Islamism', *The Journal of the Royal Anthropological Institute*, 15.1 (2009), 145–62.
5. Frédéric Volpi and Ewan Stein, 'Islamism and the State after the Arab Uprisings: Between People Power and State Power', *Democratization*, 22.2 (2015), 276–93.

6. Kamran Bokhari (n.d.), 'Jamāat-I Islami', *The Oxford Encyclopedia of the Islamic World*, Oxford Islamic Studies Online <http://www.oxfordislamicstudies.com/opr/t236/e0408> (last accessed 10 April 2012).
7. Bokhari, 'Jamāat-I Islāmī'.
8. Michaelle Browers, *Democracy and Civil Society in Arab Political Thought: Transcultural Possibilities* (Syracuse, NY: Syracuse University Press, 2006).
9. Olivier Roy, *Globalized Islam: The Search for a New Ummah* (New York: Columbia University Press, 2004).
10. Asef Bayat, 'Revolution without Movement, Movement without Revolution: Comparing Islamic Activism in Iran and Egypt', *Comparative Studies in Society and History*, 40.1 (1998), 136–69.
11. Bayat, 'Revolution without Movement'.
12. Muhammad Abduh (n.d.), 'Laws Should Change in Accordance with the Conditions of Nations and the Theology of Unity', *Oxford Islamic Studies Online* <http://www.oxfordislamicstudies.com/book/islam-9780195154672/islam-9780195154672-chapter-3> (last accessed 10 April 2012).
13. Bayat, 'Revolution without Movement'.
14. Carrie Rosefsky Wickham, *Mobilizing Islam: Religion, Activism, and Political Change in Egypt* (New York: Columbia University Press, 2002).
15. Roy, *The Failure of Political Islam*.
16. Anonymous interview with a high-ranking member of the JSM by the author, 4 May 2010, Rabat, Morocco.
17. Muhammad Darif, *Monarchie Marocaine et Acteurs Religieux [Moroccan Monarchy and Religious Actors]* (Casablanca, Morocco: Afrique Orient, 2010).
18. Malika Zeghal and Henry Munson (n.d.), 'Morocco', *The Oxford Encyclopedia of the Islamic World. Oxford Islamic Studies Online* <http://www.oxfordislamicstudies.com/article/opr/t236/e0544> (last accessed 21 July 2018).
19. Darif, *Monarchie Marocaine et Acteurs Religieux*.
20. Eva Wegner and Miquel Pellicer, 'Islamist Moderation without Democratization: The Coming of Age of the Moroccan Party of Justice and Development?', *Democratization*, 16.1 (2009), 157–75.
21. Shahrough Akhavi (n.d.), 'Qutb, Sayyid', *The Oxford Encyclopedia of the Islamic World*, Oxford Islamic Studies Online <http://www.oxfordislamicstudies.com/opr/t236/e0663> (last accessed 10 April 2012).
22. Mohamed Tozy, 'Champ et Contre Champ Politico-Religieux au Maroc' ['The Religious Field and Its Counter-Field in Morocco'] (unpublished PhD

Dissertation, Université de Droit, d'Économie et des Sciences d'Aix-Marseille, Faculte de Droit et de Science Politique, 1984).
23. Wegner and Pellicer, 'Islamist Moderation without Democratization'.
24. Darif, *Monarchie Marocaine et Acteurs Religieux*.
25. Darif, *Monarchie Marocaine et Acteurs Religieux*.
26. Darif, *Monarchie Marocaine et Acteurs Religieux*.
27. Tozy, 'Champ et Contre Champ Politico-Religieux au Maroc'.
28. Tozy, 'Champ et Contre Champ Politico-Religieux au Maroc'.
29. Tozy, 'Champ et Contre Champ Politico-Religieux au Maroc'.
30. Mohammed Boudarham (2013), 'Leaders Islamistes. Les Dix Portraits' ['Islamist Leaders: Six Portraits'], *Telquel*, 14 November, <http://telquel.ma/2013/11/14/leaders-islamistes-les-dix-portraits_9487> (last accessed 2 July 2014).
31. Anonymous interview with a former member of the Islamic Youth's preaching wing and current PJD leader by the author, 3 May 2010, Rabat, Morocco.
32. Haoues Seniguer, 'Genèse et Transformations de l'Islamisme Marocain à Travers les Noms. Le Cas Du Parti de La Justice et Du Développement' ['Genesis and Transformations of Moroccan Islamism through Party Names: The Case of Justice and Development Party'], *Mots: Les Langages Du Politique* 103 (2013): 111–20.
33. Youssef Belal, *Le Cheikh et le Calife: Sociologie Religieuse de L'Islam Politique au Maroc [The Sheikh and the Caliph: Religious Sociology of Political Islam in Morocco]* (Lyon, France: ENS Editions, 2011).
34. Mohamed Tozy, *Monarchie et Islam Politique au Maroc [Monarchy and Political Islam in Morocco]* (Paris, France: Presses de la Fondation Nationale des Sciences Politiques, 1999).
35. Khadija Mohsen-Finan and Malika Zeghal, 'Opposition Islamiste et Pouvoir Monarchique au Maroc: Le Cas du Parti de La Justice et Du Développement' ['Islamist Opposition and Monarchical Power in Morocco: The Case of the Party for Justice and Development'], *Revue Française de Science Politique*, 56 (2006), 79–119.
36. Julie E. Pruzan-Jørgensen (2010), 'Islamist Movement in Morocco: Main Actors and Regime Responses', *Academia*, <http://www.academia.edu/1892070/Islamist_Movement_in_Morocco_Main_Actors_and_Regime_Responses_DIIS_Report_2010_April_2010> (last accessed 21 July 2018).
37. Pruzan-Jørgensen, 'Islamist Movement in Morocco'.
38. Michael J. Willis, *Politics and Power in the Maghreb: Algeria, Tunisia and*

Morocco from Independence to the Arab Spring (New York: Columbia University Press, 2012).
39. Azzedine Layachi, 'Islam and Politics in North Africa', in John L. Esposito and Emad El-Din Shahin (eds), *The Oxford Handbook of Islam and Politics* (Oxford & New York: Oxford University Press, 2013), pp. 352–78.
40. Ahmed Raissouni, interview by Al Hassan Al Sarat (2006), 'Raissouni: Religious Scholars Should Participate in Governments, Parliaments', *The Muslim Brotherhood's Official English Website*, 24 November, <http://www.ikhwanweb.com/article.php?id=2999> (last accessed 21 July 2018).
41. Eva Wegner, *Islamist Opposition in Authoritarian Regimes: The Party of Justice and Development in Morocco* (Syracuse, NY: Syracuse University Press, 2011).
42. Pruzan-Jørgensen (2010), 'Islamist Movement in Morocco'.
43. Darif, *Monarchie Marocaine et Acteurs Religieux*.
44. Zeghal and Munson, 'Morocco'.
45. Darif, *Monarchie Marocaine et Acteurs Religieux*.
46. Mohsen-Finan and Zeghal, 'Opposition Islamiste et Pouvoir Monarchique au Maroc'.
47. Anonymous interview with a Moroccan researcher of political Islam by the author, 21 April 2010, Rabat, Morocco.
48. Anonymous interview with a PJD minister by the author, 19 April 2010, Rabat, Morocco.
49. Anonymous interview with a PJD minister by the author, 19 April 2010, Rabat, Morocco.
50. Ahmed Raissouni, interview by Al Hassan Al Sarat 'Raissouni: Religious Scholars Should Participate in Governments, Parliaments'.
51. Anonymous interview with a PJD minister by the author, 15 April 2010, Rabat, Morocco.
52. Anonymous interview with a PJD minister by the author, 19 April 2010, Rabat, Morocco.
53. Darif, *Monarchie Marocaine et Acteurs Religieux*.
54. Tozy, *Monarchie et Islam Politique au Maroc*.
55. Tozy, *Monarchie et Islam Politique au Maroc*.
56. Tozy, *Monarchie et Islam Politique au Maroc*.
57. Anonymous interview with a PJD minister by the author, 19 April 2010, Rabat, Morocco.
58. Anonymous interview with a PJD minister by the author, 19 April 2010, Rabat, Morocco.

59. Anonymous interview with a parliamentarian from the PJD by the author, 28 April 2010, Rabat, Morocco.
60. Ashraf Nabih El Sherif, 'Institutional and Ideological Re-Construction of the Justice and Development Party (PJD): The Question of Democratic Islamism in Morocco', *The Middle East Journal*, 66.4 (2012), 660–82.
61. Anonymous interview with a high-ranking leader of the MUR by the author, 21 April 2010, Rabat, Morocco.
62. Darif, *Monarchie Marocaine et Acteurs Religieux*.
63. Zeghal and Munson, 'Morocco'.
64. Henri Lauzière, 'Post-Islamism and the Religious Discourse of Abd Al-Salam Yasin', *International Journal of Middle East Studies*, 37.2 (2005), 241–61.
65. Lauzière, 'Post-Islamism and the Religious Discourse of Abd Al-Salam Yasin'.
66. Tozy, *Monarchie et Islam Politique au Maroc*.
67. Zeghal and Munson, 'Morocco'.
68. Mohamed Tozy (1999), 'Qui Sont Les Islamistes au Maroc' ['Who Are the Islamists in Morocco'], *Le Monde Diplomatique*, <http://www.monde-diplomatique.fr/1999/08/TOZY/12315> (last accessed 21 July 2018).
69. Amr Hamzawy (2008), 'Party for Justice and Development in Morocco: Participation and Its Discontents', *Carnegie Endowment for International Peace*, <http://www.carnegieendowment.org/files/cp93_hamzawy_pjd_final1.pdf> (last accessed 21 July 2018).
70. Zeghal and Munson, 'Morocco'.
71. Ahmet Yükleyen and Aziz Abba, 'Religious Authorization of the Justice and Spirituality Movement in Morocco', *Politics, Religion & Ideology*, 14.1 (2013), 136–53.
72. Driss Maghraoui, 'The Strengths and Limits of Religious Reforms in Morocco', *Mediterranean Politics*, 14.2 (2009), 195–211.
73. Malika Zeghal (n.d.), 'Yasin, Abdessalam', *The Oxford Encyclopedia of the Islamic World*, Oxford Islamic Studies Online, <http://www.oxfordislamicstudies.com/article/opr/t236/e0983> (last accessed 21 July 2018).
74. Lauzière, 'Post-Islamism and the Religious Discourse of Abd Al-Salam Yasin'.
75. Zeghal, 'Yasin, Abdessalam'.
76. Zeghal, 'Yasin, Abdessalam'.
77. Lauzière, 'Post-Islamism and the Religious Discourse of Abd Al-Salam Yasin'.
78. Lauzière, 'Post-Islamism and the Religious Discourse of Abd Al-Salam Yasin'.
79. Mark R. Woodward, Dale F. Eickelman, Charles C. Stewart, Rafiuddin Ahmed, John R. Bowen, Fred R. von der Mehden and Char Simons (n.d.), 'Popular

Religion', *The Oxford Encyclopedia of the Islamic World, Oxford Islamic Studies Online* <http://www.oxfordislamicstudies.com/article/opr/t236/e0642> (last accessed 21 July 2018).

80. Lauzière, 'Post-Islamism and the Religious Discourse of Abd Al-Salam Yasin'.
81. Abdessalam Yassine (2013), 'Two-Fold Renewal', *Abdessalam Yassine*, <https://yassine.net/en/2013/05/02/two-fold-renewal/> (last accessed 21 July 2018).
82. Abdessalam Yassine, *Winning the Modern World for Islam* (Iowa City, IA: Justice and Spirituality Publishing, 2000).
83. Youssef Belal, 'Mystique et Politique chez Abdessalam Yassine et Ses Adeptes' ['Mystique and Politics in Abdessalam Yassine and His Followers'], *Archives de Sciences Sociales des Religions* 135 (2006): 165–84.
84. Abdessalam Yassine, *The Muslim Mind on Trial: Divine Revelation versus Secular Rationalism* (Iowa City, IA: Justice and Spirituality Publishing, 2003).
85. Abdelhakim Hajjouji, 'Education and Values', in Maati Monjib (ed.), *Islamists versus Secularists: Confrontations and Dialogues in Morocco: Values, Democracy, Violence, Freedom, Education* (Rabat: IKV PAX, 2009).
86. Kassem Bahaji, 'Islamism in Morocco: Appeal, Impact and Implications (1969–2003)' (unpublished PhD Dissertation, Political Science, Northern Illinois University, 2007).
87. Marina Ottaway and Meredith Riley (2006), 'Morocco: From Top-Down Reform to Democratic Transition?', *Carnegie Endowment for International Peace*, <http://www.carnegieendowment.org/files/cp71_ottaway_final.pdf> (last accessed 21 July 2018).
88. Anonymous interview with a veteran Moroccan scholar of Political Islam by the author, 10 May 2010, Casablanca, Morocco.
89. Anonymous interview with a member of JSM's youth branch by the author, 10 May 2010, Casablanca, Morocco.
90. Anonymous interview with a high-ranking leader of the JSM by the author, 4 May 2010, Rabat, Morocco.
91. Tozy, *Monarchie et Islam Politique au Maroc*.
92. Sami Zemni, 'Moroccan Post-Islamism: Emerging Trend or Chimera?', in Asef Bayat (ed.), *Post-Islamism: The Changing Faces of Political Islam* (New York & Oxford: Oxford University Press, 2013), pp. 134–56.
93. Anonymous interview with an expert on political Islam in Morocco by the author, 10 May 2010, Casablanca, Morocco.
94. Ellen Lust-Okar, *Structuring Conflict in the Arab World: Incumbents, Opponents, and Institutions* (Cambridge & New York: Cambridge University Press, 2006).

95. Interview with Abdelkébir Alaoui M'Daghri (2004), 'Interview-vérité, Abdelkébir Alaoui M'Daghri: J'ai Gagné la Confiance des Islamistes' ['Interview-truth, Abdelkebir M'Daghri Alaoui: I Won the Confidence of Islamists'], *Telquel*, <http://www.telquel-online.com/archives/150/sujet4.shtml> (last accessed 10 April 2012).
96. Anonymous interview with a member of JSM's board of guidance by the author, 13 May 2010, Rabat, Morocco.
97. Anonymous interview with a member of JSM's board of guidance by the author, 13 May 2010, Rabat, Morocco.
98. Anonymous interview with a member of JSM's board of guidance by the author, 13 May 2010, Rabat, Morocco.
99. Lauzière, 'Post-Islamism and the Religious Discourse of Abd Al-Salam Yasin'.
100. Lauzière, 'Post-Islamism and the Religious Discourse of Abd Al-Salam Yasin'.
101. Nadia Yassine (2005), 'Presentation of the Justice and Spirituality Association: A Great Hello to All the Militants!', *Nadia Yassine,* <http://www.nadiayassine.net/en/page/10364.htm> (last accessed 29 March 2009).
102. Mohammed Taha Wardi, *Islamists and the Outside World: The Case of Abdessalam Yassin and Al Adl Wal Ihsan* (Ifrane, Morocco: Al Akhawayn University Press, 2003).
103. Nadia Yassine, 'Presentation of the Justice and Spirituality Association'.
104. Nadia Yassine, 'Presentation of the Justice and Spirituality Association'.
105. Abdallah Saaf and Abdelrahim Manar Al Slimi (2008), 'Morocco 1996–2007: A Decisive Decade of Reforms?', *Arab Reform Initiative,* <https://www.arab-reform.net/en/node/914> (last accessed 21 July 2018).
106. Yassine, *Winning the Modern World for Islam.*
107. Yassine, *Winning the Modern World for Islam.*
108. Yassine, *Winning the Modern World for Islam.*
109. Marlise Simons (1998), 'Morocco Finds Fundamentalism Benign but Scary', *The New York Times,* 9 April, <http://go.galegroup.com/ps/i.do?id=GALE%7CA150212737&v=2.1&u=tel_a_rhodes&it=r&p=AONE&sw=w&asid=145102eaefd295e95ab765797b517033> (last accessed 9 November 2014).
110. Anonymous interview with a high-ranking leader from the JSM by the author, 14 May 2010, Rabat, Morocco.
111. Kyle McEneaney (2008), 'Interview with Nadia Yassine of the Moroccan Justice and Charity Group', 18 August, *Carnegie Endowment for International Peace,* <https://carnegieendowment.org/sada/20813> (last accessed 21 July 2018).

112. Bruce Maddy-Weitzman, 'Islamism Moroccan-Style: The Ideas of Sheikh Yassine', *Middle East Quarterly*, 10.1 (2003), 43–51.
113. Nadia Yassine, interview by Emmanuel Martinez (2008), 'Féminisme Islamique' ['Islamic Feminism'], *Le Journal Des Alternatives*, 28 September, <http://journal.alternatives.ca/spip.php?article4140> (last accessed 24 July 2018).
114. Anonymous interview with a member of JSM's youth branch by the author, 10 May 2010, Casablanca, Morocco.
115. Anonymous interview with a member of JSM's youth branch by the author, 10 May 2010, Casablanca, Morocco.
116. Nadia Yassine (2008), 'Only the Combined Efforts of All Forces of the Nation Can Get Morocco Out of the Crisis', *Nadia Yassine*, <http://www.nadiayassine.net/en/page/12400.htm> (last accessed 19 April 2009).
117. Anonymous interview with a high-ranking member of the JSM by the author, 4 May 2010, Rabat, Morocco.
118. Anonymous interview with a member of JSM's youth branch by the author, 10 May 2010, Casablanca, Morocco.
119. 'M. Arsalan: Le Mouvement a Un Vaste Projet de Société Qui Touche à Toutes Les Catégories et Répond à Tous Les Soucis et Dont Le Centre d'intérêt Est l'Homme [Mr. Arsalan: The Movement Has a Broad Vision of Society That Affects All Classes and Meets All the Worries and Whose Focus Is the Man],' (2009) *Justice and Spirituality Movement's Webpage*, <http://www.aljamaa.net/fr/document/1405.shtml> (last accessed 23 April 2013).
120. Nadia Yassine, 'Only the Combined Efforts of All Forces of the Nation Can Get Morocco Out of the Crisis'.
121. Halil Inalcık, 'Tarihsel Bağlamda Sivil Toplum ve Tarikatlar' ['Civil Society and Religious Orders in Historical Perspective'], in Emin Fuat Keyman and Ali Yaşar Sarıbay (eds), *Global Yerel Eksende Türkiye [Turkey within the Global-Local Axis]* (Istanbul: Alfa Yayınları, 2000), pp. 593–616.
122. Because Islamic Orders are widespread across a vast geography, they are run by 'lodges' at the local level.
123. Kemal H. Karpat, *The Politicization of Islam: Reconstructing Identity, State, Faith, and Community in the Late Ottoman State* (New York: Oxford University Press, 2001).
124. Arda Can Kumbaracıbaşı, *Turkish Politics and the Rise of the AKP: Dilemmas of Institutionalization and Leadership Strategy* (London & New York: Routledge, 2009).

125. Şerif Mardin, 'The Nakshibendi Order of Turkey', in Martin Marty and R. Scott Appleby (eds), *Fundamentalisms and the State: Remaking Polities, Economies, and Militance* (Chicago, IL: University of Chicago Press, 1993), pp. 204–32.
126. Emin Yaşar, 'Dergâh'tan Parti'ye, Vakıftan Şirkete Bir Kimliğin Oluşumu ve Dönüşümü: Iskenderpaşa Cemaati' ['Identity Formation and Transformation from Lodge to Party, from Foundation to Company: Iskenderpaşa Congregation'], in Yasin Aktay (ed.), *Modern Türkiye'de Siyasi Düşünce, Cilt 6: Islamcılık [Political Thought in Modern Turkey, Volume 6: Islamism]* (Istanbul: Iletişim Yayınları, 2004), pp. 321–40.
127. Ruşen Çakır, *Ayet ve Slogan: Türkiye'de Islamcı Oluşumlar [Verse and Slogan: Islamic Formations in Turkey]* (Istanbul: Metis Yayınları, 2002).
128. Anonymous interview with a high-ranking NOM leader by the author, 29 May 2010, Istanbul, Turkey.
129. Anonymous interview with a founder of the NOM by the author, 5 June 2010, Bolu, Turkey.
130. Oral Çalışlar and Tolga Çelik, *Islamcılığın Üç Kolu [Three Branches of Islamism]* (Istanbul: Güncel Yayıncılık, 2006).
131. Süleyman Arif Emre, *Siyasette 35 Yıl [35 Years in Politics]* (Istanbul: Keşif Yayınları, 2002).
132. Emre, *Siyasette 35 Yıl*.
133. Emre, *Siyasette 35 Yıl*.
134. Ruşen Çakır, 'Milli Görüş Hareketi' ['National Outlook Movement'], in Yasin Aktay (ed.), *Modern Türkiye'de Siyasi Düşünce, Cilt 6: Islamcılık [Political Thought in Modern Turkey, Volume 6: Islamism]* (Istanbul: Iletişim Yayınları, 2004), pp. 544–603.
135. Anonymous interview with a veteran parliamentarian from the NOM by the author, 18 June 2009, Ankara, Turkey.
136. Oral Çalışlar, *Refah Partisi, Nereden Nereye [Welfare Party, from/to Where]* (Istanbul: Pencere Yayıncılık, 1995).
137. Fehmi Çalmuk, 'Necmettin Erbakan', in Yasin Aktay (ed.), *Modern Türkiye'de Siyasi Düşünce, Cilt 6: Islamcılık [Political Thought in Modern Turkey, Volume 6: Islamism]* (Istanbul: Iletişim Yayınları, 2004), pp. 550–67.
138. Oral Çalışlar and Tolga Çelik, *Erbakan – Fethullah Gülen Kavgası: Cemaat ve Tarikatların Siyasetteki 40 Yılı [Erbakan-Fethullah Gülen Fight: 40 Years of Religious Communities and Orders in Politics]* (Istanbul: Sıfır Noktası Yayınları, 2000).

139. Çalışlar and Çelik, *Erbakan – Fethullah Gülen Kavgası*.
140. The only link between Erbakan and the Order was Erbakan's previous employment in a company (*Gümüş Motor*) owned by the Order.
141. Çakır, *Ayet ve Slogan*.
142. Menderes Çınar, 'Kemalist Cumhuriyetçilik ve Islamcı Kemalizm' ['Kemalist Republicanism and Islamist Kemalism'], in Yasin Aktay (ed.), *Modern Türkiye'de Siyasi Düşünce, Cilt 6: Islamcılık [Political Thought in Modern Turkey, Volume 6: Islamism]* (Istanbul: Iletişim Yayınları, 2005), pp. 157–77.
143. Anonymous interview with a veteran Turkish journalist by the author, 2 July 2009, Istanbul, Turkey.
144. Ali Bulaç, *Din, Kent ve Cemaat: Fethullah Gülen Örneği [Religion, City and Religious Community: The Example of Fethullah Gülen]* (Istanbul: Ufuk Kitap, 2007).
145. Necmettin Erbakan (n.d.), 'Erbakan Milli Görüş'ü Tarif Ediyor' ['Erbakan Describes National Outlook'], *National Outlook Movement Germany's Erbakan Page* <http://erbakan.vze.com/> (last accessed 23 September 2009).
146. Ali Bulaç, 'The Most Recent Reviver in the 'Ulama Tradition: The Intellectual 'Alim Fethullah Gülen', in Robert A. Hunt and Yüksel A. Aslandoğan (eds), *Muslim Citizens of the Globalized World: Contributions of the Gülen Movement* (Houston, TX: Tughra Books, 2010), pp. 101–20.
147. Bulaç, *Din, Kent ve Cemaat*.
148. Ali Bulaç, *Göçün ve Kentin Siyaseti -MNP'den SP'ye Milli Görüş Partileri [Politics of Migration and the City: National Outlook Parties from the National Order Party to the Felicity Party.]* (Istanbul: Çıra Yayınları, 2009).
149. Çınar, 'Kemalist Cumhuriyetçilik ve Islamcı Kemalizm'.
150. Erbakan, 'Erbakan Milli Görüş'ü Tarif Ediyor'.
151. Çınar, 'Kemalist Cumhuriyetçilik ve Islamcı Kemalizm'.
152. Erbakan, 'Erbakan Milli Görüş'ü Tarif Ediyor'.
153. Anonymous interview with a founder of the NOM by the author, 5 June 2010, Bolu, Turkey.
154. Anonymous interview with a founder of the NOM by the author, 5 June 2010, Bolu, Turkey.
155. Soner Yalçın, *Hangi Erbakan [Which Erbakan]* (Ankara: Başak Yayınları, 1999).
156. Yalçın, *Hangi Erbakan*.
157. Fulya Atacan, 'Explaining Religious Politics at the Crossroad: AKP-SP', in Ali

Çarkoğlu and Barry Rubin (eds), *Religion and Politics in Turkey* (London & New York: Routledge, 2006), pp. 45–58.
158. Yaşar, 'Dergâh'tan Parti'ye, Vakıftan Şirkete Bir Kimliğin Oluşumu ve Dönüşümü'.
159. Emre, *Siyasette 35 Yıl*.
160. Anonymous interview with a veteran parliamentarian from the NOM by the author, 18 June 2009, Ankara, Turkey.
161. Emre, *Siyasette 35 Yıl*.
162. 'Milli Nizam Partisi: Program ve Tüzük' ['National Order Party: Programme and Regulations'] (1970), *Türkiye Büyük Millet Meclisi Resmi İnternet Sitesi [Official Website of the Grand National Assembly of Turkey]*, <http://www.tbmm.gov.tr/develop/owa/e_yayin.eser_bilgi_q?ptip=SIYASI%20PARTI%20YAYINLARI&pdemirbas=197600505> (last accessed 25 July 2018).
163. Gülen Institute, 'A Brief Biography of Fethullah Gülen', 2010, *Gülen Institute*, <http://www.guleninstitute.org/index.php/Biography.html> (last accessed 10 November 2010).
164. Gülen Institute, 'A Brief Biography of Fethullah Gülen'.
165. Gülen Institute, 'A Brief Biography of Fethullah Gülen'.
166. İştar B. Gözaydın, 'The Fethullah Gülen Movement and Politics in Turkey: A Chance for Democratization or a Trojan Horse?', *Democratization*, 16.6 (2009), 1214–36.
167. Marcia Hermansen, 'The Cultivation of Memory in the Gülen Community', in Ihsan Yilmaz (ed.), *Muslim World in Transition: Contributions of the Gülen Movement* (Leeds Metropolitan University Press, 2007), pp. 60–76.
168. Pelin Turgut (2010), 'The Turkish Imam and His Global Educational Mission', *Time Magazine*, 26 April, <http://content.time.com/time/magazine/article/0,9171,1969290,00.html> (last accessed 25 July 2018).
169. Hakan M. Yavuz and Rasim Koç, 'The Turkish Coup Attempt: The Gülen Movement vs. the State', *Middle East Policy* 23.4 (2016), 136-148.
170. Gazeteciler ve Yazarlar Vakfı (2013), 'Gündeme Dair: Gazeteciler ve Yazarlar Vakfı'ndan Hizmet Hareketi'ne Yönelik İddialara Cevaplar' ['About Current News: Journalists and Writers Foundation's Response to Accusations against the Hizmet Movement'], *Gazeteciler ve Yazarlar Vakfı [Journalists and Writers Foundation]*, 13 August, <http://gyv.org.tr/Haberler/Detay/2454/> (last accessed 1 July 2014).
171. Ahmet Şık, *Paralel Yürüdük Biz Bu Yollarda [We Walked Parallel on these Roads]* (Istanbul: Postacı Yayınevi, 2014); Nedim Şener, *Ergenekon Belgelerinde*

Fethullah Gülen ve Cemaat [*Fethullah Gülen and His Religious Community in Ergenekon Documents*] (Istanbul: Destek Yayınevi, 2014).
172. Çakır, *Ayet ve Slogan*.
173. Ahmet T. Kuru, 'Globalization and Diversification of Islamic Movements: Three Turkish Cases', *Political Science Quarterly*, 120.2 (2005), 253–74.
174. Hakan M. Yavuz, *Toward an Islamic Enlightenment: The Gülen Movement* (Oxford & New York: Oxford University Press, 2013).
175. Elizabeth Özdalga, 'Secularizing Trends in Fethullah Gülen's Movement: Impasse or Opportunity for Further Renewal?', *Middle East Critique*, 12.1 (2003), 61–73.
176. Şerif Mardin (n.d.), 'Nurculuk', *The Oxford Encyclopedia of the Islamic World*, Oxford Islamic Studies Online, <http://www.oxfordislamicstudies.com/opr/t236/e0517> (last accessed 12 April 2012).
177. Joshua D. Hendrick (n.d.), 'Gülen Movement', *Oxford Islamic Studies Online*, <http://www.oxfordislamicstudies.com/opr/t343/e0178> (last accessed 25 July 2018).
178. Yavuz, *Toward an Islamic Enlightenment*.
179. Fethullah Gülen, *Toward a Global Civilization of Love and Tolerance* (Somerset, NJ: Light, Inc., 2004).
180. Hakan M. Yavuz, 'The Three Stages of the Gülen Movement: From Pietistic Weeping Movement to Power-Obsessed Structure', in Bayram Balcı and Hakan M. Yavuz (eds), *Turkey's July 15th Coup: What Happened and Why* (Salt Lake City, UT: The University of Utah Press, 2018), pp. 20–45.
181. Rachel Sharon-Krespin, 'Fethullah Gülen's Grand Ambition Turkey's Islamist Danger', *Middle East Quarterly*, 16.1 (2009), 55–66.
182. Yavuz, *Toward an Islamic Enlightenment*.
183. Çakır, *Ayet ve Slogan*.
184. Çakır, *Ayet ve Slogan*.
185. Anonymous interview with a high-ranking leader of the Gülen-linked Journalists and Writers Foundation by the author, 1 June 2010, Istanbul, Turkey.
186. Anonymous interview with a researcher at the Journalists and Writers Foundation, 1 June 2010, Istanbul, Turkey.
187. Anonymous interview with a researcher at the Journalists and Writers Foundation, 1 June 2010, Istanbul, Turkey.
188. Anonymous interview with an official at the Journalists and Writers Foundation, 1 June 2010, Istanbul, Turkey.

189. Yavuz, 'The Three Stages of the Gülen Movement'.
190. Yavuz, *Toward an Islamic Enlightenment*.
191. Yavuz, 'The Three Stages of the Gülen Movement'.
192. Yavuz, *Toward an Islamic Enlightenment*.
193. Yavuz, 'The Three Stages of the Gülen Movement'.
194. Yavuz, *Toward an Islamic Enlightenment*.
195. Ruşen Çakır (2013), 'Gülen Cemaatinin "Sivil" Kanadı' ['Gülen Religious Community's "Civilian" Wing'], *Vatan*, 13 December, <http://www.rusencakir.com/Gulen-cemaatinin-sivil-kanadi/2332> (last accessed 25 July 2018).
196. Joshua D. Hendrick, *Gülen: The Ambiguous Politics of Market Islam in Turkey and the World* (New York: NYU Press, 2013).
197. 'Mardin: Gülen Cemaatini Çözemedim' ['Mardin: I Could Not Figure out the Gülen Religious Community'] (2010), *NTV*, 17 September, <https://www.ntv.com.tr/turkiye/mardin-gulen-cemaatini-cozemedim,9vq9a2cFe0m-8KvMU5cpuoQ> (last accessed 24 July 2018).
198. Uğur Kömeçoğlu, 'Kutsal ile Kamusal: Fethullah Gülen Cemaat Hareketi' ['Sacred and Public: Fethullah Gülen Religious Community Movement'], in Nilüfer Göle (ed.), *Islam'ın Yeni Kamusal Yüzleri: Islam ve Kamusal Alan Üzerine Bir Atölye Çalışması [New Public Faces of Islam: A Workshop on Islam and Public Space]* (Istanbul: Metis Yayınları, 2000), pp. 148–94.
199. 'Prof. İsmail Kara ile Gülen Cemaati-AKP Hükümeti Savaşı Üzerine Söyleşi' ['A Conversation about the Gülen Religious Community-AKP Government War with Prof. Ismail Kara'], *Ruşen Çakır*, 27 December 2014, <http://rusencakir.com/Prof-Ismail-Kara-ile-Gulen-cemaati-AKP-hukumeti-savasi-uzerine-soylesi-tam-metin/4039> (last accessed 25 July 2018).
200. Çakır, *Ayet ve Slogan*.
201. Çakır, *Ayet ve Slogan*.
202. Berna Turam, *Between Islam and the State: The Politics of Engagement* (Stanford, CA: Stanford University Press, 2007).
203. Faruk Mercan, *Fethullah Gülen* (Istanbul: Doğan Egmont Yayıncılık ve Yapımcılık A.Ş., 2009).
204. Hakan M. Yavuz, 'Neo-Nurcular: Gülen Hareketi' ['The Neo-Nurcus: The Gülen Movement'], in Yasin Aktay (ed.), *Modern Türkiye'de Siyasi Düşünce, Cilt 6: Islamcılık [Political Thought in Modern Turkey, Volume 6: Islamism]* (Istanbul: Iletişim Yayınları, 2004), pp. 295–307.
205. Yavuz, 'Neo-Nurcular'.
206. Bulaç, *Din, Kent ve Cemaat*.

207. Gülen, *Toward a Global Civilization of Love and Tolerance*.
208. Shmuel Bar, *The Muslim Brotherhood in Jordan* (Tel Aviv, Israel: The Moshe Dayan Center for Middle Eastern and African Studies, 1998).
209. Maan Abu Nowar, *The Struggle for Independence 1939—1947: A History of the Hashemite Kingdom of Jordan* (Reading: Ithaca Press, 2001).
210. Mohammad S. Abu Rumman and Hassan Abu Hanieh, *The 'Islamic Solution' in Jordan: Islamists, the State, and the Ventures of Democracy and Security* (Amman, Jordan: Friedrich-Ebert-Stiftung, 2013).
211. Carrie Rosefsky Wickham, *The Muslim Brotherhood: Evolution of an Islamist Movement* (Princeton, NJ: Princeton University Press, 2013).
212. Wickham, *The Muslim Brotherhood*.
213. Quintan Wiktorowicz, *The Management of Islamic Activism: Salafis, the Muslim Brotherhood, and State Power in Jordan* (Albany, NY: State University of New York Press, 2001).
214. Anonymous interview with a leading member of the JMB/IAF by the author, 25 February 2010, Amman, Jordan.
215. Hamed El Said and James E. Rauch, 'Education, Political Participation, and Islamist Parties: The Case of Jordan's Islamic Action Front', *The Middle East Journal*, 69.1 (2015), 51–73.
216. Mohammad Al-Fodeilat, (2012), 'How Jordan's Islamists Came to Dominate Society: An Evolution', *Al Monitor*, 10 September, <https://archive.li/mJ7yq> (last accessed 25 July 2018).
217. Mohammad S. Abu Rumman, *The Muslim Brotherhood in the 2007 Jordanian Parliamentary Elections: A Passing 'Political Setback' or Diminished Popularity* (Amman, Jordan: Friedrich-Ebert-Stiftung, 2007).
218. Ryan, 'Islamist Political Activism in Jordan'.
219. Ibrahim Gharaibeh, *Jama-a Ikhwan Muslimin fi al-Urdun (1946–1996) [Muslim Brotherhood in Jordan (1946–1996)]*. (Amman, Jordan: Al-Urdun al-Jadid Research Center, 1997).
220. Hassan Abu Hanieh, *Women and Politics: From the Perspective of Islamic Movements in Jordan* (Amman, Jordan: Friedrich-Ebert-Stiftung, 2008).
221. Umar Khrawish Hamayil, 'Institutional Characteristics of the Jordanian Professional Associations', in Warwick M. Knowled (ed.), *Professional Associations and the Challenges of Democratic Transformation in Jordan: Proceedings and Workshops* (Amman, Jordan: Al-Urdun al-Jadid Research Center, 2000).

222. Curtis R. Ryan, *Jordan in Transition: From Hussein to Abdullah* (Boulder, CO: Lynne Rienner Publishers, 2002).
223. Anonymous interview with a former Executive Committee Member of the JMB by the author, 7 February 2010, Amman, Jordan.
224. Ibrahim Gharaibeh, *Jama-a Ikhwan Muslimin fi al-Urdun*.
225. Ibrahim Gharaibeh, *Jama-a Ikhwan Muslimin fi al-Urdun*.
226. Atallah Abu Latifeh, 'Die Muslimbruderschaft in Jordanien zwischen Ideologie und Pragmatischer Anpassung' ['The Muslim Brotherhood in Jordan between Ideology and Pragmatic Adjustments'] (unpublished Doctoral Dissertation, Freie Universität Berlin Fachbereich Politische Wissenschaft [Freie University Berlin Political Science Department], 1997).
227. Hani Hourani, Sa'eda Kilani, Taleb Awad, and Hamed Dabbas, *Islamic Action Front Party* (Amman, Jordan: Al-Urdun al-Jadid Research Center, 1993).
228. Al-Fodeilat, 'How Jordan's Islamists Came to Dominate Society'.
229. Ibrahim Gharaibeh, *Jama-a Ikhwan Muslimin fi al-Urdun*.
230. Wickham, *Mobilizing Islam: Religion, Activism, and Political Change in Egypt*.
231. El Said and Rauch, 'Education, Political Participation, and Islamist Parties'.
232. El Said and Rauch, 'Education, Political Participation, and Islamist Parties'.
233. El Said and Rauch, 'Education, Political Participation, and Islamist Parties'.
234. Shadi Hamid, *Temptations of Power: Islamists and Illiberal Democracy in a New Middle East* (Oxford & New York: Oxford University Press, 2014).
235. Abu Rumman and Abu Hanieh, *The 'Islamic Solution' in Jordan*.
236. Mohammad Abu Faris, *Al-Musharaka fi al-Wizara fi al-Anthima al-Jahiliyya [Participation in the Cabinet of the Jahili (Pre-Islamic/Ignorant) Systems]* (Amman, Jordan: Dar Al Furqan, 1991). Cited in: Abu Rumman and Abu Hanieh, *The 'Islamic Solution' in Jordan*.
237. Omar Suleiman Al-Ashqar, *Hukm al-Musharaka fi al-Wizara wa al-Majalis al-Niyabiya [The Ruling on Participation in the Cabinet Government and Municipal Councils]* (Amman, Jordan: Dar Al Nafa'is, 1992). Cited in: Abu Rumman and Abu Hanieh, *The 'Islamic Solution' in Jordan*.
238. Abu Rumman and Abu Hanieh, *The 'Islamic Solution' in Jordan*.
239. As'ad Ghanem and Mohanad Mustafa, 'Strategies of Electoral Participation by Islamic Movements: The Muslim Brotherhood and Parliamentary Elections in Egypt and Jordan', *Contemporary Politics*, 17.4 (2011), 393–409.

240. Ghanem and Mustafa, 'Strategies of Electoral Participation by Islamic Movements'.
241. These factions within the Brotherhood have also been called 'the hawks versus the doves'.
242. Ibrahim Gharaibeh, *Jama-a Ikhwan Muslimin fi al-Urdun*.
243. Abu Rumman, *The Muslim Brotherhood in the 2007 Jordanian Parliamentary Elections*.
244. Anonymous interview with a former Executive Committee Member of the JMB by the author, 21 February 2010, Amman, Jordan.
245. Marion Boulby, *The Muslim Brotherhood and the Kings of Jordan, 1945–1993* (Atlanta, GA: Scholars Press, 1999).
246. Sayyid Qutb, *Milestones* (Indianapolis, IN: American Trust, 1990).
247. Qutb, *Milestones*.
248. Qutb, *Milestones*.
249. Ibrahim Gharaibeh, *Jama-a Ikhwan Muslimin fi al-Urdun*.
250. Ibrahim Gharaibeh, *Jama-a Ikhwan Muslimin fi al-Urdun*.
251. Abu Rumman and Abu Hanieh, *The 'Islamic Solution' in Jordan*.
252. Mustafa Abdelwahid, *The Rise of the Islamic Movement in Sudan (1945–1989)* (Lampeter: The Edwin Mellen Press Ltd, 2008).
253. Abdelwahid, *The Rise of the Islamic Movement in Sudan*.
254. Abdelwahid, *The Rise of the Islamic Movement in Sudan*.
255. Abdelwahid, *The Rise of the Islamic Movement in Sudan*.
256. Abdelwahab El Affendi, *Turabi's Revolution: Islam and Power in Sudan* (London: Grey Seal Books, 1991).
257. Millard Burr and Robert Oakley Collins, *Revolutionary Sudan: Hasan Al Turabi and the Islamist State, 1989–2000* (Leiden: Brill, 2003).
258. Anonymous interview with a former Executive Committee Member of the JMB by the author, 7 February 2010, Amman, Jordan.
259. Al-Fodeilat, 'How Jordan's Islamists Came to Dominate Society'.
260. Abu Latifeh, 'Die Muslimbruderschaft in Jordanien zwischen Ideologie und Pragmatischer Anpassung'.
261. Al-Fodeilat, 'How Jordan's Islamists Came to Dominate Society'.
262. Bar, *The Muslim Brotherhood in Jordan*.
263. Abu Latifeh, 'Die Muslimbruderschaft in Jordanien zwischen Ideologie und Pragmatischer Anpassung'.
264. Abu Latifeh, 'Die Muslimbruderschaft in Jordanien zwischen Ideologie und Pragmatischer Anpassung'.

265. Hourani, Kilani, Awad, and Dabbas, *Islamic Action Front Party*.
266. Anonymous interview with a former Deputy from the IAF by the author, 8 February 2010, Amman, Jordan.
267. Anonymous interview with a former Deputy from the IAF by the author, 24 February 2010, Amman, Jordan.
268. Anonymous interview with a former Deputy from the IAF by the author, 1 March 2010, Amman, Jordan.
269. Anonymous interview with a high-ranking leader of the JMB by the author, 16 February 2010, Amman, Jordan.
270. Anonymous interview with a former Executive Committee Member of the JMB by the author, 7 February 2010, Amman, Jorxdan.
271. Jillian Schwedler, *Faith in Moderation: Islamist Parties in Jordan and Yemen* (Cambridge & New York: Cambridge University Press, 2007).
272. Anonymous interview with a former Deputy from the IAF by the author, 8 February 2010, Amman, Jordan.
273. Anonymous interview with a former Deputy from the IAF by the author, 24 February 2010, Amman, Jordan.
274. Anonymous interview with a high-ranking leader of the JMB by the author, 16 February 2010, Amman, Jordan.
275. Ahmad Jamil Azem, 'The Islamic Action Front Party', in Hani Hurani, Jillian Schwedler, and George A. Musleh (eds), *Islamic Movements in Jordan* (Amman, Jordan: Al-Urdun al-Jadid Research Center & Friedrich Ebert Stiftung, 1997), pp. 95–144.
276. Anonymous interview with a leading member of the JMB/IAF by the author, 23 February 2010, Amman, Jordan.
277. Ruheil Gharaibeh (2004), 'Islamists and Political Development in Jordan: A Vision and an Experience', *Al Quds Research Center*, <http://alqudscenter.org/english/pages.php?local_type=128&local_details=2&id1=543&menu_id=19&program_id=6&cat_id=24> (last accessed 12 February 2010).
278. Anonymous interview with a former Deputy from the IAF by the author, 24 February 2010, Amman, Jordan.
279. Anonymous interview with a former Executive Committee Member of the JMB by the author, 21 February 2010, Amman, Jordan.
280. Anonymous interview with a former member of the JMB and IAF by the author, 10 March 2010, Amman, Jordan.
281. Schwedler, *Faith in Moderation*.
282. Ibrahim Gharaibeh, 'The Political Performance and the Organization of the

Muslim Brotherhood', in Hani Hourani (ed.), *Islamic Movements in Jordan* (Amman, Jordan: Al-Urdun al-Jadid Research Center, 1997), pp. 47-80.
283. Anonymous interview with a Jordanian scholar by the author, 17 February 2010, Amman, Jordan.
284. Schwedler, *Faith in Moderation*.
285. Azem, 'The Islamic Action Front Party'.
286. Boulby, *The Muslim Brotherhood and the Kings of Jordan*.
287. Abu Rumman and Abu Hanieh, *The 'Islamic Solution' in Jordan*.
288. 'Brotherhood to Take Part in Elections through IAF', *Al Dustur*, 27 August 1993.
289. Azem, 'The Islamic Action Front Party'.
290. Azem, 'The Islamic Action Front Party'.
291. Wiktorowicz, *The Management of Islamic Activism*.
292. Wiktorowicz, *The Management of Islamic Activism*.
293. Quintan Wiktorowicz, 'The Salafi Movement in Jordan', *International Journal of Middle East Studies*, 32.2 (2000), 219–40.
294. Wiktorowicz, 'The Salafi Movement in Jordan'.
295. Wiktorowicz, 'The Salafi Movement in Jordan'.
296. Wiktorowicz, *The Management of Islamic Activism*.
297. Wiktorowicz, 'The Salafi Movement in Jordan'.
298. Wiktorowicz, 'The Salafi Movement in Jordan'.
299. Wiktorowicz, 'The Salafi Movement in Jordan'.
300. Wiktorowicz, 'The Salafi Movement in Jordan'.
301. Wiktorowicz, *The Management of Islamic Activism*.
302. Wiktorowicz, 'The Salafi Movement in Jordan'.
303. Abu Rumman and Abu Hanieh, *The 'Islamic Solution' in Jordan*.
304. Jacob Olidort (2015), 'The Politics of "Quietist" Salafism', *Brookings Institution*, <https://www.brookings.edu/wp-content/uploads/2016/07/Brookings-Analysis-Paper_Jacob-Olidort-Inside_Final_Web.pdf> (last accessed 25 July 2018).
305. Joas Wagemakers, *Salafism in Jordan: Political Islam in a Quietist Community* (Cambridge & New York: Cambridge University Press, 2016).
306. Wiktorowicz, 'The Salafi Movement in Jordan'.
307. Abu Rumman and Abu Hanieh, *The 'Islamic Solution' in Jordan*.
308. Wiktorowicz, 'The Salafi Movement in Jordan'.
309. Wiktorowicz, 'The Salafi Movement in Jordan'.
310. Wagemakers, *Salafism in Jordan*.

311. Abu Rumman and Abu Hanieh, *The 'Islamic Solution' in Jordan*.
312. Mohammad S. Abu Rumman and Hassan Abu Hanieh, *Jordanian Salafism: A Strategy for the 'Islamization of Society' and an Ambiguous Relationship with the State* (Amman, Jordan: Friedrich-Ebert-Stiftung, 2010).
313. Abu Rumman and Abu Hanieh, *The 'Islamic Solution' in Jordan*.
314. Abu Rumman and Abu Hanieh, *The 'Islamic Solution' in Jordan*.
315. Abu Rumman and Abu Hanieh, *The 'Islamic Solution' in Jordan*.
316. Olidort, 'The Politics of "Quietist" Salafism'.
317. Olidort, 'The Politics of "Quietist" Salafism'.
318. Wagemakers, *Salafism in Jordan*.
319. Wagemakers, *Salafism in Jordan*.
320. Wagemakers, *Salafism in Jordan*.
321. Wagemakers, *Salafism in Jordan*.
322. Abu Rumman and Abu Hanieh, *The 'Islamic Solution' in Jordan*.
323. Abu Rumman and Abu Hanieh, *The 'Islamic Solution' in Jordan*.
324. Abu Rumman and Abu Hanieh, *The 'Islamic Solution' in Jordan*.
325. Wiktorowicz, 'The Salafi Movement in Jordan'.
326. Wagemakers, *Salafism in Jordan*.
327. Wiktorowicz, 'The Salafi Movement in Jordan'.

4

TWO PATHS,
SIX DIFFERENT OUTCOMES,
THREE NEW POLITICAL CENTRES

The city of Ouarzazate in Southern Morocco and the Ksar of Ait-Ben-Haddou, a fortress made of red mud bricks next to Ouarzazate, both sit on the foothills of the High Atlas Mountains and the Sahara Desert. For centuries, they served as a stopover on the Trans-Saharan trade route for traders involved in the exchange of gold and salt. Translating from Berber as the city 'without noise', Ouarzazate also hosted a lively Jewish community at one point in its history together with a shrine dedicated to a Sufi saint. In the world of the television drama *Game of Thrones*, Ouarzazate and the Ksar, however, are better known as the city of Yunkai, a city run by slave traders, destroyed later on by three fire-breathing dragons flying over the city. In contrast to its fictional representation where justice is served rather poetically, in reality, the city houses one of the world's largest film studios that at times provides 'Oriental(ist)' sceneries for Hollywood.

Much like Ouarzazate, Istanbul is a city both similar to and different from its fictional self. Straddling Asia and Europe, Istanbul has served as the capital to two empires, the Byzantine and the Ottoman Empires, but its history is much older dating back 6,000 years. Over the centuries, the city has not only withstood the rise and fall of empires, but also plagues, wars, economic crises, and urbanisation. Today, it is the cultural centre of Turkey hosting cinema, art, music, and theatre festivals all year around, but also a massive construction site as a result of the city's greedy growth absorbing neighbourhoods at its edges. On the screens, however, the city and its architectural silhouette with its mosques, churches, bazaars, bridges, and towers —as well as its popular image as a Muslim-yet-Western city – forms the backdrop to Turkish soap operas, such as *Noor and Muhannad* (*Gümüş*) and *Forbidden Love* (*Aşk-ı Memnu*), which have become some of the country's biggest exports to the Middle East. Although Istanbul, similar to its fictional self in soap operas, sees itself as a place where its Muslim and Western selves amicably co-exist, the reality is closer to a cautious and anxious relationship between these two identities.

Like the Ouarzazate and Istanbul, Wadi Rum, or the Valley of the Moon, in Jordan houses a historical and an imaginary world. Wadi Rum is located near the border with Saudi Arabia and is often described as the most beautiful desert in the world because of its red sands and out-of-place rocks that give the impression one has ended up inside of a computer animation. The valley has been occupied by humans for over 10,000 years, who have inscribed their history, thoughts and feelings into more than 25,000 rock carvings. It also is where Colonel Thomas Edward Lawrence would become Lawrence of Arabia playing a major role in the colonisation of the Middle East. In stark contrast to its actual history, Wadi Rum has often served as a setting to space movies. Recently, it 'was' the planet of Mars in the movie *The Martian* and the sacred moon of Jedha in the movie *Rogue One: A Star Wars Story*. Unlike the heroic acts of such an imaginary world, in reality the lines between 'good' and 'evil' are not so simple in a country surrounded by conflict on all sides.

Islamic movements in Morocco, Turkey, and Jordan are not so different from Ouarzazate, Istanbul, and Wadi Rum in that they all have an imagined world to which they aspire, yet they also face historical and contextual realities to which they need adjusting. As a result, although the six Islamic movements under study in this book have chosen one of two political paths, that of participation or non-participation, they have ended up with different outcomes from the one they expected. And in the process, they have redefined the political centre of the countries in which they were born. Such distinct transformations of six Islamic movements and the political centre in these three countries are the subject of this chapter.

Islamic Movements and the Regime after the Decision to Participate

While Islamic movements become more realistic about the menu of options available to them as a result of years of strategising in light of their strategic objectives, the regime closes in on them in order to preserve its ideological hegemony in the society thereby redefining the political centre in the country. This third hypothesis of this book, firstly, suggests that Islamic movements become more realistic about the menu of options available to them as a result of years of strategising in light of their strategic objectives. Here, 'becoming more realistic' means that Islamic movements grasp what they can and cannot achieve within the parameters of their political choices after years of working towards the achievement of their strategic objectives. Hence, strategic objectives are not just the independent variables of this study explaining the decision to enter (or not) party politics, but also end goals which Islamic movements seek to achieve. Thus, participation/non-participation in party politics is not just the dependent variable of this study but also the means through which Islamic movements expect to achieve their strategic objectives.

Within this understanding, vanguard movements will want to maximise the benefits of their political choice to participate in party politics, namely to have a top-down influence and to reach new constituents, and to minimise its costs, that is co-optation. To this end, they may choose to 'moderate' their political agenda by adapting less controversial, less openly Islamic, more widely accepted, and more pragmatic policies, and accommodate the regime by doing so.[1] In other words, they may choose 'loyalty' from Hirschman's 'exit, voice, loyalty' options.[2] Such moderation or loyalty may, in return, help these vanguard movements to connect their vanguards with new supporters beyond their ideological niche and to acquire an increased role within the government as a result. In other words, moderation may help vanguard movements to achieve their strategic objectives. However, as 'subversive parties' aiming at a wholesale transformation of the state and society,[3] such 'moderation/loyalty' may also risk diluting ideals, namely co-optation, in its 'watering down' of Islamic ideals for strategic ends.

Alternatively, vanguard movements may choose to remain 'immoderate' by continuing to advocate for their ideological/Islamic agendas, and in doing so choose to 'exit'[4] party politics by remaining at the margins of party politics.[5] Although such a stance may avoid co-optation in its immoderation, it may also prevent these movements from achieving their strategic objectives to gain top-down influence and reach more supporters. After all, such a niche party can only play a limited role in the party system and can only appeal to an ideological core.

As a result, vanguard movements will need to walk a delicate line between moderation and immoderation following their participation in the party system. In this, they will want to 'voice'[6] their demands as the main opposition party within the party system, because such an oppositional voice will position vanguard movements not only as the 'vanguards' to new socio-political constituents but also empower them as their representative. Such a stance will also avoid co-optation in its oppositional integrity. As a matter of fact, vanguard movements have often seen the risks of loyalty as so high that they have chosen 'to lose on purpose' to protect their ideological core from co-optation.[7] Thus, even if vanguard movements may experiment with moderation and immoderation, over time they will become more realistic about the opportunities and limits of the party system, and thus start playing hard opposition.

While vanguard movements may become more realistic within party politics, grassroots movements will want to maximise the benefits of their political choice to eschew party politics, namely to have more bottom-up influence and to protect their organisational core, and to minimise its costs, that is political stagnancy. To this end, they may continue what they are doing; namely, continue to engage in grassroots activism through informal channels. The problem with this strategy, nonetheless, is that it can risk political stagnancy as a result of decades of work without seeing the results of it. Although Islamic movements claim to work in decades rather than by the electoral cycle, such political stagnancy in return may limit the societal growth of a grassroots movement in its failure to recruit and in its inability to protect the organisation from regime repressions. In other words, not changing anything in the movement may hurt grassroots movements in its failure to achieve the movement's strategic objectives.

Consequently, grassroots movements may need to break the cycle of political stagnancy by pursuing various options. To this end, they may, for instance, look to build transnational alliances to bypass regime repressions at home through the 'boomerang effect',[8] wherein international actors put pressure on domestic governments to open up their political space, not only to empower their bottom-up calls for change but also to protect their organisations from regime repressions. They may also look for alliances with other opposition groups in the country to strengthen their calls for regime reconstitution. Alternatively, they may search for partnerships with the regime by ironically allying themselves with the regime to protect themselves from its repressions. In short, grassroots movements may choose to proactively avoid political stagnancy and to work towards the achievement of their strategic objectives by becoming more realistic about what they can and cannot do outside of party politics.

In addition to such expected realism, the third hypothesis of this book also suggests that the regime will close in on Islamic movements in order to preserve its ideological hegemony in the society. After all, the contention between the regime and Islamic movements is one of ideological power. As Migdal[9] states, regime–society relations are paradoxical. On the one hand, the regime aims to mould society into its ideals. On the other hand, the regime also needs to legitimise its existence in the society. As a result, the regime's engagement with the society is a process of 'mutual transformation of the state and society [that] create[s] contending coalitions that [...] cut across and blur the lines between them'.[10] Thus, the regime is '(and ha[s] to be) always in a process of becoming'.[11]

Within this framework, Islamic movements, foremost pose a threat to the regime's legitimacy, which 'involves an acceptance of the state's rule of the game, its social control as true and right [and which] means the acceptance of the symbolic order associated with the idea of the state as people's own system of meaning',[12] in their critical stance towards the concept of a nation-state. Furthermore, Islamic movements challenge the regime's legitimacy in practical terms in their unprecedented growth. Islamic movements have over time grown so much that they have started to function as a 'state within a state'[13] with their own welfare services and economic businesses. Meanwhile, the regime itself has witnessed 'growing disconnects between an already fractured political community and an increasingly illegitimate state', which in turn 'provide[d] Islamists the opening to capture key institutions in civil society or to create alternative avenues of communal identity, participation, and civic action'.[14] As a result, both the regime and Islamic movements compete to influence and to control 'the behaviour of the same population living in the same territory'.[15] Last but not least, Islamic movements challenge the regime's legitimacy ideologically. As Casanova argues, modern religions are 'similar to the classical, republican, and feminist critiques' of modernity in that they can intervene, critique, and inform civil society from a position within modernity.[16] Hence, Islamic movements challenge the regime's legitimacy by offering solidarity in the face of economic deterioration and/or by providing spiritual guidance in the face of rapid urbanisation.

In addition to such contending regime–Islamic movement relations, unforeseeable external developments and external shocks, such as a changing regional context or external conflicts, may take place beyond the control of both the regime and the Islamic movements, to which both actors need adjusting. For instance, as Al-Anani argues 'the Arab Spring has rebuilt the relationship between (and within) Islamist movements to become more complex, fluid and sometimes confrontational'.[17] Thus, although structures define an Islamic actor's 'menu of options', structures themselves are subject to change. Decisions are sometimes made in the face of changing and hence uncertain socio-political transformations; and at other times, they are made in the face of political stagnancy and the exhaustion of political alternatives. For instance, while Islamic movements in countries that have undergone regime change during the events of the Arab Spring are facing uncertain socio-political transformations, their counterparts in countries that have *not* experienced a regime change during the events of the Arab Spring are making decisions in the face of regime persistence.

Given such competition over legitimacy and changing external factors, the regime will need to close in on Islamic movements. They may do so by increasing the levels of repression to control the religio-political field. The regime may also go in the opposite direction and co-opt some Islamic movements in the hopes to divide-and-rule the political field. Alternatively, the regime itself may become more Islamic; emphasising its Islamic characteristics to re-legitimise itself in the public eye and to steal away from Islamic movements' 'Islamic' legitimacy. No matter how the regime adjusts to Islamic movements to preserve or regain its legitimacy, by closing in on Islamic movements, it will redefine regime–Islamic movement relations and thus the political centre in the country.

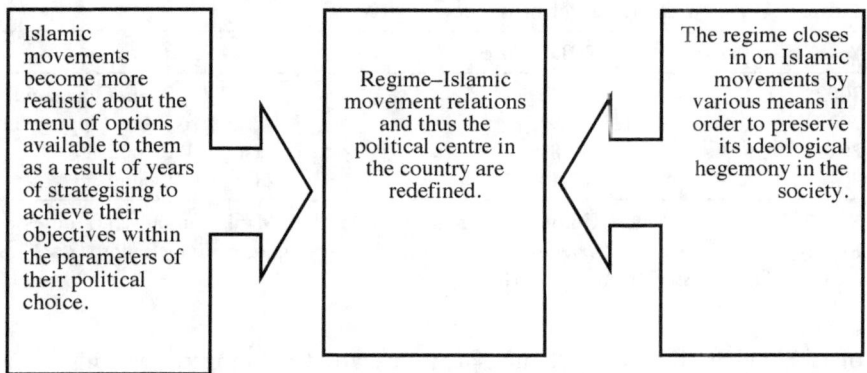

Figure 4.1 Evolution of Islamic Movement–Regime Relations

The following pages will look at these evolving Islamic movement–regime relations (Figure 4.1) after the decision to participate or not to participate in the party system, starting with Morocco.

Morocco

Following their important decisions over party politics in the mid-1990s, both Islamic movements in Morocco strategised to minimise the costs of their political choices and to maximise the benefits throughout the 2000s to realistically achieve their strategic objectives within the pragmatist authoritarian context of the Moroccan regime. To begin with, the PJD, to achieve its ideological priority of attaining top-down political influence while also avoiding co-optation within the process, walked a careful line between accommodating a repressive yet pragmatist regime and challenging it from within the parliament. To this end, the PJD, foremost, 'endorse[d] various government policies' to create relations of trust with the Moroccan regime, 'and at the same time criticise[d] other positions of the government to appear as a platform for protest' among its ideological hardliners.[8] In doing so, the PJD, on the one hand, brought attention to new political issues, such as the corruption and nepotism of the *Makhzen*, thereby increasing its top-down influence in the society, but on the other hand, also retained its loyalty to the Moroccan regime by avoiding criticising the King and the royal family and thereby avoiding regime repression.

Furthermore, the PJD carefully altered its Islamic characteristics. Instead

Table 4.1 PJD's Electoral Performance

Year	PJD's Votes	PJD Status
2002	12.92%	3rd Party/Main Opposition
2007	10.9%	2nd Party/Main Opposition
2011	22.8%	1st Party/Incumbent
2016	27.14%	1st Party/Incumbent

Source: Inter-Parliamentary Union Database (n.d.), 'Morocco: Majliss-annouwab (House of Representatives)', *Inter-Parliamentary Union*, <http://www.ipu.org/parline-e/reports/2221_arc.htm> (last accessed 10 August 2018).

of labelling itself as an 'Islamic' Party, it started defining its position as 'a political party with an Islamic frame of reference'.[19] This avoidance of direct Islamic references was also visible in the Party's political rhetoric. Instead of 'Islam is the solution', PJD started calling for political reforms and social justice.[20] In doing so, the Party demanded change, but without directly challenging the King's monopoly over the religio-political field. As a result, the PJD became the only viable opposition party in the Moroccan parliament in the 2000s (Table 4.1) and started achieving its ideological mission of top-down influence in the society with minimal levels of co-optation. For this latter end, the PJD even avoided running enough candidates to win the elections.[21]

To connect its vanguards with a wider audience the Party divorced itself from its mother movement, the MUR. In the end, the MUR, as an Islamic movement engaged in *daʿwa*, could only appeal to an ideological niche. Nonetheless, the PJD, as a political party eager to win elections, needed to appeal to a wider constituency beyond an ideological niche. As a result, MUR–PJD relations altered throughout the 2000s. According to a Minister from the PJD, the MUR and the PJD first went from full cooperation to 'coordinating partnership' in 1998 after the PJD's participation in the party system, and later into a phase of 'clear differentiation between the movement and the party' in 2004.[22] Today the two organisations define their partnership as one 'based on strategic cooperation on long-term goals, and real separation in terms of functions'.[23] This decision was made official in a 'document of complementarity', which stated that the PJD would serve as the political organisation dealing with all political issues of the country and defend Islamic causes in its institutions, while the MUR would focus on *daʿwa* and education.[24] Thus, by separating the two organisations, the PJD has resisted the regime's 'divide and rule' policy by 'dividing to survive'.[25] As a result of these strategic measures, the PJD achieved its organisational need to connect its vanguards with new societal constituents while also preserving its existing core/ideological supporter base within the MUR framework.

Like the MUR/PJD, the JSM also engaged in strategic measures to minimise the costs of its non-participation and to maximise its benefits. Foremost, the JSM went transnational in the 2000s to strengthen its ideological quest for bottom-up influence vis-à-vis the repressive pragmatist regime of Morocco. The Movement established United States headquarters in Iowa, launched two branches devoted to the publication of their literature in Great Britain and the United States under the 'Justice and Spirituality Publishing', and sent JSM leaders Nadia Yassine and Fathallah Arsalane to give lectures across the United States in venues as prominent as Harvard and Berkeley.[26] The Movement also launched a website that published in English and French.[27] The Movement transnationalised, because, according to a high-ranking leader of the JSM, globalisation and global civil society opened up a new venue to fight for the JSM.[28] Transnationalisation also protected the JSM from repression, according to a Moroccan scholar of political Islam.[29] For instance, when Nadia Yassine was tried for an interview she gave in 2005 in which she criticised the Moroccan regime and called for a republican form of government, the US and French ambassadors intervened, and she was set free. Within this understanding, the JSM 'realised that to win the battle on the domestic front, they had to put pressure on the monarchy from abroad'.[30] As a result, the JSM empowered its ideological mission for bottom-up influence with the help of transnational civil society.

Organisationally, to preserve its core supporter base while also avoiding the cost of non-participation, namely political stagnancy, the Movement formed alliances with secular forces. The Movement believed that such an alliance would not only empower the JSM's calls for bottom-up change but also its organisational integrity as the Movement's organisation, and thus relations *within* the organisation, would *not* change as a result of an alliance. According to JSM leader Abdessalam Yassine, this was a strategic move:

> There is no harm if we are to co-operate passionately with others to further the dignity and self-esteem of individuals [...] one of the virtues we deem

essential in our relations with others is the love of the nation, that is to say, to be faithful to the country and proud to serve it. Hence, we are willing to co-operate with those who are skilful and have virtues.[31]

To realise this alliance, the JSM advocated for the formation of a national charter:

> a comprehensive document that gathers under its wings the best among those who have a vision and free will, because the crisis is bigger than any party, movement or individual, no matter how capable.[32]

As a result, the JSM preserved its organisational solidarity while taking further steps towards the accomplishment of its grassroots mission.

While both Islamic movements were becoming more realistic about the discontents of their chosen political path, they entered a phase of new political opportunities in 2011 when mass protests inspired by the Arab Spring mobilised on the streets with the February 20 Movement (F20M). In response, the Moroccan King, as an authoritarian yet pragmatist leader, announced constitutional changes limiting his control over the party system. Specifically, with the new Moroccan Constitution of 2011, the King could no longer appoint the Prime Minister according to his will but had to do so based on electoral results. However, although the King could no longer preside over the executive, he still maintained absolute power over major policy choices. Hence, the regime remained a repressive pragmatist one.

Both Islamic movements in Morocco seized this moment with open arms yet ended up being disappointed by it as they realised the limits of their chosen political paths. In particular, with the first post-Arab Spring elections of 2011, the PJD became Morocco's incumbent party, leading the coalition government. Hence, for a moment, it looked like the PJD finally had the chance to achieve its strategic objective to lead political reform top-down under its vanguards. However, the reality was not so simple. Although leading the new government, the PJD was unable to introduce the top-down reforms it intended to when *Makhzen* technocrats 'supervising' government decisions halted the PJD's reform initiatives. For instance, in May 2012, the PJD Minister of Equipment and Transport, Abdelaziz Rabbah, to show the PJD's commitment to fighting corruption in Morocco, 'started to publish lists of individuals benefiting from inter-city transport licenses – many of which [were] granted as royal favours'.[33] However, other than garnering widespread publicity, this move did not change much as none of the individuals on the list were prosecuted. Furthermore, the cost of participation got higher when the PJD took a leading role in forming a government. Within the pragmatist reality of party politics, which requires ideological flexibility, avoiding co-optation was near impossible. Specifically, the PJD, after the withdrawal of its principal coalition partner, the *Istiqlal* Party, was forced to form a new coalition with the *Rassemblement National des Indépendants* (National Rally of Independents —RNI), 'a party of businessmen who did not care about ideology'.[34] This was a compromising alliance for the PJD because RNI leaders were accused of corruption and the PJD was forming a coalition with such a party while also claiming to fight corruption. In short, although the PJD achieved the highest position it could attain through participation, namely the position of an incumbent party, it still could not meet its strategic objective of top-down reform under its vanguards given the repressive pragmatism of the Moroccan regime.

Similarly, in the immediate aftermath of the F20M in Morocco, the JSM seemed, for a brief moment, to have achieved its strategic objective of bottom-up regime reconstitution through grassroots activism. Hence it joined the F20M in the hopes of introducing bottom-up change together with secular actors. However, the JSM's hopes quickly diminished when the F20M withered away while the Moroccan regime remained intact. These developments showed the limitations of the JSM's non-participation strategy. Foremost, these developments showed the difficulty of achieving the JSM's last stage of bottom-up regime reconstitution. Initially, the JSM welcomed the F20M and hoped that these protests would lead to regime reconstitution as they did elsewhere during the events of the Arab Spring. Hence, JSM's official declarations to join the F20M stated, 'this political and social congestion requires the solidarity of all the free consciences of our people [...] setting aside ideological and political considerations'.[35] Nonetheless, the JSM soon realised that the protests had reached their peak without having changed the system.

Moreover, in JSM's grassroots vision, the Movement was going to achieve its goals in coalition with secular forces. Nevertheless, internal disagreements within the F20M, between the JSM and the secularists, in particular, showed the difficulty of putting such an organisational expectation into practice and thus were cited as a major reason for the JSM's withdrawal from the F20M. Whereas secularists worried about the JSM taking over the F20M, the JSM was dissatisfied with the limited demands the secularists were making.[36] Thus, after ten months of collaboration, the JSM left the F20M in December 2011 stating that they 'wanted to act in a movement that aspired real change and not in a movement that builds on popular anger'.[37] As a result, the JSM was pushed into political stagnancy. Although this was not a new cost for the JSM, it coincided with the electoral rise of its Islamic contender, the PJD, and thus it risked a greater cost: losing supporters to the PJD, which now had governing power.

Despite learning the limits of their political choices to realise their strategic objectives after the F20M, both movements also achieved partial success towards the realisation of their strategic objectives. Although the PJD's incumbency remained ineffective for improving the institutional framework of Moroccan politics and risked co-optation in its political flexibility, the PJD also became Morocco's dominant party and redefined the 'political centre' in Morocco thereby compensating its limited top-down influence within institutional channels with its influence over the political landscape. In particular, opposition parties reformulated their political discourse to keep up with the PJD. Like the PJD, which uses a populist language of reform and criticises the *Makhzen* in heavy tones, new populist leaders using similar discourses emerged amongst opposition parties.[38] For instance, the PJD's former coalition partner, the *Istiqlal*, withdrew from the coalition claiming that the PJD's policies were hurting the Moroccan people.[39] In this, *Istiqlal* started emulating the PJD's success by aiming to become 'the government's top opponent' to garner mass popularity.[40] Hence, although the PJD, as the dominant party in the system, was itself subject to co-optation, it also controlled the language of this political landscape and thus the frameworks of co-optation of 'other' players in the system.

Organisationally, although the PJD suffered a loss in its initial popularity, it nevertheless achieved its organisational goal of extending its supporter base beyond a small ideological niche. Ironically, the voters' acknowledgment of the limited role the PJD can play within an authoritarian regime like in

Morocco allowed the PJD to become one of the best organised parties at the local level. In this, the PJD's decentralisation of its organisation and its new access to state resources helped the Party to engage in widespread recruitment activities and voter mobilisation.[41] Moreover, the PJD's commitment to providing stability, especially in the face of post-Arab Spring turmoil in Egypt and Syria, widened the Party's appeal amongst new societal classes. Hence, 'although historically, the PJD was dominated by educated middle-class engineers, doctors, lawyers, and professors, it increasingly open[ed] up to and incorporat[ed] wealthier businessmen'.[42] Furthermore, the PJD's pragmatism, especially in local politics, garnered widespread appeal. For instance, it launched a campaign in which it organised 'a series of town hall-style meetings held in villages and cities to communicate directly with citizens, allowing legislators to explain their experiences in government and the problems they face'.[43] This campaign, in turn, allowed the PJD to introduce itself to rural voters. As a result, the PJD succeeded in extending its vanguard organisation to a wider audience, while also changing the actors within the system through participation.

Like the PJD, the JSM also partially achieved its strategic objectives. Ideologically, the JSM proved that top-down reforms were impossible within a system prone to co-optation, where not even the governing party, the PJD, could engage in deep-seated reforms. This realisation, in turn, demonstrated that even if the JSM's vision would take time, its vision still was more likely to bring fundamental changes to Morocco than the alternative of engaging in non-essential reforms within the party system.

Organisationally, the JSM's non-participation also allowed the Movement to establish relations of solidarity within the Movement outside of the fragmenting context of party politics. These relations of trust in turn allowed the JSM to overcome two significant organisational obstacles. Firstly, the Movement survived the failure of the F20M and the electoral success of its Islamic contender, the PJD. It did not see major internal splits or differences over the Movement's course of action even though these historic events showed the limitations of the JSM's strategy of non-participation. Secondly, the Movement survived the death of its charismatic leader without any major splits. After Yassine had passed away in late 2012, religious scholar Mohammed Abbadi began serving as the elected secretary-general, and

Fatallah Arsalane, the long-time spokesperson of the JSM, became the deputy secretary-general.[44] 'The speed with which a new leadership was announced suggest[ed] that a formula for nominations and elections [...] had all been prepared before Yassine's death'.[45] As a result, the JSM succeeded in creating and maintaining organisational solidarity by remaining outside the party system – a key to success that was reiterated by Yassine in his last testament: 'I advise of righteous companionship and building a community, and of righteous companionship within that community'.[46]

While the PJD and the JSM were becoming more realistic as to what they could and could not achieve through participation and non-participation respectively, the Moroccan regime was closing in on them, too. Specifically, the Moroccan regime was starting to promote an 'official Moroccan Islam' by increasing the public visibility of the King's role as the Commander of the Believers, and by extending the powers and the geographical scope of the Ministry of Islamic Affairs.[47] The King was protecting and promoting an 'official Moroccan Islam' through 'non-political religious organisations, such as da^cwa associations [... and ...] the Council of 'Ulama'', and through 'the enactment of a conservative Code of Personal Status (*Mudawana*), the creation of Qur'anic schools, and the imposition of prayer in school'.[48] He also had empowered the Minister of Islamic Affairs, who in turn led various religious councils at the national and local levels,[49] and controlled 'traditional education that produces Imams and preachers'.[50] All of these engagements in the religious sphere, in turn, were helping the King 'to establish a personal bond and link with the ordinary Moroccan people'.[51]

In this, as Maghraoui explains: 'Broad concepts, such as "moderation", "tolerance", "openness", "cultural coexistence" and "reconciliation", [were becoming] part of the lexicon of the official discourse about what Islam is about in Morocco'.[52] In doing so, according to Belal, the King as 'the guarantor of Morocco's Islamic identity [was] constantly "refresh[ing]" his role as the spiritual guide'.[53] Moreover, the King had started promoting a religious identity for himself as the 'King of the Poor' by competing with the charities run by Islamic movements through his charities.[54]

The King was also using Maghrebi Sufism, a key component of Moroccan Islam. For instance, he was encouraging Sufism's moderate and often apolitical calls through festivals and TV shows.[55] He also had appointed a Sufi scholar, Ahmed Taoufiq, as the Minister of Islamic Affairs replacing 'the longstanding minister Abdelkebir Alaoui Mdaghri who was seen as being too close to the Salafis'.[56] Furthermore, the monarchy had formed the Supreme Council of the Ulama to oversee suspicious activities outside the scope of 'official Moroccan Islam'.[57] This Council had closed down a number of mosques associated with extremism, and had started educating the society in line with 'official Moroccan Islam' (1) by engaging in activities such as 'holding meetings in mosques or in people's homes, as well as in universities', and (2) by encouraging the formation of 'legal mosques' through tax exemptions, financial support, and training of local Imams.[58] Hence, today the Moroccan regime has closed in on the MUR/PJD and the JSM by reemphasising its Islamic role and legitimacy and thereby has redefined the political centre of Morocco towards a more openly Islamic one yet one controlled by the regime.

Meanwhile, in Turkey, Islamic movements have redefined the political centre of the country by altering the parameters of laicism.

Turkey

By the 1970s, while the NOM was pursuing party politics, the GM was staying out of it. They were working to minimise the costs of their political choices and to maximise the benefits in light of the Turkish regime's civilising mission and thus its profound distrust towards political Islam. This was a regime watching Islamic movements carefully to close in on them early on. Within this context, the NOM faced serious setbacks in party politics. Firstly, the laic Turkish regime was institutionally blocking the NOM's political parties: the NOM's first party, the National Order Party (*Milli Nizam Partisi*), was closed down in its very first year for promoting Islamism, and its second party, the National Salvation Party (*Milli Selamet Partisi*), would be closed down a few years later with the 1980 military coup. In later years, two more parties associated with the NOM would also be closed down (Table 4.2). Secondly, the NOM was facing strong contenders in Turkish party politics. Existing mainstream parties, the Justice Party (*Adalet Partisi*) on the centre-right and the Republican People's Party (*Cumhuriyet Halk Partisi*) on the centre-left, were electorally and politically dominating the party system gathering together around seventy percent of the votes. Consequently,

Table 4.2 Parties Related to the NOM

Party Name	Years Active
National Order Party (*Milli Nizam Partisi*)	1970–1971
National Salvation Party (*Milli Selamet Partisi*)	1972–1980
Welfare Party (*Refah Partisi*)	1983–1998
Virtue Party (*Fazilet Partisi*)	1998–2001
Felicity Party (*Saadet Partisi*)	2001–
Justice and Development Party (*Adalet ve Kalkınma Partisi*)	2001–

the NOM's early experience within the party system was a disappointment for its vanguards expecting to swipe elections immediately after their participation.

Given such restrictive circumstances, the NOM could either moderate its Islamism to embrace laicism thereby co-opting its ideals or it could remain immoderate and continue to advocate for a greater role for Islam in party politics. In its early years, the NOM chose to remain immoderate in order to avoid co-optation. To this end, the NOM, unlike PJD's cautious calls for reform in Morocco, strategically adapted an immoderate rhetoric throughout the 1970s.[59] In particular, it criticised Turkey's quest for secularisation as being a tool of foreign powers to intervene in Turkish politics, and advocated for the introduction of a new economic system called the 'Just Order' (*Adil Düzen*) based on Islamic finance to replace and to rival Westernisation.[60] Under this new socio-economic order, the NOM promised (1) to minimise the influence of Istanbul-based big corporations and Western companies in the economy in favour of small businesses and state-owned heavy industry, and (2) to ban interest-based banking in favour of Islamic finance.[61] As a result of such an immoderate rhetoric, the NOM started to form a small yet devoted ideological appeal amongst 'the homogeneous Sunni-Muslim base of farmers and the conservative petty bourgeoisie of shopkeepers, small merchants, and artisans from provincial towns and cities'.[62] Turning this niche appeal into a political asset, the NOM took on the role of a kingmaker party to form coalitions with mainstream parties[63] (Table 4.3). By doing so, the NOM thrived, having more influence than its votes, and taking over vital ministries as a minor coalition partner. In particular, the National Salvation Party became the minor coalition partner (1) of the centre-left Republican People's Party in 1974, controlling the Ministries of Justice, Internal Affairs,

Table 4.3 NOM Related Parties' Electoral Performance

Year	NOM Party Name	Votes (%)	Status
1973	National Salvation Party	11.8%	4th Party/Minor Coalition Partner
1977	National Salvation Party	8.6%	3rd Party/Minor Coalition Partner
1987	Welfare Party	7.16%	No seats
1991	Welfare Party	16.88%	4th Party/Opposition Party
1995	Welfare Party	21.33%	1st Party/Coalition Partner
1999	Virtue Party	15.47%	3rd Party/Opposition Party
2002	Justice and Development Party	34.17%	1st Party/Incumbent Party
2007	Justice and Development Party	46.52%	1st Party/Incumbent Party
2011	Justice and Development Party	49.90%	1st Party/Incumbent Party
2015 (June)	Justice and Development Party	40.87%	1st Party/Early Elections
2015 (Nov.)	Justice and Development Party	49.50%	1st Party/Incumbent Party

Source: Inter-Parliamentary Union Database (n.d.), 'Turkey: Türkiye Büyük Millet Meclisi (T.B.M.M) (Grand National Assembly of Turkey)', *Inter-Parliamentary Union*, <http://archive.ipu.org/parline-e/reports/2323_arc.htm> (last accessed 10 August 2018).

and Industry and Technology, (2) of the centre-right Justice Party in 1975–1977, occupying the Ministries of Justice and Internal Affairs, and (3) of the centre-right Justice Party again in 1977–1978, this time controlling the Ministries of Internal Affairs and Industry and Technology.

Starting in the 1980s, in addition to its strategic use of an immoderate rhetoric to achieve its ideological mission for top-down influence, the NOM also tried to connect its vanguards with the masses. Firstly, in the late 1980s and under its third party, the Welfare Party (*Refah Partisi*), the NOM started targeting the urban poor. As Dağı explains, the NOM:

> came to realise the need for turning the party into a mass political movement, adopting an agenda that put stress on social problems rather than on religious themes, using modern propaganda methods. It mainly tried to mobilise the urban poor, who suffered from the liberalisation policies of the 1980s that had a negative impact on peripheral social and economic groups.[64]

Secondly, in the early 1990s the NOM 'invented the concept of the "social municipality" *(sosyal belediyecilik)* to deal with poverty by creating horizontal networks of aid to the needy'.[65] They 'linked citizens to the city administration and responded to the pressing questions and inquiries of ordinary folk', while also emphasising their Islamic character.[66] By targeting the urban poor and creating direct links with people at the local level, the NOM started attracting followers beyond its ideological niche in the early 1990s. With their support, the Welfare Party won the 1994 municipal elections in Ankara and Istanbul, the two biggest cities in Turkey, came out as the winning party in the 1995 general elections, and formed a coalition government with the centre-right True Path Party (*Doğru Yol Partisi*) in 1996–1977.

In the meantime, the NOM also avoided co-optation by adapting an exclusive organisation around a few leaders. In this way, the organisation, like the PJD in Morocco, separated from its mother movement, the *Nakşibendi* Order after the Nakşi leader Kotku died in 1980 and the NOM leader Erbakan stood against the new head of the Order, Esad Coşan, forcing the *Nakşibendi*s out of the NOM.[67] Furthermore, its leading cadre, its 'vanguards', remained constant for forty years and have together embraced the ups and downs of Turkish party politics including party closures as well as taking up leading positions in coalition governments.[68]

Unlike the NOM, which operated in the open as a political party up until the 1980s, the GM was rather an unknown quantity to the general Turkish public. In the 1980s however, the GM started becoming more public in order to take advantage of the liberalisation process spearheaded by then-Prime Minister Turgut Özal and his incumbent centre-right Motherland Party (*Anavatan Partisi*).[69] With the economic liberalisation of Turkey, the GM and its wealthy patrons and followers' assets grew, allowing the Movement to expand exponentially. The GM also continued to stay close to the incumbent parties in the 1990s by lending support to the centre-left Democratic Left Party (*Demokratik Sol Parti*) under Bülent Ecevit's leadership. While the JSM in Morocco was being persecuted by the Moroccan regime, the GM was able to extend its grassroots activism in the realm of education and the media in and beyond Turkey through its high-level connection. In the field of education, it was

> estimated that some 75 percent of Turkey's two million preparatory school students [were] enrolled in Gülen institutions. He control[led] thousands of top-tier secondary schools, colleges, and student dormitories throughout

Turkey, as well as private universities, the largest being [the] Fatih University in Istanbul. Outside Turkey, his movement [ran] hundreds of secondary schools and dozens of universities in 110 countries worldwide.[70]

In the realm of media, the GM operated

> a media network, including *Samanyolu*, a television channel with a global satellite outreach; several local and national radio stations; *Zaman*, a newspaper published in twelve different countries; *Aksiyon*, a news magazine; *The Fountain*, an international magazine in English; and about ten other magazines, which cover issues ranging from ecology, literature, and theology to popular science.[71]

It was estimated that all these engagements in education and media together with the Movement's business ventures were worth $20 billion.[72]

The GM, like the Moroccan JSM's transnationalisation, was also growing beyond Turkey in the 1990s, especially in the Turkic Republics of Central Asia and the Caucasus that had just gained their independence after the fall of the Soviet Union. In particular, the GM was opening schools in these countries with the financial backing of its 'pious capitalist' followers. Consequently, the GM came to operate 'twenty-nine schools in Kazakhstan, twelve in Uzbekistan, fifteen in Turkmenistan, twelve in Kyrgyzstan, five in Tajikistan and another twelve in Azerbaijan'.[73] Together they were educating about 20,000 students.[74] These schools benefited the GM in two ways. Firstly, the GM and its followers were gaining economic entry into these newly opening markets.[75] Secondly, these schools were striking a nationalist cord within the laic establishments in their prioritisation of Turkish nationalism abroad.

The GM, going beyond its counterpart to the JSM's transnationalisation, was also becoming more publicly visible through its academic seminars in Turkey and abroad. In Turkey the GM was organising the 'Abant Platforms', bringing various scholars, think tanks, intellectuals, politicians, and civil society organisations together. Abroad, the Movement was hosting academic conferences on topics such as interfaith dialogue and on the GM itself to introduce the Movement to international scholars. Such academic engagements in return were helping the GM to portray itself as an alternative to Islamic fundamentalism domestically and internationally and thus was allowing the Movement to mobilise freely.

On February 28, 1997, however, the growth of both the NOM and the GM was put on hold when the Turkish military under the leadership of the National Security Council (*Milli Güvenlik Kurulu*), in a memorandum dubbed a 'post-modern coup',[76] called for a curbing down of Islamic influence in politics and society. This memo resulted in the closing down of the NOM's Welfare Party (*Refah Partisi*), which at the time was a coalition partner to the incumbent government, while the GM remained under suspicion because, although the GM did not directly participate in party politics or challenge the regime's laicism, questions remained over the long-term political intentions of such a successful Islamic movement and its presence within state institutions. As the Turkish regime closed in on both Islamic movements, the costs of posing a political challenge to laic establishments were getting higher. Hence, unlike Morocco's opening political opportunities in light of the F20M, political opportunities in Turkey were closing down for Islamic movements forcing them to re-evaluate their strategies.

Within this political context, both Islamic movements faced their greatest fear: while co-optation became a reality for the NOM, political stagnancy defined the GM. To begin with, co-optation became a reality for the NOM when, after the closure of NOM's fourth party Virtue Party (*Fazilet Partisi*) in 2001, some younger leaders within the NOM 'realised that they could also win national elections if they lowered their ideological commitments and stressed pragmatic policy solutions'.[77] Thus, unlike its Moroccan counterpart, after the closure of NOM's Welfare Party, an internal split erupted within the NOM resulting in the establishment of the Justice and Development Party (*Adalet ve Kalkınma Partisi*) (AKP) in 2001 when the younger generation within the NOM, Abdullah Gül and Recep Tayyip Erodoğan, left the NOM to form this new party. Unlike their predecessors in the NOM, this new Party situated itself at the political centre as a new centre-right party embracing secularism thereby co-opting the NOM's strategic objectives. Firstly, this new Party, like the Moroccan PJD, redefined itself as a 'conservative democratic' party without any Islamic associations left in its official documents. Secondly, instead of claiming that they were the vanguards of Turkish society, leading it towards Islam, the new leaders of the pro-Islamic movement claimed that they were the representatives of a pious majority that was barred from decision-making by laicist elites for decades. Within this framework, both democratisation and European Union (EU) membership were presented as complementary components allowing freedom of religious exercise.[78]

Lastly, the AKP prioritised economic liberalisation instead of an Islamic 'Just Order'.[79] Ironically, such co-optation also distinguished the AKP from the PJD in Morocco and made this new Party the 'dominant party' of Turkish politics: 'a party that outdistances all the others (and thus) is significantly stronger than others'.[80] The reasons for the AKP's new political orientation away from its roots in the NOM[81] as well as for its electoral success[82] has been addressed in books and articles taking up many bookshelves, most of which focus on the demise of governing/mainstream centre-right and centre-left parties after the 2001 economic crisis and the AKP's promise of an economic recovery.[83] However, what matters for this study is that ironically by co-opting their Islamism to accommodate the laic Turkish regime, the NOM's successor, the AKP, achieved the NOM's twin objectives of widening its supporter base and becoming a dominant party with top-down influence over policymaking. Today, the AKP has been the sole incumbent party of Turkey for over a decade. Meanwhile, the NOM and its new (fifth) party, the Felicity Party (*Saadet Partisi*) failed in both regards after this split. Since it is the AKP that took over the NOM's mission and constituency, this study will talk about the AKP as the NOM successor from hereon.

Similarly, for the GM, like the JSM after the F20M in Morocco, political stagnancy became the norm after the February 28 process. Within a year of the memo, Fethullah Gülen, citing his health treatment, relocated to the US, where he still resides, and thereby avoided being tried in person for Islamism and clandestine networking, and the Movement entered a period of political stagnancy by laying low in order to protect its grassroots organisation from political pressures.

Despite such accommodation by both Islamic movements, the Turkish regime's laic pressures increased as the regime aimed to close in on Islamic movements with an iron grip. First, on 27 April 2007, the military made an

'E-memorandum' and tried to limit AKP's governing abilities by protesting the candidacy of Abdullah Gül from the AKP to the position of the President, a position that was seen by many as the guardian of laicism in Turkey. The next year, in 2008, the Turkish Constitutional Court discussed charges against AKP's secular commitment and debated whether it was necessary to close down the Party. Although the decision dismissed demands for AKP's closure, that the decision was made with one vote difference is very telling in itself. Meanwhile, 'a series of secret military plans were leaked to the public' that accused the GM of having links to coordinated efforts to build a 'parallel state' within state institutions.[84]

As a result of such rising repression, both Islamic movements, like their Moroccan counterparts after the F20M, realised the limits to their political paths. Although AKP's vanguards had finally achieved a position of top-down influence as the sole governing party, they were not fully able to translate these achievements into practice given the control of laic establishments. Similarly, although the GM had built the most powerful Islamic network in the country through years of grassroots activism, it still could not engage in the bottom-up transformation it was seeking, as it remained under the thumb of the laic establishments in its occasional designation as an Islamic threat to the state.

Despite such drawbacks, nevertheless, both actors had also accumulated vital political capital over the years to an extent unparalleled by their Moroccan counterparts. The AKP, unlike the PJD in Morocco, had engaged, in the Party's own words, in a 'silent revolution' by using its position not only as the sole incumbent party of Turkey but also as the dominant party of Turkey that has the support of half the population.[85] Until the E-memo, the Party had already passed eight reform packages for EU accession and increased civilian (their) control over the military: in 2003, the number of civilians was raised in the National Security Council, which is responsible for developing the country's security policies,[86] in 2004, the National Security Council's role was reduced to a consultative role,[87] and in 2006, the Military Criminal Code was amended wherein civilians could not be tried by the military court anymore.[88] With these changes, the AKP not only received the support of its own constituency but also of liberal segments of society, who saw these reforms favourably as a step en route to democratisation and of businesspeople benefiting from such openings. Meanwhile, the Party had also increased its voteshare from 34% to 49% in consecutive elections (2002–2015), and no other political party came even close to challenging its electoral strength. The AKP's main political rivals within the same time span, the Republican People's Party (*Cumhuriyet Halk Partisi*) and the Nationalist Action Party (*Milliyetçi Hareket Partisi*), only increased their votes from 19% to 25% and from 8% to 12%, respectively. Although there was certainly societal opposition outside formal institutions, as showcased by the Gezi Protests of 2013, in the absence of an organised opposition, they remained too fragmented to counter the AKP. As a result, the AKP's incumbency started becoming unrivaled within the Parliament to pass and to administer its desired legislations. Adding to this, the Party also consolidated its political dominance through its control of the executive, legislature, and the presidency. As a result, the secular military tutelage in Turkey started weakening.

The GM, unlike the JSM in Morocco, on the other hand, already possessed socio-economic power through its dominance in education, media, and business circles within and beyond Turkey. Furthermore, in these circumstances, the GM and the AKP, despite coming from different Islamic movements and thus diverse political paths, also shared a number of similarities: both actors were persecuted by the same laic military tutelage, and had a similar societal base appealing to pious segments of the society hailing from small and mid-size towns.[89] These similarities, however, according to Kara, were not based on 'ideational consensus, or relations of love'.[90] On the contrary, these two Islamic trends diverged significantly in their outlook towards the Kurdish issue, Israel, and Iran.[91]

Regardless of such vital differences, the GM started openly supporting the AKP's incumbency against the laic military tutelage. Although this was not a first in GM's history, since the GM had supported incumbent parties in the past, it was the first time the Movement was supporting a party from an Islamic origin and was doing so publicly. Within this framework, the GM rallied its grassroots power behind the AKP. Its media outlets supported the government's policies and criticised its opposition.[92] Moreover, during the *Ergenekon* and *Balyoz* (Sledgehammer) trials, military officers, journalists and opposition lawmakers were alleged as being part of a laic clandestine organisation called 'Ergenekon' and were charged with scheming against the AKP government by 'attempting to incite turbulence in society and preparing the conditions for the military to intervene'.[93] During these trials, the GM enthusiastically supported the trials in its own media and has 'presented the prosecutions as a deep cleaning of state institutions, ridding them of terrorist organisations, coup mongers (*darbeci*), and secular-Kemalist bureaucrats'.[94] Going beyond the media support, there were also allegations that the GM was behind these trials. According to Yavuz and Balcı, for instance, 'the chief prosecutor in the Ergenekon case, and some key police officials [...] were Gülen sympathisers',[95] and with these trials they aimed to 'remove secular and nationalist officers in order to promote Gülen or pro-Gülen sympathisers in the military'.[96] Similarly, in their investigation of these trials, Doğan and Rodrik, have also argued that these trials were mostly based on fabricated evidence provided by prosecutors and police close to the GM.[97] At the end of these trials, 275 defendants, including Ilker Basbuğ, former Chief of the Armed Forces, were convicted. Although the convictions of these Kafkaesque trials were overturned by the Appeals Court in a few years, which cited that 'evidence had been collected illegally',[98] what is clear regardless of the nebulous process of these trials is that during the five years that they went on, they hurt the public image of the laic military and diminished its political prestige. Today, these trials are considered to be one of the vital turning points for the laic military tutelage in Turkey.

Another turning point for the laic tutelage was the 2010 constitutional referendum proposed by the AKP incumbency to alter the structure of the Judiciary by increasing the number of civilian-appointed judges to the Constitutional Court. To support the AKP in this referendum, Fethullah Gülen made a video that aired in the popular media announcing his 'personal' support for a yes vote by saying 'if circumstances would allow, even those in the grave shall be woken up to vote yes'.[99] Such judicial changes weakened the laic tutelage further. As a result, unlike their Moroccan counterparts, which were unable to challenge the Moroccan regime's religio-political power inside or outside the party system, Islamic movements in Turkey succeeded in weakening the laic tutelage and thus redefining the political centre in Turkish politics. Today, it is not Islamic movements that need to adapt to an existing political centre but other political actors that need to adapt.

In Jordan, in the meantime, the Brotherhood and the Quietist Salafis stagnated within the tolerant authoritarian context of the regime there.

Table 4.4 IAF's Electoral Performance

Year	JMB/IAF's Votes	JMB/IAF's Status
1989	20 Seats (out of 80)	1st Party/Part of Coalition
1993	16 seats (out of 80)	1st Party/Opposition
1997	N/A	Boycotted
2003	17 seats (out of 104)	1st Party/Opposition
2007	6 seats (out of 110)	Rejected results
2010	N/A	Boycotted
2013	N/A	Boycotted
2016	15 seats (out of 130)	Ran with Christian candidates under the 'National Coalition for Reform'

Source: Inter-Parliamentary Union Database (n.d.), 'Jordan: Majlis Al-Nuwaab (House of Representatives)', *Inter-Parliamentary Union*, <http://archive.ipu.crg/parline-e/reports/2163_arc.htm> (last accessed 10 August 2018).

Jordan

Unlike their counterparts in Morocco and Turkey, Islamic movements in Jordan stagnated inside and outside the party system as the tolerant authoritarian regime of Jordan closed in on them by redefining its dominance in the religio-political field. The JMB's options within the party system were limited because decades-long friendly relations between the Jordanian regime and the Muslim Brotherhood deteriorated after the formation of the IAF when the Brotherhood became electorally more successful than the regime expected. In the 1989 elections, the Brotherhood won 22 seats out of 80, and in the 1993 elections, the IAF won 17 out of 80 seats becoming the biggest party in the Jordanian Parliament (Table 4.4). This electoral victory was the first warning sign for the Jordanian regime. In the words of a regime loyalist Jordanian Senator, even though Jordan had '16 parties, all of them together, with all due respect to them, [could not] move the streets like them [the Brotherhood]'.[100] Hence, unlike its counterparts in Morocco or Turkey, both of which started as minor parties, the IAF started out as a dominant party in the party system, putting the Jordanian regime on high alert.

The second warning sign was the way in which the Brotherhood acted as a member of the 1990/91 Badran coalition. Specifically, the Brotherhood saw its electoral victory as a sign to pursue its ideological goals in the society top-down and introduced controversial moral policies. For instance, the

Brotherhood proposed to ban 'male hairdressers from working in women's beauty salons', and 'fathers from attending their daughters' sporting events'.[101] These proposals not only alienated more secular segments of the Jordanian society but also shattered the perception within the Jordanian regime that the Brotherhood was a *moderate* Islamic actor. Hence, while the PJD in Morocco was trying to convince power-holders of its moderation, the Brotherhood was alienating the Jordanian regime in its immoderation.

As a result, the Jordanian regime started seeing the Brotherhood as a counter-hegemonic force that the regime needed to limit if it wanted to control its tactical political opening process. Hence, the regime, like its Moroccan counterpart, started promoting its 'official Islam' not only to counterbalance the rise of the Islamic opposition but also to consolidate its political legitimacy as a Hashemite Kingdom claiming prophetic descent.[102] Furthermore, the regime introduced a series of legal changes to limit the Brotherhood's political options. In particular, the regime, like its Turkish counterpart limiting Islamic movements through institutional frameworks, introduced a new electoral system in 1992, the 'one man, one vote' system under which 'each voter could cast a ballot for only one person' rather than for all the seats in their district.[103] In effect, this increased the vote share of rural areas, where pro-monarchy tribes form the majority, for urban areas, where the IAF was powerful.[104] Hence, the IAF boycotted the 1997 elections when it became apparent that their participation under such an engineered electoral system was futile to the achievement of their strategic objectives. According to a former deputy from the JMB, they learned that they 'do not have actual democracy, it is decoration'.[105]

The Brotherhood could also not strategise to work outside the party system to support its strategic objectives when the regime revised the law on preaching at mosques to control for the JMB-affiliated imams by demanding that each sermon be officially approved.[106] They 'shut down newspapers associated with the movement, and in 1993 it issued a decree enacting restrictive press law'.[107] The regime also banned 'Brotherhood activists [from engaging in] demonstrations and mass public events'.[108] In this, different from Morocco and Turkey where Islamic movements faced a repressive regime, for the JMB regime repression was a new cost when the regime started seeing the Brotherhood, its former ally, as the main rival to its hegemony.

Two external shocks strained JMB–regime relations further in the 2000s, thus limiting the Brotherhood's extra-parliamentary activities. Firstly, in 2005, radical Islamists bombed hotels around Amman. Secondly, in 2006, Hamas won the Palestinian Legislative Elections. While the latter event instilled fear in the Jordanian regime and hope in the JMB for an increased Islamic role in party politics, the former event justified further repression against Islamic actors on the part of the regime. Brotherhood establishments, such as the Islamic Hospital and the Islamic Centre, both of which formed the backbone to the JMB's grassroots activities with more than $1.5 billion in assets,[109] were seized by the regime to control for the Brotherhood's expansion. Between 2001 and 2011, the King of Jordan, Abdullah II, did not even meet with the leaders of the JMB/IAF.[110] Within this domestic isolation, the Brotherhood, unlike the JSM in Morocco or the GM in Turkey, found itself also isolated internationally. According to an ex-JMB member,

> at that time we thought that the West, or the Americans and the Europeans are supporting us and the region to go through democratisation. That is why we thought we are 50-50 between our expectations and the real position.[111]

However, the West did not deliver on their expectations. A journalist from the Islamist daily *Assabeel*[112] recalls that they had many meetings with the leaders of the Western world explaining their positions and their desire for human rights and democracy but the West 'chose' not to understand them. As a result, unlike the GM in Turkey or the JSM in Morocco, the Brotherhood could not use transnational networks to strengthen its calls in Jordan. In short, the Brotherhood, in the face of such deteriorating domestic and international relations, did not even have a strategic trade-off to choose from between participation and non-participation as it could neither have top-down influence within party politics nor bottom-up influence outside of it.

The Brotherhood could also not make any progress on its organisational needs as it could neither widen its mass appeal nor protect its existing supporter base. Foremost, the Brotherhood could not expand its mass appeal to new constituents as the IAF did not develop into a new political party but remained the political wing of the Muslim Brotherhood. Unlike the PJD–MUR separation in Morocco or AKP's divorce from the NOM, until

2013, the IAF head was elected by the JMB and the IAF had to consult the Brotherhood on its decisions.[113] As a result, the IAF did not reach out and appeal beyond the Brotherhood's mass base.

More importantly, the Brotherhood failed to attract Transjordanians. Historically, the Brotherhood had a strong presence amongst the Palestinians in Jordan. After the establishment of Israel in 1948, Jordan had annexed the West Bank and had 'restructured its parliament to provide for seats equally divided between the West Bank and the East Bank populations'.[114] However, a lot had changed since then: the second and third generation Palestinian refugees had become the urban poor without access to state resources, and after 'Jordan formally severed legal and administrative ties with the West Bank in July 1988', West Bank Palestinians could not vote anymore.[115] In the meantime, the Brotherhood, with the support of the Jordanian regime, had filled in the Palestine Liberation Organisation's (PLO) vacuum after its expulsion from Jordan in 1970 by working in Palestinian refugee camps.[116] Hence, the Brotherhood had historically been the only political organisation in Jordan integrating Palestinians into its ranks without resorting to Palestinian nationalism.[117] According to a Brotherhood leader, whereas Palestinians were family-based, Jordanians were tribe-based, and thus Palestinians, because they lacked such tribal connections, could not get networked, and the JMB served as their network instead.[118]

Moreover, Hamas and the JMB came from the same ideological and organisational framework of the International Muslim Brotherhood, and many Brotherhood leaders were of Palestinian origin.[119] As a result, the Brotherhood was supported by Palestinians as well as by 'Jordanians of Palestinian descent'.[120] In light of these internal divisions, if the Brotherhood strategised to win new constituents, then it had to become a 'Jordanian movement'. This transformation, nonetheless, would risk losing its Palestinian base – a significant base given that with the new 'one man, one vote' system, the IAF had already lost its power amongst the Transjordanian/East Bank electorate and had increasingly started relying on Jordanian voters of Palestinian descent.[122] However, not doing so also would lead to electoral failures in the absence of Transjordanian votes for the Brotherhood.

Preserving its organisational strength also proved difficult given the Brotherhood's internal disagreements. Unlike the JSM under Yassine or the

GM under Gülen, the IAF established an internal structure, where 'party leaders [were] elected by the membership, and there [was] a regular turnover in top positions'.[122] Nonetheless, such democratic turnover in leadership also led to constant shifts between the reformists and hardliners and thus to shifts in policies and strategies leading to political inconsistencies. In short, the Brotherhood failed to reach a wider audience but also failed to preserve a strong union internally.

In light of such failures, political stagnation became a reality for the Brotherhood as the IAF's strategising faltered and it followed an ambiguous policy between boycotting elections and running in elections throughout the late 1990s and 2000s. The IAF boycotted the 1997 and 2010 elections and ran in the 2003 and 2007 elections (Table 4.4). In 2003, the Brotherhood participated in elections and encouraged its constituencies to go to the polls. Despite such enthusiasm, they only won 17 seats out of 110. This electoral decline continued with the 2007 elections when IAF's seats dropped to 6. As a result, the IAF boycotted the 2010 elections in the belief that its electoral failure was due to the one-person-one vote system and to election manipulations.[123] During these years, although the Brotherhood avoided co-optation by boycotting the new electoral laws designed to limit its influence, it also entered a long phase of political stagnancy, where the Brotherhood's participation as well as non-participation were fruitless. In this, unlike its Moroccan or Turkish counterparts, the Brotherhood failed to formulate a strategic course of action.

As regime–Brotherhood relations deteriorated, regime–Quietist Salafi relations improved as the regime saw Quietist Salafism as a medium to control the religio-political field. Firstly, because Quietist Salafis rejected party politics, direct political engagements, and open opposition to the state, and because they pledged allegiance and obedience to the state, they were not seen as an immediate threat to the Jordanian regime.[124] In other words, the Jordanian regime, unlike its position towards the Brotherhood, did not see the Quietist Salafis as a threat to its socio-political hegemony. On the contrary, the Jordanian regime saw Quietist Salafis as a counterbalance to the Brotherhood's societal strength. Hence, while the regime banned the Brotherhood from public engagements in mosques and closed down its charities, it encouraged Quietist Salafis to organise freely.[125] Secondly, after the 2006 Amman hotel bombings, Quietist Salafis were also seen as a counterbalance to Jihadi Salafism by the regime. In particular, the Jordanian regime 'benefited from the *fatwas*, lectures, sermons and discourse' of the Quietist Salafis against radical currents.[126] Lastly, by encouraging Quietist Salafism, the regime was able to divide the Islamic political field internally.[127]

In this political climate, unlike the JMB/IAF, which could neither work within the party system nor take action outside of it, Quietist Salafis grew in strength as they widened the scope of their grassroots activities. Foremost, they, like the JSM in Morocco and the GM in Turkey, strategically utilised new channels of communications to support their strategic objective of bottom-up grassroots change. Specifically, they opened up new television channels, such as the *al-Athar* [The Impact], *al-Nass* [The People] and *al-Rahmeh* [The Mercy], with the spread of satellite stations.[128] They also made use of the internet for recruitment. For instance, 'the *Kul al-salafiyyin* [All the Salafists] forum and website, which is overseen by Ali al-Halaby, and which is playing a critical and major role in creating a communications network and platform for ongoing dialogue between the individuals in this current', disseminated Quietist Salafi ideas more widely in Jordan.[129] As a result, Quietist Salafism in Jordan grew exponentially.[130]

In all these new grassroots engagements, unlike the self-financing Islamic movements of Morocco and Turkey, Saudi financing played a vital role as well. 'Saudi Arabian money provide[d] all the funding for Jordanian Salafists to produce, publish and distribute tapes and books. These funds [were] also used to encourage preaching and other 'missionary' activities'.[131] For instance, the *Al-Kitab wal-sunnah* [The Book and the Sunnah] Association funded by Saudi Arabia provided funds for the poor.[132] It also helped that Jordanian expatriates and students in Saudi Arabia and other Gulf states brought Salafi beliefs and Saudi money back with them.[133] In short, while the JMB/IAF entered a period of political stagnancy to achieve its strategic objectives, the Quietist Salafis entered a period of growth towards the achievement of their strategic objective to engage in grassroots bottom-up change.

In 2011, the Arab Spring swept across the region and changed calculations on all sides. Arab Spring-inspired protests in Jordan brought various groups together ranging from the JMB to leftist parties around calls for economic reforms, social justice, anti-corruption measures, and changes in the electoral law.[134] Unlike previous protests, Transjordanians, the pillars of the Jordanian regime, joined the protests given their increasingly deteriorating economic wellbeing.[135] Hence, it looked like a new political opportunity was opening up for Islamic movements in Jordan.

In light of these new developments, the King of Jordan promised new political openings under the National Dialogue Committee, which was composed of various political actors from across the Jordanian political spectrum. In 1989, the Brotherhood had participated in such a Committee quite willingly. Nonetheless, now in 2011, it rejected entering this Committee.[136] Instead, the Brotherhood became more involved in 'street politics'. During the Arab Spring protests, the Brotherhood organised weekly protests and joined forces with smaller leftist groups.[137] This rejection was a strategic one informed by the failure of both participation and non-participation in Jordan.

Such a perception was further supported when the Jordanian regime, once again, in 2012 limited the political openings of the Arab Spring: new laws limiting the press and online media freedoms were introduced,[138] and the new electoral law was altered to be more restrictive so that 'no party [was] permitted to take more than five seats'.[139] Hence, unlike the Moroccan regime, which engaged in political liberalisations, the Jordanian regime, like its Turkish counterparts closing down on Islamic movements through the military and the judiciary, closed down political liberalisations within a year after the Arab Spring. Furthermore, the regime started using the language of centrism in Islam claiming to represent a centrist Islam. Within this framework, King Abdullah II called the Brotherhood a 'Masonic cult [...] run by wolves in sheep's clothing',[140] and the Brotherhood's headquarters and other offices in Madaba, Karak, and Mafraq were raided in 2015.[141] Also, given the violent turmoil of the Arab Spring's transitions of Egypt, Syria, and Yemen, the Jordanian public became more reluctant to engage in a new set of protests.[142] In other words, 1989 was repeating itself for the Brotherhood.

In this political climate, the Brotherhood became more realistic as to what it could achieve in Jordan. In particular, the Brotherhood realised that, unlike its Moroccan and Turkish counterparts, it could neither pursue top-down influence nor bottom-up influence within or outside Jordanian party politics. This realisation led the Brotherhood to re-evaluate its ideological priorities and to target the wholesale transformation of the Jordanian regime instead. Consequently, unlike its Moroccan and Turkish counterparts that accommodated the regime, the Brotherhood, instead of calling for Islamic policies as a 'loyal opposition', started directly calling for political reforms as a 'hard opposition'.[143]

The Brotherhood refused to run in the first post-Arab Spring elections in 2013, demanding 'broader political representation and a more democratic parliament'.[144] Nimer al-Assaf, deputy secretary general of the IAF, stated that there was 'no way [they were] going to accept anymore that one person rules over 6 million people and nobody [could] ask him about what he does'.[145] In this, the JMB did not condemn calls for the fall of the Jordanian regime made during the Arab Spring-inspired protests. Bani Irsheid, a senior leader of the Brotherhood, stated 'Those who [were] calling for the fall of the regime [were] increasing', and that 'this [could not] and should not be ignored'.[146] Hence, the Brotherhood started calling for (1) the reduction of the King's powers, (2) the majority party to form the government instead of an appointed (by the King) technocrat, and for (3) the transformation of the House of Senate, which is also appointed by the King, 'into an elected body'.[147]

In addition to changes in its ideological priorities, the Brotherhood also changed its organisational objectives. Instead of either prioritising new recruitments or the protection of core supporters, the Brotherhood started prioritising reaching out to younger generations. Firstly, the IAF, after two years of preparations, announced a new economic programme called 'Jordan Tomorrow 2020' in 2014. This economic plan proposed to decrease Jordan's foreign aid dependency by 2020 by focusing on developing domestic industries.[148] With this new programme, the IAF aimed to win younger generations over to its side. Secondly, the IAF also announced new programmes to expand its membership base. According to Tayseer Fityani, the head of the IAF's inner court, it was political learning that pushed them towards this new political direction, to 'focus on young people and be more open'.[149] To do so the organisation decided to go after socio-economic challenges and announced 'two national campaigns against the rising costs of living and corruption'.[150] With the 'Let Us Live' campaign, the IAF sought 'to highlight the various economic challenges facing the Kingdom in light of the global economic crisis',[151] while with the 'We Are Enough' campaign, the organisation aimed to combat corruption in the public sector.[152] In short, the Brotherhood and the IAF became more realistic about their strategic objectives in the face of a persistently repressive Jordanian regime.

While the Brotherhood was becoming more realistic about what it can achieve in Jordan, the Quietist Salafis were realising their limits. Foremost, Quietist Salafis had witnessed internal splits after the death of their founding father, Albani, in 1999, over who would be their next leader.[153] In particular, Muhammad Abu Shaqra, who was educated at the Al-Azhar University in Egypt, and Ali Hasan Al-Halabi, who was a civil servant in Jordan, started competing for leadership.[154] Furthermore, the absence of a formal organisation had given way to fluidity between various Salafi currents. The most 'institutionalised' structure within the Movement was the Imam Al-Albani Scholarly Research and Study Centre, which 'produced the "*al-Asala*" Magazine', '"approved" *fatwas*', and 'organised and conducted seminars and lectures'.[155] However, this semi-formal organisation did not prevent followers from switching between various Salafi trends in Jordan. As Abu Rumman and Abu Hanieh describe:

> there is one, solid, common doctrinal and intellectual ground between all of them; and, if an individual finds himself in conflict with the political stance of the current he is in, moving from one current such as the Conservative or Reform Salafist current to another such as the Jihadi Salafist current, is quite easy.[156]

As a result, the absence of a formal organisation and the presence of organisational fluidity, which were organisational characteristics that protected Quietist Salafis from regime repressions, had also made Quietist Salafism vulnerable to organisational fragility. Hence, unlike the strong unity presented within the Moroccan JSM under Yassine and the Turkish GM under Gülen, the disunity of Quietist Salafis in Jordan had limited their attempts to achieve bottom-up grassroots change through non-participation. In this context, Quietist Salafis were realising the pragmatic implications of their idealistic stance in the form of organisational and thus political weakness.

By closing in on both the Brotherhood and the Quietist Salafis and thereby limiting the scope of their socio-political influence, the Jordanian regime itself has redefined the political centre of Jordan today. Whereas in the past the Jordanian regime, in contrast to the Moroccan and Turkish regimes which both maintained an iron grip on Islamic movements, was known for its tolerant authoritarianism and minimum interference into the religious field, the Jordanian regime today has become more repressive formally and informally. Formally, the Jordanian regime, through various electoral laws, has turned the Jordanian party system into an ineffective institution to which no one pays attention. Informally, the Jordanian regime has retaken control of the religious field by encouraging internal divisions within the Brotherhood and the Salafis. Firstly, the regime has supported the internal split within the Brotherhood. An initiative within the Brotherhood, led by Abdel Hamid Thneibat, formally requested to register the JMB as a 'political association under the umbrella of [the] Ministry of Political Development' separate from the international Muslim Brotherhood network, as a precaution against a potential designation of the JMB as a terrorist organisation as had been done in Egypt in 2013.[157] To support such internal divisions, the Jordan regime

> granted the new license on March 2, 2015, and the [Brotherhood] responded by expelling Thneibat and ten other members. Thus, two Muslim Brotherhood entities are operating in Jordan today: the one led by the general overseer, and the newly registered one.[158]

Going further, the regime also prevented

> the old Brotherhood from holding its 70th-anniversary rally, [...] transferring ownership of properties that were worth millions from the old Muslim Brotherhood group to the new wing, [...and by banning the JMB] from holding internal election.[159]

Secondly, the regime has kept an eye on Quietist Salafi activism through strict surveillance and monitoring so that the Movement did not 'deviate from the red lines defined by the security interests of the state, and so that none become a source of threat or danger to the security and the political regime in the future'.[160] In short, the Jordanian regime has regained the control of the religio-political field by leaving no room to breathe for any real opposition group and thereby redefining the political centre in Jordan.

Summary

How does participation and non-participation progress? This chapter has addressed how both vanguard movements which choose to participate, and grassroots movements which choose not to do so have adjusted to the limits of their political choices and strategised to make the most of them. In particular, this chapter has addressed how Islamic movements have become the main opposition figures in their countries. It has discussed how these Islamic movements have acquired a more visible presence in the society and a louder voice in politics. This chapter has also addressed how the regimes have responded to such socio-political influence, by, for instance, becoming more Islamic or by becoming more repressive, to regain their ideological hegemony.

In consequence, what this chapter has found is that, although they have resulted in six different outcomes, these Islamic movements have each altered the regime's status quo. While the Moroccan regime started out as a repressive pragmatist regime where the King was also the 'Commander of the Believers', after years of strategising and counter-strategising, the Moroccan regime has ended up becoming more openly Islamic and owning the King's role as the Commander of the Believers more publicly. In Turkey, the regime started out as a militantly laic regime with a civilising mission to socially engineer society towards Westernisation and has ended up with a redefined pro-Islamic political centre. Meanwhile, the Jordanian regime started out as a tolerant authoritarian regime with ceremonies of religious involvement and yet has turned into a repressive regime reclaiming religio-political monopoly in Jordan.

The final chapter will address the consequence of these redefinitions of the political centre for Islamic movements.

Notes

1. Güneş Murat Tezcür, 'The Moderation Theory Revisited: The Case of Islamic Political Actors', *Party Politics*, 16.1 (2009), 69–88.
2. Albert O. Hirschman, *Exit, Voice, and Loyalty: Responses to Decline in Firms, Organizations, and States* (Cambridge, MA: Harvard University Press, 1970).
3. Shadi Hamid, 'Arab Islamist Parties: Losing on Purpose?', *Journal of Democracy*, 22.1 (2011), 68–80.

4. Hirschman, *Exit, Voice, and Loyalty*.
5. Esen Kirdiş, 'Immoderation: Comparing the Christian Right in the US and Pro-Islamic Movement-Parties in Turkey', *Democratization*, 23.3 (2016), 417–36.
6. Hirschman, *Exit, Voice, and Loyalty*.
7. Hamid, 'Arab Islamist Parties: Losing on Purpose'.
8. Margaret E. Keck and Kathryn Sikkink, *Activists Beyond Borders: Advocacy Networks in International Politics* (Ithaca, NY: Cornell University Press, 1998).
9. Joel S. Migdal, *State in Society: Studying How States and Societies Transform and Constitute One Another* (New York: Cambridge University Press, 2007).
10. Migdal, *State in Society*.
11. David Campbell, *Writing Security: United States Foreign Policy and the Politics of Identity* (Minneapolis, MN: University of Minnesota Press, 1992).
12. Migdal, *State in Society*.
13. Carrie Rosefsky Wickham, *Mobilizing Islam: Religion, Activism, and Political Change in Egypt* (New York: Columbia University Press, 2002).
14. Mustapha Pasha Kamal, 'Predatory Globalisation and Democracy in the Islamic World', *The Annals of the American Academy of Political and Social Science*, 581 (2002), 121–32.
15. Abdallah Ahmad An-Naim, *Islam and the Secular State: Negotiating the Future of Shari`a* (Cambridge, MA: Harvard University Press, 2008).
16. José Casanova, *Public Religions in the Modern World* (Chicago, IL: University of Chicago Press, 1994).
17. Khalil Al-Anani, 'Islamist Parties Post-Arab Spring', *Mediterranean Politics*, 17.3 (2012), 466–72.
18. Samir Amghar (2007), 'Political Islam in Morocco', *CEPS Working Document*, <http://aei.pitt.edu/11725/1/1510.pdf> (last accessed 28 July 2018).
19. Malika Zeghal, *Islamism in Morocco: Religion, Authoritarianism, and Electoral Politics* (Princeton, NJ: Markus Wiener Publishing, 2009).
20. Esen Kirdiş and Amina Drhimeur, 'The Rise of Populism? Comparing Incumbent Pro-Islamic Parties in Turkey and Morocco', *Turkish Studies*, 17.4 (2016), 599–617.
21. Michael Willis, 'Morocco's Islamists and the Legislative Elections of 2002: The Strange Case of the Party that Did not Want to Win', *Mediterranean Politics*, 9.1 (2004), 53–81.
22. Anonymous interview with a PJD minister by the author, 19 April 2010, Rabat, Morocco.

23. Anonymous interview with a PJD minister by the author, 19 April 2010, Rabat, Morocco.
24. Eva Wegner and Miquel Pellicer, 'Islamist Moderation without Democratization: The Coming of Age of the Moroccan Party of Justice and Development?', *Democratization*, 16.1 (2009), 157–75.
25. Khadija Mohsen-Finan and Malika Zeghal, 'Opposition Islamiste et Pouvoir Monarchique au Maroc. Le Cas du Parti de La Justice et Du Developpement' ['Islamist Opposition and Monarchical Power in Morocco: The Case of the Party for Justice and Development'], *Revue Française de Science Politique*, 56 (2006), 79–119.
26. Abdellatif El Azizi (2006), 'Al Adl Wal Ihsane, L'Internationale Islamiste' ['Justice and Spirituality, and International Islamist'], *Telquel*, <http://www.telquel-online.com/185/sujet1.shtml> (last accessed 1 June 2010).
27. See: http://www.yassine.net/en/
28. Anonymous interview with a high-ranking leader from the JSM by the author, 14 May 2010, Rabat, Morocco.
29. Anonymous interview with a Moroccan scholar of political Islam by the author, 16 April 2010, Rabat, Morocco.
30. El Azizi, 'Al Adl Wal Ihsane, L'Internationale Islamiste'.
31. Rochdi Bouyibri, 'Towards a Society that Rejects Violence', in Maâti Monjib (ed.), *Islamists versus Secularists: Confrontations and Dialogues in Morocco – Values, Democracy, Violence, Freedom, Education* (Rabat: IKV PAX, 2009).
32. Abdallah Saaf and Abdelrahim Manar Al Slimi (2008), 'Morocco 1996-2007: A Decisive Decade of Reforms?', *Arab Reform Initiative*, <https://www.arab-reform.net/en/node/914> (last accessed 21 July 2018).
33. Mohammed Masbah (2014), 'Morocco's Slow Motion Reform Process', *Stiftung Wissenschaft und Politik*, <http://www.swp-berlin.org/en/publications/swp-comments-en/swp-aktuelle-details/article/moroccos_slow_motion_reform_process.html> (last accessed 19 July 2018).
34. Masbah (2014), 'Morocco's Slow Motion Reform Process'.
35. 'La Jeunesse d'Al Adl Wal Ihsane Participe aux Protestations du 20 Février 2011' ['The Youth of Al Adl Wal Ihsane Participates in the Protests of 20 February 2011'] (2011), *Al Jamaa*, <http://www.aljamaa.net/fr/document/2484.shtml> (last accessed 3 July 2014).
36. Ahmed Benchemsi, 'Morocco's Makhzen and the Haphazard Activists', in Lina Khatib and Ellen Lust (eds), *Taking to the Streets: The Transformation of*

Arab Activism (Baltimore, MD: Johns Hopkins University Press, 2014), pp. 199–235.
37. 'Al Adl Wal Ihsane Annonce Son Retrait du Mouvement du 20 Février: La Fin de La Lune de Miel' ['Al Adl Wal Ihsane Announces Its Withdrawal From February the 20th Movement: The End of the Honeymoon'] (2011), *Aufait*, 19 December <http://www.aufaitmaroc.com/actualites/maroc/2011/12/18/la-fin-de-la-lune-de-miel#.U7UMmqj1uSZ> (last accessed 3 July 2014).
38. Mohamed Jalid (2012), 'The Rise of Populists in Moroccan Politics', *Carnegie Endowment for International Peace*, <http://carnegieendowment.org/sada/?fa=50182> (last accessed 2 July 2014).
39. 'Istiqlal Party Quits Morocco's Islamist-Led Government' (2013), *BBC News*, 9 July, <http://www.bbc.com/news/world-africa-23250370> (last accessed 2 July 2014).
40. Souleïman Bencheikh (2013), 'Morocco's Cabinet Crisis', *Al Monitor*, 17 July, <http://www.al-monitor.com/pulse/politics/2013/07/morocco-istiqlal-withdrawal-replacement-rni.html#> (last accessed 2 July 2014).
41. Masbah (2014), 'Morocco's Slow Motion Reform Process'.
42. Mohammed Masbah (2012), 'The Party Just In (and Developing)', *Carnegie Endowment for International Peace*, <http://carnegieendowment.org/sada/2012/07/03/party-just-in-and-developing/d31e> (last accessed 2 July 2014).
43. Mohammed Masbah (2013), 'The PJD's Balancing Act', *Carnegie Endowment for International Peace*, <http://carnegieendowment.org/sada/2013/05/01/pjd-s-balancing-act/g1uy> (last accessed 2 July 2014).
44. Consultative Council of the JSM (2012), 'Closing Communiqué of the Consultative [Shūrā] Council of the Movement Al Adl Wal Iḥsān', *Abdessalam Yassine*, <https://yassine.net/en/2012/12/27/closing-communique-of-the-consultative-shura-council-of-the-movement-al-adl-wal-i%E1%B8%A5san/> (last accessed 28 July 2018).
45. Mohammed Masbah (2013), 'In Yassine's Footsteps', *Carnegie Endowment for International Peace*, <http://carnegieendowment.org/sada/2013/01/10/in-yassine-s-footsteps/f0nj> (last accessed 3 July 2014).
46. Abdessalam Yassine (2013), 'The Last Testament of Imam Abdessalam Yassine', *Abdessalam Yassine*, <https://yassine.net/en/2013/05/04/the-last-testament-of-imam-abdessalam-yassine/> (last accessed 28 July 2018).
47. Mohammed El Katiri, 'The Institutionalisation of Religious Affairs: Religious Reform in Morocco', *The Journal of North African Studies*, 18.1 (2013), 53–69.
48. Azzedine Layachi, 'Islam and Politics in North Africa', in John L. Esposito and

Emad El-Din Shahin (eds), *The Oxford Handbook of Islam and Politics* (Oxford & New York: Oxford University Press, 2013), pp. 352–78.
49. Julie E. Pruzan-Jørgensen (2010), 'Islamist Movement in Morocco: Main Actors and Regime Responses', *Academia*, <http://www.academia.edu/1892070/Islamist_Movement_in_Morocco_Main_Actors_and_Regime_Responses_DIIS_Report_2010_April_2010> (last accessed 21 July 2018).
50. El Katiri, 'The Institutionalisation of Religious Affairs'.
51. Michael J. Willis, *Politics and Power in the Maghreb: Algeria, Tunisia and Morocco from Independence to the Arab Spring* (New York: Columbia University Press, 2012).
52. Driss Maghraoui, 'The Strengths and Limits of Religious Reforms in Morocco', *Mediterranean Politics*, 14.2 (2009), 195–211.
53. Youssef Belal, *Le Cheikh et le Calife: Sociologie Religieuse de L'Islam Politique au Maroc [The Sheikh and the Caliph: Religious Sociology of Political Islam in Morocco]* (Lyon: ENS Editions, 2011).
54. Layachi, 'Islam and Politics in North Africa'.
55. Maghraoui, 'The Strengths and Limits of Religious Reforms in Morocco'.
56. Maghraoui, 'The Strengths and Limits of Religious Reforms in Morocco'.
57. Maghraoui, 'The Strengths and Limits of Religious Reforms in Morocco'.
58. Maghraoui, 'The Strengths and Limits of Religious Reforms in Morocco'.
59. Kirdiş, 'Immoderation'.
60. Necmettin Erbakan, *Adil Ekonomik Düzen [Just Economic Order]* (Ankara: Anadolu Matbaacılık, 1991).
61. Erbakan, *Adil Ekonomik Düzen*.
62. Hakan M. Yavuz, *Secularism and Muslim Democracy in Turkey* (Cambridge & New York: Cambridge University Press, 2009).
63. Kirdiş, 'Immoderation'.
64. Ihsan Dağı, 'Transformation of Islamic Political Identity in Turkey: Rethinking the West and Westernization', *Turkish Studies*, 6.1 (2005), 21–37.
65. Yavuz, *Secularism and Muslim Democracy in Turkey*.
66. Yavuz, *Secularism and Muslim Democracy in Turkey*.
67. Ruşen Çakır, *Ayet ve Slogan: Türkiye'de Islamcı Oluşumlar [Verse and Slogan: Islamic Formations in Turkey]* (Istanbul: Metis Yayınları, 2002).
68. Oral Çalışlar and Tolga Çelik, *Islamcılığın Üç Kolu [Three Branches of Islamism]* (Istanbul: Guncel Yayıncılık, 2006).
69. Hakan M. Yavuz, 'The Three Stages of the Gülen Movement: From Pietistic Weeping Movement to Power-Obsessed Structure', in Bayram Balcı and

Hakan M. Yavuz (eds), *Turkey's July 15th Coup: What Happened and Why* (Salt Lake City, UT: The University of Utah Press, 2018), pp. 20–45.
70. Rachel Sharon-Krespin, 'Fethullah Gülen's Grand Ambition: Turkey's Islamist Danger', *Middle East Quarterly*, 16.1 (2009), 55–66.
71. Ahmet T. Kuru, 'Globalization and Diversification of Islamic Movements: Three Turkish Cases', *Political Science Quarterly*, 120.2 (2005), 253–74.
72. Mujeeb R. Khan, 'The July 15th Coup: A Critical Institutional Framework for Analysis', in Bayram Balcı and Hakan M. Yavuz (eds), *Turkey's July 15th Coup: What Happened and Why* (Salt Lake City, UT: The University of Utah Press, 2018), pp. 46–77.
73. Arthur Bonner, 'An Islamic Reformation in Turkey', *Middle East Policy*, 11.1 (2004), 84–97.
74. Bonner, 'An Islamic Reformation in Turkey'.
75. 'Prof. İsmail Kara ile Gülen Cemaati-AKP Hükümeti Savaşı Üzerine Söyleşi' ['A Conversation about the Gülen Religious Community-AKP Government War with Prof. Ismail Kara'] (2014), *Ruşen Çakır*, 27 December, <http://rusencakir.com/Prof-Ismail-Kara-ile-Gulen-cemaati-AKP-hukumeti-savasi-uzerine-soylesi-tam-metin/4039> (last accessed 25 July 2018).
76. Hulki Cevizoğlu, *Generalinden 28 Şubat İtirafı: Postmodern Darbe [February 28 Confession from Its General: Post-Modern Coup]* (Istanbul: Ceviz Kabuğu Yayınları, 2001).
77. Yavuz, *Secularism and Muslim Democracy in Turkey*.
78. Kirdiş, 'Immoderation'.
79. Saban Tanıyıcı, 'Transformation of Political Islam in Turkey: Islamist Welfare Party's Pro-EU Turn', *Party Politics*, 9.4 (2003), 463–83.
80. Ali Çarkoğlu, 'Turkey's 2011 General Elections: Towards a Dominant Party System?', *Insight Turkey*, 13.3 (2011), 43–62.
81. See: Şebnem Gümüşçü, 'Class, Status, and Party: The Changing Face of Political Islam in Turkey and Egypt', *Comparative Political Studies*, 43.7 (2010), 835–61; R. Quinn Mecham, 'From the Ashes of Virtue, a Promise of Light: The Transformation of Political Islam in Turkey', *Third World Quarterly*, 25.2 (2004), 339–58; Sultan Tepe, 'Moderation of Religious Parties: Electoral Constraints, Ideological Commitments, and the Democratic Capacities of Religious Parties in Israel and Turkey', *Political Research Quarterly*, 65.3 (2012), 467–85; Ziya Öniş and Emin Fuat Keyman, 'A New Path Emerges', *Journal of Democracy*, 14.2 (2003), 95–107; Gamze Çavdar, 'Islamist New Thinking in Turkey: A Model for Political Learning?', *Political Science Quarterly*, 121.3 (2006), 477–97.

82. See: Çarkoğlu, 'Turkey's 2011 General Elections'; Ziya Öniş, 'The Triumph of Conservative Globalism: The Political Economy of the AKP Era', *Turkish Studies*, 13.2 (2012), 135–52; William M. Hale and Ergun Özbudun, *Islamism, Democracy and Liberalism in Turkey: The Case of the AKP* (Abingdon & New York: Routledge, 2010); Ali Çarkoğlu and Ersin Kalaycıoğlu, *The Rising Tide of Conservatism in Turkey* (New York: Palgrave Macmillan, 2009).
83. Öniş and Keyman, 'A New Path Emerges'.
84. Hakan M. Yavuz, *Toward an Islamic Enlightenment: The Gülen Movement* (Oxford & New York: Oxford University Press, 2013).
85. '2002–2014 Sessiz Devrim: Türkiye'nin Demokratik Değişim ve Dönüşüm Envanteri' ['2002–2014 Silent Revolution: Turkey's Democratic Change and Transformation Inventory'] (2015), *Official Website of the AKP*, 1 August, <https://www.akparti.org.tr/site/haberler/sessiz-devrim/77738#1> (last accessed 30 July 2018).
86. European Commission (2003), '2003 Regular Report on Turkey's Progress towards Accession', *EU Publications*, <https://publications.europa.eu/en/publication-detail/-/publication/deffe767-febd-4228-8c07-657380ffa3cf/language-en> (last accessed 28 July 2018).
87. European Commission (2004), '2004 Regular Report on Turkey's Progress towards Accession', *European Parliament*, <http://www.europarl.europa.eu/meetdocs/2004_2009/documents/sec/com_sec(2004)1201_/com_sec(2004)1201_en.pdf> (last accessed 28 July 2018).
88. European Commission (2006), 'Commission Staff Working Document – Turkey 2006 Progress Report', *Access to European Union Law*, <https://eur-lex.europa.eu/legal-content/EN/TXT/?uri=celex%3A52006SC1390> (last accessed 28 July 2018).
89. Yavuz, 'The Three Stages of the Gülen Movement'.
90. Ruşen Çakır (2013), 'Cemaat-Hükümet Meydan Muharebesi: Kim Kazanır?' ['Religious Community-Government Field Battle: Who Would Win'], *Vatan*, 16 December, <http://www.rusencakir.com/Cemaat-hukumet-meydan-muharebesi-Kim-kazanir/2335> (last accessed 28 July 2018).
91. Bayram Balcı and Hakan M. Yavuz, *Turkey's July 15th Coup: What Happened and Why* (Salt Lake City, UT: The University of Utah Press, 2018).
92. Hakan M. Yavuz and Rasim Koç, 'The Turkish Coup Attempt: The Gülen Movement vs. the State', *Middle East Policy*, 23.4 (2016), 136–48.
93. Yaprak Gürsoy, 'The Final Curtain for the Turkish Armed Forces? Civil-

Military Relations in View of the 2011 General Elections', *Turkish Studies*, 13.2 (2012), 191–211.
94. Yavuz, 'The Three Stages of the Gülen Movement'.
95. Balcı and Yavuz, *Turkey's July 15th Coup*.
96. Hakan M. Yavuz and Bayram Balcı, 'Introduction: The Gülen Movement and the Coup', in Bayram Balcı and Hakan M. Yavuz (eds), *Turkey's July 15th Coup: What Happened and Why* (Salt Lake City, UT: The University of Utah Press, 2018), pp. 1–19.
97. Pınar Doğan and Dani Rodrik, *Yargı, Cemaat ve Bir Darbe Kurgusunun İçyüzü [Judiciary, Religious Community, and Behind the Scenes of a Coup Fabrication]* (Istanbul: Destek Yayınevi).
98. Gulsen Solaker (2016), 'Turkish Appeals Court Overturns "Ergenekon" Coup Plot Convictions', *Reuters*, 21 April, <https://www.reuters.com/article/us-turkey-coup-trial/turkish-appeals-court-overturns-ergenekon-coup-plot-convictions-idUSKCN0XI1WS> (last accessed 2 August 2018).
99. 'Mezardakiler Bile Referandum İçin Kaldırılmalı' ['Even those in the Grave Shall be Woken Up for the Referendum'] (2010), *Cumhuriyet*, 1 August, <http://www.cumhuriyet.com.tr/haber/diger/167646/_Mezardakiler_bile_referandum_icin_kaldirilmali_.html> (last accessed 4 August 2018).
100. Anonymous interview with a loyalist member of Jordanian Senate by the author, 9 February 2010, Amman, Jordan.
101. Shadi Hamid, *Temptations of Power: Islamists and Illiberal Democracy in a New Middle East* (Oxford & New York: Oxford University Press, 2014).
102. Michael Robbins and Lawrence Rubin, 'The Rise of Official Islam in Jordan', *Politics, Religion & Ideology*, 14.1 (2013), 59–74.
103. Hamid, *Temptations of Power*.
104. Hamid, *Temptations of Power*.
105. Anonymous interview with a deputy from the JMB by the author, 1 March 2010, Amman, Jordan.
106. Nathan J. Brown (2006), 'Jordan and Its Islamic Movement: The Limits of Inclusion?', *Carnegie Papers 74* , <https://carnegieendowment.org/files/cp_74_brown_final.pdf> (last accessed 19 July 2018).
107. Nathan J. Brown and Amr Hamzawy, *Between Religion and Politics* (Washington, DC: Carnegie Endowment for International Peace, 2010).
108. As'ad Ghanem and Mohanad Mustafa, 'Strategies of Electoral Participation by Islamic Movements: The Muslim Brotherhood and Parliamentary Elections in Egypt and Jordan', *Contemporary Politics*, 17.4 (2011), 393–409.

109. Mohammad Al-Fodeilat (2012), 'How Jordan's Islamists Came to Dominate Society: An Evolution', *Al Monitor*, 10 September, <https://archive.li/mJ7yq> (last accessed 25 July 2018).
110. Hassan Hafidh (2011), 'Jordan's King, Islamists Meet After Nearly 10-Year Hiatus', *The Wall Street Journal*, 4 February, <https://www.wsj.com/articles/SB10001424052748703652104576121773416123228?mod=ITP_pageone_3> (last accessed 28 July 2018).
111. Anonymous interview with a former member of the JMB and IAF by the author, 10 March 2010, Amman, Jordan.
112. Anonymous interview with a journalist from the Islamist daily *Assabeel* by the author, 9 March 2010, Amman, Jordan.
113. Neven Bondokji (2015), 'The Muslim Brotherhood in Jordan: Time to Reform', *Brookings Doha Center Publications*, <https://www.brookings.edu/wp-content/uploads/2016/06/en-muslim-brotherhood-in-jordan.pdf> (last accessed 28 July 2018).
114. Jillian Schwedler (n.d.), 'Jordan', *Oxford Islamic Studies Online*, <http://www.oxfordislamicstudies.com/opr/t236/e0422> (last accessed 28 July 2018).
115. Schwedler, 'Jordan'.
116. Mohammad S. Abu Rumman and Hassan Abu Hanieh, *The 'Islamic Solution' in Jordan: Islamists, the State, and the Ventures of Democracy and Security* (Amman: Friedrich-Ebert-Stiftung, 2013).
117. Glenn E. Robinson, 'Defensive Democratization in Jordan', *International Journal of Middle East Studies*, 30.3 (1998), 387–410.
118. Anonymous interview with a JMB leader by the author, 15 February 2010, Amman, Jordan.
119. Abu Rumman and Abu Hanieh, *The 'Islamic Solution' in Jordan*.
120. Abu Rumman and Abu Hanieh, *The 'Islamic Solution' in Jordan*.
121. David Siddhartha Patel (2015), 'The More Things Change, the More They Stay the Same: Jordanian Islamist Responses in Spring and Fall', *Brookings Institution*, <https://www.brookings.edu/wp-content/uploads/2016/07/Jordan_Patel-FINALE.pdf> (last accessed 28 July 2018).
122. Brown, 'Jordan and Its Islamic Movement'.
123. Ghanem and Mustafa, 'Strategies of Electoral Participation by Islamic Movements'.
124. Mohammad S. Abu Rumman and Hassan Abu Hanieh, *Jordanian Salafism: A Strategy for the 'Islamization of Society' and an Ambiguous Relationship with the State* (Amman: Friedrich-Ebert-Stiftung, 2010).

125. Abu Rumman and Abu Hanieh, *Jordanian Salafism*.
126. Abu Rumman and Abu Hanieh, *Jordanian Salafism*.
127. Abu Rumman and Abu Hanieh, *Jordanian Salafism*.
128. Abu Rumman and Abu Hanieh, *Jordanian Salafism*.
129. Abu Rumman and Abu Hanieh, *Jordanian Salafism*.
130. Joas Wagemakers, *Salafism in Jordan: Political Islam in a Quietist Community* (New York: Cambridge University Press, 2016).
131. Abu Rumman and Abu Hanieh, *Jordanian Salafism*.
132. Al-Fodeilat, 'How Jordan's Islamists Came to Dominate Society'.
133. Abu Rumman and Abu Hanieh, *Jordanian Salafism*.
134. Bondokji, 'The Muslim Brotherhood in Jordan'.
135. Abu Rumman and Abu Hanieh, *The 'Islamic Solution' in Jordan*.
136. Tareq Al-Naimat (2014), 'The Jordanian Regime and the Muslim Brotherhood: A Tug of War', *Wilson Center*, <https://www.wilsoncenter.org/sites/default/files/jordanian_regime_muslim_brotherhood_tug_of_war.pdf> (last accessed 28 July 2018).
137. Al-Naimat, 'The Jordanian Regime and the Muslim Brotherhood'.
138. David Fox and Katrina Sammour (2012), 'Disquiet on the Jordanian Front', *Carnegie Endowment for International Peace*, September 27, <http://carnegieendowment.org/sada/49500> (last accessed 28 July 2018).
139. Curtis R. Ryan (2012), 'The Implications of Jordan's New Electoral Law', *Foreign Policy*, 13 April, <https://foreignpolicy.com/2012/04/13/the-implications-of-jordans-new-electoral-law/> (last accessed 28 July 2018).
140. Jeffrey Goldberg (2013), 'The Modern King in the Arab Spring', *The Atlantic*, <https://www.theatlantic.com/magazine/archive/2013/04/monarch-in-the-middle/309270/> (last accessed 28 July 2018).
141. Aaron Magid (2016), 'The King and the Islamists', *Foreign Affairs*, 3 May, <https://www.foreignaffairs.com/articles/jordan/2016-05-03/king-and-islamists> (last accessed 28 July 2018).
142. Bondokji, 'The Muslim Brotherhood in Jordan'.
143. Esen Kirdiş, 'From Loyal to Hard Opposition: The Political Transformation of the Jordanian Muslim Brotherhood', *Politics, Religion & Ideology*, 17.2/3 (2016), 121–42.
144. 'Jordan's King Abdullah Swears in Caretaker Government' (2012), *BBC News*, 12 October <http://www.bbc.com/news/world-middle-east-19924672> (last accessed 28 July 2018).
145. Sara Sidner and Ashley Fantz (2012), 'Thousands Rally for Political Change in

Jordan', *CNN*, 5 October <http://edition.cnn.com/2012/10/05/world/jordan-protest/> (last accessed 28 July 2018).
146. Shadi Hamid (n.d.), 'The Islamic Action Front in Jordan', *The Oxford Handbook of Islam and Politics, Oxford Islamic Studies Online,* <http://www.oxfordislamicstudies.com/article/opr/t9001/e008> (last accessed 28 July 2018).
147. Al-Naimat, 'The Jordanian Regime and the Muslim Brotherhood'.
148. Dana Al-Emam (2014), 'Economists Discuss Muslim Brotherhood's Proposed Economic Strategy', *Jordan Times*, 22 July, <http://www.jordantimes.com/news/local/economists-discuss-muslim-brotherhood%E2%80%99s-proposed-economic-strategy> (last accessed 28 July 2018).
149. 'Islamic Action Front Approves Four-Year Strategy to Increase Membership Base', *Jordan Times*, 9 January 2011.
150. Islamic Action Front Approves Four-Year Strategy to Increase Membership Base', *Jordan Times*, 9 January 2011.
151. 'Islamic Action Front Approves Four-Year Strategy to Increase Membership Base', *Jordan Times*, 9 January 2011.
152. 'Islamic Action Front Approves Four-Year Strategy to Increase Membership Base', *Jordan Times*, 9 January 2011.
153. Joas Wagemakers, 'Contesting Religious Authority in Jordanian Salafi Networks', in Marko Milosevic and Kacper Rekawek (eds), *Perseverance of Terrorism: Focus on Leaders* (Amsterdam: IOS Press, 2014), pp. 111–25.
154. Wagemakers, *Salafism in Jordan*.
155. Abu Rumman and Abu Hanieh, *The 'Islamic Solution' in Jordan*.
156. Abu Rumman and Abu Hanieh, *Jordanian Salafism*.
157. Bondokji, 'The Muslim Brotherhood in Jordan'.
158. Bondokji, 'The Muslim Brotherhood in Jordan'.
159. Magid, 'The King and the Islamists'.
160. Abu Rumman and Abu Hanieh, *The 'Islamic Solution' in Jordan*.

5

CONCLUSION: THE RISE OF ISLAMIC POLITICAL MOVEMENTS AND PARTIES

In his 'Mirror Paintings' series, the artist Michelangelo Pistoletto prints life-size images of people engaged in action, such as a protest or a conversation, with their backs turned to the viewer, on polished stainless steel surfaces that function as a mirror and thereby allow the viewer to see their own reflections within the paintings and thus become part of the narrative in the mirror painting. As the viewers interact with these mirror paintings, interpretations as multiple as the viewers emerge. Like these mirror paintings, Islamic movements at once reflect their socio-political context and also give new meanings to this context. As discussed in chapter two, the political opportunity and threat structures of the socio-political context within which Islamic movements emerge, 'the mirror paintings', define the 'menu of options' for Islamic movements. Nonetheless, Islamic movements, as discussed in chapter three, also give new meanings to this 'menu of options' as they, like the viewers looking at their own reflections within the mirror paintings and interpreting the paintings through the lenses of their own experiences, evaluate and strategise about their options in light of their strategic objectives defined by their ideological priorities and organisational needs. Through these interactions between the structures and Islamic movements (agents), like the interactions between the mirror paintings and the viewers, new meanings are born, as discussed in chapter four, which in turn leads to multiple redefinitions of the political status quo.

In line with these discussions on such Islamic diversity, this last chapter will conclude this book with a look at the rise of Islamic political movements and parties.

Islamic Movements and Parties between Reform and Transformation

How has the decision regarding participation versus non-participation in the party system contributed to Islamic movement differentiation? In particular, what has this decision meant for the political agenda of Islamic movements? What kinds of changes have these decisions triggered internally within Islamic movements? And ultimately, have these Islamic movements succeeded in altering the socio-political structures they face?

To begin with, this book discussed how the decision to participate in party politics has been taken by vanguard Islamic movements seeking top-down Islamic revival under the leadership of their small vanguard organisations. Looking back at the evolution of such vanguard Islamic movements as discussed throughout this book, it seems that their political agenda has become more pro-status quo oriented and less reformist as they have gotten closer to power. Firstly, when vanguard Islamic movements seeking state power started out their journey in party politics under a small group of leaders without mass recognition, they started out from a position of relative weakness vis-à-vis the regime and other political opponents. Hence, they needed to work with the regime and the (secular) opposition, and to accommodate them. And accommodation has hardly been a reformist act since it has involved 'accept[ing] limited reforms that protect the power bases of the current elites'.[1] Secondly, in order to succeed in elections without co-opting their long-term ideals, vanguard Islamic movements have moderated their political agenda 'behaviourally' by advocating more pragmatic but less structural, and more oppositional but less fundamental policies in order to appeal to the lowest common denominator amongst the electorate, thereby expand their constituency, and thus increase their chances to win elections.[2] Thirdly, once in political power, there was hardly any reason for these vanguard Islamic movements to seek reform since they wanted to consolidate the status quo that brought them into power. To this end, they have started upholding traditional moral values in the society. As a result, vanguard Islamic movements seeking top-down political power within the party system have been more likely to become part of the status quo the closer they got to power.

While vanguard Islamic movements have came closer to power and adapted 'safer' political agendas to come into and remain in power, they have also tended to become more rigid politically foregoing internal and external pressures for change. Internally, vanguard Islamic movements were organisationally composed of a small group of like-minded individuals willing to devote their lives to the socio-political mission of their organisation.[3] This, in turn, gave way to groupthink and peer pressures wherein individuals thinking alike became even more convinced of their beliefs within the vanguard organisations.[4] And in the absence of self-criticism, these organisations became more convinced of their moral superiority.

Externally, vanguard Islamic movements, in order to avoid the biggest pitfall of participation in party politics, namely co-optation, have become more defensive towards outsiders. After all, these were self-selective organisations where new members abided by the vanguards' thorough guidelines, dedicated their lives to the movement's cause, and accepted the decisions of the leadership without faltering.[5] Through such internal discipline, freeriders who diluted the organisation's resources by benefiting from its services without putting in material or non-material contributions were eliminated, while remaining followers were rewarded for their dedication by experiencing stronger community ties within the organisation,[6] leading to even more ideological unity within the movement. Hence, as these vanguard Islamic movements became more uniform ideologically and organisationally, they were unable to trust or to work with anyone else leading to a tribe-like 'us versus them' perspective and to an intolerance of 'others'.[7] Consequently, vanguard Islamic movements have become more defensive towards political transformations.

As vanguard Islamic movements have become less reformist and more defensive once they attained political power, grassroots Islamic movements eschewing party politics seem to have adapted a more reformist political agenda aiming at a wholesale restructuring of the state and society. Grassroots Islamic movements, unlike vanguard Islamic movements, have not sought top-down political power but rather aimed to jumpstart a gradual reform process through their grassroots activism that would eventually lead to a reconstitution of the socio-political system. Therefore, unlike vanguard Islamic movements seeking accommodation, they 'demand[ed] substantive systemic change and strongly oppose[d] the power configurations of the status quo'.[8] Moreover, grassroots Islamic movements, unlike their vanguard counterparts, did not aim to win elections by appealing to a wide range of voters through 'behavioural moderation' but rather aimed to protect their supporter base by all means necessary. Sometimes this involved opposing power-holders and at other times it involved working with them in order to achieve political change. It also involved at times publicly working towards their goals, and at other times doing so silently by staying under the regime's radar. Lastly, grassroots Islamic movements, in contrast to the safe pragmatism of vanguard Islamic movements, have in essence been idealists aimed at redefining the status quo in order to reconstitute a new society and state, in line with their own Islam interpretations. Such idealism, however, has not necessarily meant an idealistic quest for democratic reformism. Rather, it has meant a desire to alter existing structures rather than working towards their consolidation.

Whilst seeking such reformism, grassroots Islamic movements eschewing party politics, unlike vanguard Islamic movements participating in party politics, have also been more open to political transformations. Internally, grassroots Islamic movements eschewing party politics, unlike their vanguard counterparts, have been organisationally diverse as a result of their mass following. Such a mass following also gave rise to multiple factions with different demands and beliefs about the movement's future direction over time. Such an organisation in return has necessitated balancing each faction's demands and interests to keep the movement unified. Hence, grassroots movements, in contrast to the prevalent groupthink within their vanguard counterparts, have been more likely to engage in internal debate and self-reflection. Externally, grassroots Islamic movements, in order to avoid the main cost of non-participation, namely political stagnancy, have also been more likely to interact with other political organisations at the grassroots and transnational levels and with a diverse populace. Thus, they, unlike the potential tribalism of their vanguard counterparts, have been more open to political learning because, through such interactions, they engaged in dialogue, negotiations, and compromise leading potentially to a political transformation.[9] As a result, grassroots Islamic movements have tended to be more open to change.

Nonetheless, grassroots Islamic movements eschewing party politics have also been more opaque in their internal workings compared to their vanguard counterparts, which have accepted to open their organisations to public accountability. In this way, because grassroots Islamic movements have survived regime repressions for decades by building strong internal bonds between their followers and by socialising their followers from childhood onwards, they have also been more protective of their organisations and thus have often closed off their organisation to public eyes. Additionally, grassroots Islamic movement's organisation around a charismatic founding figure has also added to their organisational ambiguity. Consequently, political transformations within grassroots Islamic movements have often taken place behind closed doors, only becoming visible if the movement chose to make these transformations public. What this meant in practical terms is that the political transformations grassroots Islamic movements underwent have not necessarily been political transformations towards political pluralism but more often than not have been transformations to survive and to thrive outside the party system in order to avoid political stagnation.

The diversity of the six Islamic movements in Morocco, Turkey, and Jordan illustrates such differentiation within political Islam.

Morocco

The MUR and the PJD, after their decision to participate in party politics in order to engage in top-down Islamic revival under their vanguards, have consolidated the status quo in various ways. Firstly, as discussed in detail in the last chapter, both the MUR and the PJD have accommodated the Moroccan regime. In this, they have assumed the role of a 'loyal opposition' criticising the regime but never asking for the reconstitution of the monarchy itself. To recount a few instances, the PJD lost elections on purpose by nominating fewer candidates to avoid a clash with the regime,[10] neither the PJD nor the MUR joined the Arab Spring inspired F20M, which asked for democratic reforms, and the PJD only criticised the *Makhzen* but never the King. Secondly, the PJD, in order to appeal to a wider constituency, has proposed 'thin-centred'[11] policies, on the one hand, continuing the neoliberal policies of the *Makhzen* and thus consolidating the grip of power-holders in the economy, and on the other hand, voicing an anti-elitist and populist critique of the same power-holders.[12] By doing so, it appealed to educated urban populations as well as to middle-class voters 'interested in incremental change'.[13] Thirdly, during its incumbency, the PJD has ignored persisting problems requiring deep-seated structural reforms, such as socio-economic inequalities over which protests erupted in the Riff region and minority problems with the Amazigh and Western Sahara. Instead, the Party's incumbency focused on moral policies that in the end consolidated theirs and the regime's hold on power.

In particular, during the PJD's tenure, 'popular committees' have risen in some cities to fight against immoral behaviour, which included several members of the PJD and organised sit-ins in front of department stores that were selling alcoholic beverages.[14] The PJD has also pushed for having a *mufti*, a Muslim cleric, on TV programmes about youth and social issues,[15] issued new regulations for public television, banned advertisements for the lottery, and made it mandatory to have 80% of the TV broadcasts to be in Arabic,[16] and to broadcast the five daily calls to prayer and the Friday sermon.[17] According to Communications Minister El Khalfi, they engaged in such new regulations to 'reconcile Moroccans with public stations, and by making TV near [them]'.[18] Its understanding of Islam also remained focused on moral behaviour rather than on structural reform. For instance, the PJD continued to punish public eating during Ramadan, extra-marital relations, and blasphemy.[19] It also rejected to revise the Family Code for greater gender equality.[20] According to a Moroccan journalist, the PJD, by focusing on such morality issues, has avoided talking about real politics.[21] In sum, the PJD has engaged in the promotion of top-down moral policies centred on an individual's moral character under its vanguards and in doing so defended the status quo rather than changing it.

In addition to the pursuit of such top-down moral policies, the PJD has also remained politically unchanged as a result of its vanguard organisation. Internally, the PJD's vanguard leadership, composed of roughly 20 individuals, has remained stable. Although leadership positions have altered back and forth between various leaders, such as the position of party leader between Saadeddin Othmani and Abdelilah Benkirane, the organisation remained in the hands of a few vanguards. Furthermore, internal elections were designed to 'limit the risk of undesired outcomes' through 'lengthy and complicated but transparent procedures'.[22] In particular, the PJD has administered an exclusive two-stage membership system. In this recruitment system, two party members first recommend a candidate as a 'participatory member'.[23] During this stage, the candidate has no access to any of the party's legislative or executive bodies. Then, in the second stage, after a year of performance evaluation and background screening, the member becomes a 'working member' with an increasing role in the Party's decision-making.[24] By doing so, the PJD has kept the Party under the control of its vanguards and avoided co-optation. As a result, even if the PJD leadership disagreed on certain issues from time to time, once a decision was taken, all Party vanguards stood by this decision in unity.

Externally, such a tight organisation prevented the PJD's political transformation, because although the organisation was united internally, it also tended to view politics tribally, seeing the political field as a zero-sum game. To illustrate, with the 2011 Constitutional amendments, civil society actors in Morocco were given 'the right to submit petitions, make legislative proposals, and to contribute in shaping public policy'.[25] However, the PJD government instead proposed to introduce financial supervisions on civil society organisations in the name of providing transparency, which conveniently allowed the PJD to limit the influence of the secular civil society and to empower the PJD-linked civil society by turning them into the PJD's sub-contractors.[26] By adopting such an 'us versus them' approach to conducting government affairs, the PJD solidified its internal monism and closed off its incumbency to outsiders.

In contrast to the PJD, the JSM has been unapologetically reformist in its non-participation in party politics. In particular, the JSM, unlike the PJD, has not sought top-down political power but a gradual reconstitution of the Moroccan regime. To this end, the Movement not only joined the F20M but also supported the Riff protests in 2016/17 by asking for structural changes in Moroccan politics.[27] Hence, the JSM foresaw a revolutionary change and worked towards this ideal by supporting mass movements demanding the restructuring of existing political and socio-economic systems. Furthermore, the JSM, unlike the PJD and its behavioural moderation to appeal to a wider constituency, has not moderated its political agenda either. On the contrary, the JSM still rejects the King's religio-political legitimacy as the Commander of the Believers, and thus is officially an illegal organisation, which costs them potential recruits but also solidifies the Movement's stance with its existing supporters. To maintain such oppositional integrity, the JSM boycotted the last local elections in 2015 and the general elections of 2016, because, in JSM member Omar Iherchane's words:

> The system [was] too corrupt. [...] The interior ministry control[led] an electoral map that guarantee[d] the regime's best interests – which [were] far from what the people need[ed]. Elections should guarantee freedom but the atmosphere in Morocco [was] everything but free.[28]

Although the JSM has been subjected to harassment by Moroccan authorities as a result of such an idealistic and counter-hegemonic stance,[29] the Movement also raised bigger questions about the legitimacy of the monarchy and its supporting structures – questions the PJD failed to raise despite being an incumbent. Consequently, the JSM has continued its reformist political agenda by posing a genuine opposition to the Moroccan regime.

While pursuing such reformism, the JSM itself has also transformed. Internally, the JSM, unlike the PJD and its internal monism, as a grassroots Islamic movement, had a diverse organisation composed of old guard leaders, often Islamic scholars, who have been close associates of Abdessalam Yassine as well of those who have been active on the ground through women and youth branches. In order to balance the various demands of these branches, the JSM has also undergone a reorganisation since Yassine's death in 2012. Specifically, the Movement organisationally separated its religious outreach activities from its political activities. While Mohamed Abbadi took over the leadership of the religious outreach, Fathallah Arsalane took over the political circle.[30] In this reorganization, the Movement also decided 'internal consensus would be required before any action was taken'.[31] In a sense, this separation signified the secularisation of the Movement's strategic objectives.

Externally, the JSM, in contrast to the PJD's tribalist approach to politics, has started participating in new alliances in order to avoid political stagnancy in its non-participation. For instance, in October 2014, the Movement participated in trade unions and their general strike to show solidarity with civil society organisations.[32] It also supported the Riff protests since 2016.[33] In these engagements, the JSM also learned from its past mistakes within the

F20M and its failure to build trust with secular opposition forces. Hence, the JSM started to be more transparent in its organisation. In particular, its political department started releasing reports of its meetings, publishing public statements on policy issues, 'reactivating its website, launching an online channel, and holding regular briefings with independent print media'.[34] In short, the JSM engaged in self-reflection and adjusted its strategies to internal and external necessities.

Turkey

Similar to their Moroccan counterparts, Islamic movements in Turkey have also presented diverse approaches to political Islam. To begin with, like the PJD accommodating the Moroccan regime by assuming the role of a loyal opposition, the NOM and its successor the AKP both have walked a line between accommodating the Turkish regime and reforming it from within. While the NOM criticised the Turkish regime's laicism, it also never questioned the legitimacy of the state, never considered radicalisation despite the closure of its multiple political parties, and never called for a revolutionary takeover of the regime. The AKP, similar to the PJD in Morocco and going further than its predecessor, the NOM, has accommodated the Turkish regime by divorcing itself from the NOM and by repositioning itself as a conservative-democratic centre-right party. Both the NOM and the AKP, like the MUR and the PJD in Morocco, have also engaged in behavioural moderation. While in the 1990s the NOM started providing pragmatic rather than ideological services through municipalities, and thus started attracting new constituents, the AKP's behavioural moderation into a conservative-democratic party consolidated its widespread appeal. Like the PJD's thin-centred policies, the AKP's advocacy of pro-EU reforms and democratisation appealed both to liberals and conservatives,[35] its neoliberal economic policies appealed to businessmen, and its use of municipalities for redistribution to the urban poor.[36]

En route to such electoral power, whilst the NOM never attained the political power the AKP has attained as an incumbent, its political agenda was nevertheless more reformist than that of the AKP because the NOM parties demanded the complete restructuring of the political and socio-economic system in line with the 'Just Order' worldview Erbakan proposed wherein a

Muslim world alliance based on an Islamic socio-economic system would rival that of secular Western neo-liberalism.[37] As the AKP consolidated its dominance electorally and politically, however, like the PJD in Morocco, it became less reformist. In the early years of its incumbency, the AKP was reformist insofar as it engaged in a speedy EU accession process. However, once the Party consolidated its political dominance, it became less interested in socio-economic reform, which was its major focus in its first two terms in office, and like its Moroccan counterpart, became more interested in pursuing top-down policies aimed to administer the demands of a 'moral majority'. For instance, the Party halted theatre plays and art exhibitions because it found them to be 'too vulgar',[38] and introduced limits to the sale of alcohol.[39] Furthermore, the party became more entangled in the advocacy of conservative values. Reproductive issues, such as abortion, caesarean section, and encouragement of three kids – issues that historically have not carried much political importance – [were] politicised on the grounds that 'foreign' forces [were] trying to control Turkey's population growth.[40] Going further, party leaders, who once reiterated their support for political liberalism, announced that they wanted to revise the education system to construct a 'pious generation'.[41] The *Diyanet*, the Directorate of Religious Affairs, was also 'transformed into a pliable state apparatus geared towards implementing the political ideology of the ruling cadre'.[42] In short, reforms to consolidate power replaced the Party's pro-EU reformism of its early years.

Similar to this reformism, the Turkish vanguard movement has also played hot and cold with political transformations over the years. Internally, although the NOM started out as a vanguard organised around a few leaders, with its societal outreach in the 1990s, it became organisationally more pluralistic. Hence, the younger generations within the NOM, as discussed in the last chapter, wanted to change the Movement's political goals. Nonetheless, the old vanguards resisted such calls for transformation, leading today's AKP founders to split from the NOM to form their own party. As a result, in its early years, the AKP was an umbrella organisation to various political groups ranging from Islamists to liberals and from centre-right politicians to former NOM members.[43] But, as the AKP consolidated its dominance in Turkish politics, the 'iron law of oligarchy'[44] took hold over the party organisation. In particular, as the Party gained more power and became the definer of the status quo, it also lost its organisational vibrancy. The need for internal discipline in order to carry out the task of being the sole incumbent led them to become increasingly hierarchical. Such a return to a vanguard organisation resulted in the departure of high profile leaders, such as of the AKP founder and former Minister of State Abdüllatif Şener, right-wing nationalist Murat Başeskioğlu, and the centre-right politician Erkan Mumcu. Even founders of the AKP with roots in the NOM, such as former President Abdullah Gül and Bülent Arınç, have found themselves marginalised within the Party. As a result, the AKP's umbrella organisation dismantled as the organisation increasingly returned to its vanguard organisation around a small group of leaders. In practice, like with the PJD in Morocco, this meant the disappearance of internal debate and thus of political transformations.

As Party leadership became more homogenous, the NOM vanguards' defensive rhetoric made a comeback externally. For instance, in contrast to past announcements of being the party of all and not just that of their own constituency, the AKP leaders started referring to opposition parties as potential traitors.[45] Within this framework, the Party periodically reminded its constituents that they needed to stick together and to defend themselves against unseen enemies inside and outside of Turkey.[46] Similarly, in the lead up to the contested 2017 referendum that approved Turkey's switch from parliamentarism to presidentialism, the opposition worried that this switch advocated by the AKP would risk further centralization of power. Instead of calming their fears and/or compromising into a middle ground, the incumbent party accused them of being on the same side as terrorist organisations.[47] Such polarised politics, like in Morocco and the PJD, led to a quest to conserve the Party at any cost and closed off the party to external critiques and to political learning thereof.

Meanwhile, the GM, like its Moroccan counterpart the JSM, pursued a reformist agenda to alter the socio-political fabric of Turkey, but unlike the JSM has done so by working with power-holders. As discussed in previous chapters, the GM tried retaining friendly relations both with secular elites as well as with incumbent parties to secure itself a safe space to conduct its bottom-up grassroots activities. Hence, unlike the JSM in Morocco, which aimed to reform Morocco through its oppositional stance, the GM aimed to reform Turkey by working with power-holders. Furthermore, unlike the

JSM, the GM adapted a rather ambiguous attitude towards moderation. On the one hand, the GM expanded its grassroots activism through a rhetoric of moderation, interfaith dialogue, and a commitment to liberal democracy. By doing so, the GM won the sympathies of leading liberals inside and outside of Turkey. On the other hand, however, the GM was also critical towards other political trends in Turkish political history. Specifically, it has been critical of other Islamic movements, leftist political activists, and of the Kurdish movement.[48] As a result, the GM's moderation can be understood as a 'behavioural' one aimed at protecting its organisation by winning the sympathies of power-holders in the state as well as of opinion leaders in the society in order carry out its reforms and protect its base, but not necessarily an 'ideological' one 'from a relatively closed and rigid worldview to one more open and tolerant of alternative perspectives'[49] allowing other political actors also to demand reform.

Starting roughly in 2010, the GM became more critical towards the incumbent AKP. Political disagreements over Syria, the Kurds, Israel, and the West as well as over the staffing of the bureaucracy have been cited as reasons for such a change in behaviour.[50] Within a few years, tensions between the GM and the incumbent party slowly increased, eventually reaching their peak on 15 July 2016 when junior military officers allegedly close to the GM attempted to overthrow the AKP-led government. While the GM denied any responsibility in this coup attempt,[51] observers across the Turkish political spectrum have disputed such denials.[52]

Like its engagements with the regime, the GM's political transformations over the years have also been curious. Internally, the GM remained a hierarchical organisation under Fethullah Gülen. Up until very recently, not much internal debate was visible, at least to outsiders. Externally, today, however, since the 2016 coup attempt, the GM is at a critical juncture point as it has been declared a terrorist organisation by the Turkish state and is subject to a purge wherein the government has confiscated its business ventures, schools, and media. Such external changes seem to have initiated internal debates and self-reflections within the GM after the coup attempt where some have started criticising the GM leader Fethullah Gülen, which was unthinkable previously.[53] One would expect such internal reflections and external pressures to turn into political learning and political transformation over time.

Jordan

Like in Morocco and Turkey, Islamic movements in Jordan have taken different approaches to political reform and transformations. But, unlike the MUR/PJD in Morocco and the NOM/AKP in Turkey, both of which started their political careers from a position of weakness vis-à-vis the regime, the Muslim Brotherhood in Jordan started the party politics chapter of its long political career from a position of dominance. With such proximity to power, the JMB, as discussed in the previous chapter, pursued moral policies such as gender segregations, rather than policies demanding structural reform, such as the reform of the monarchy. Furthermore, because the Brotherhood, unlike its Moroccan and Turkish counterparts, started its party system journey as the dominant party, it did not need to engage in behavioural moderation to attract a wider constituency. Although in principle it formed the IAF to attract a wider constituency, given the symbiotic relations between the IAF and the JMB, such aims never materialised. As a result, different to Morocco and Turkey, the Jordanian regime saw such dominance and behavioural immoderation as a threat and thus closed in on the Brotherhood leaving no breathing room for the Brotherhood to engage in political activism neither inside nor outside the party system. Hence, the Brotherhood, unlike the PJD and the AKP both of which acquired positions of power allowing them to consolidate their socio-political dominance, had to turn into a 'hard opposition' stance demanding structural reforms in order to remain a vital political player. As a result, younger Brotherhood members became more reformist in regards to the Jordanian regime.

In particular, these younger generations organised under the name of the 'Zamzam Initiative' sought 'to develop "a modern civil state" in Jordan' and aimed to widen the Brotherhood's appeal by 'reach[ing] a consensus across Jordanian society over the country's political future, which [was] entering a "transition period".'[54] Under the leadership of Ruheil Gharaibeh, the Initiative dedicated itself to offer a third way[55] by prioritising socio-economic reform.[56] In this, it called to 'build a good relationship with all state institutions based on cooperation and active participation in various fields',[57] and emphasised the 'need to adopt the principle of gradual transition toward democracy within the framework of reform plans, which must be implemented based on national consensus and popular participation in the reform project'.[58] In short, in contrast to its Moroccan and Turkish counterparts, more reformist voices started coming out of the JMB neither seeking accommodation with the regime nor its downfall but its reconstitution as a genuine constitutional monarchy.

Such a reformist transformation was not the only transformation the Brotherhood underwent in the last few years. What has differentiated the Brotherhood from its vanguard counterparts in Morocco and Turkey has been the presence of internal diversity within the Brotherhood between the hardliners and the pragmatists. As a consequence, the Brotherhood, unlike the PJD or the AKP, has not been subject to groupthink, and has instead been able to engage in internal debate and transform its strategic objectives. In particular, the Brotherhood has altered its ideological priorities. Instead of seeking top-down Islamic revival, the Brotherhood today has started debating the status of the civil state and pluralism in Islam. In this, the JMB leaders indicated that they were looking at the Constitution of Medina as well as at the writings of Rachid Ghannouchi on these subjects.[59] Furthermore, the Brotherhood has altered its organisational priorities and started debating the prioritisation of Jordanian problems over Arab, regional and even Palestinian problems. Hence, the younger generation within the Brotherhood today is advocating that, 'a strong Jordan is better for others than a weak Jordan'.[60]

Externally, the Brotherhood, unlike its vanguard counterparts in Morocco and Turkey who came to dominate party politics, had to form alliances with political actors across the political spectrum as a result of its repression by the Jordanian regime. To do so, it ran in the 2016 general elections as part of the National Coalition for Reform together with tribal, nationalist and Christian political groups. This Coalition, instead of running under the banner of 'Islam is the solution', 'offered a civic, nonreligious approach to dealing with the country's economic and social challenges'.[61] The splinter group from the JMB, the new Muslim Brotherhood Society in particular, also participated in the 2016 general elections by fielding candidates across the political spectrum and by emphasising the need for democratic and economic reforms.[62] In short, the Brotherhood's strategic objectives transformed as a result of political learning through socialisation with political actors across the spectrum.

Meanwhile, Quietist Salafis, like the JSM in Morocco and the GM in

Turkey, have always been reformist even though they chose to pursue reform through obedience to the monarchy. Within this understanding, the Quietist Salafis have separated themselves from the rest of the society in order to start their reformed communities independently of the state but without posing a direct challenge to the state either. In this, the Quietist Salafis have found an appeal amongst a niche aiming to gradually alter the status quo. They have also continued to have strict codes of behaviour, such as dress codes, for followers, thereby avoiding behavioural moderation and instead attracting those few but devoted individuals who are willing to dedicate their lives to Salafi reform. Nonetheless, the Quietist Salafis' ideological project has also gone beyond morality and dress codes. In the end, the Quietist Salafis are ultimately expecting a total reconstitution of the society and eventually of the state and think such wholesale reform will start with the reform of the individual and grow through grassroots activism. In short, the Quietist Salafis, like their Moroccan and Turkish counterparts, have been pursuing reform but unlike them have done so quietly.

In this 'quiet' reformism, the Quietist Salafis, like their Moroccan and Turkish counterparts, have also been transforming politically. Internally, the organisational fluidity and thus the vibrancy of Quietist Salafism in Jordan, as discussed in the last chapter, has resulted in a new space of debate and thus a differentiation of Salafi demands. Externally, in order to differentiate themselves from more radical Salafi trends and to fill in the historical role of the JMB, they have started allying themselves with the Jordanian regime. As a result of such internal debates and new alliances, some Quietist Salafis have started becoming more politically vocal.[63] Although this does not mean that the Salafis are going to engage in active politics anytime soon, it does signify a potential transformation within the Salafi current.[64] Such a slow turn towards open politicisation, and the eventual alliances of interests it brings, will most likely lead to some major transformations within the Quietist Salafi current in Jordan in the near future.

The Rise of Islamic Political Movements and Parties

After years of political activism inside and outside party politics, how much have these six Islamic political movements and parties (agents) succeeded in altering the socio-political structures they face? In their prominent book, *Acts of Faith*, Stark and Finke[65] ask why religion is on the rise in a religiously pluralist liberal democracy like the US. They argue that religious pluralism gives the society a wide array of choices in matters of religion, and thus gives way to a 'religious market', wherein 'customers' can choose from a spectrum of religious organisations.[66] More so, they argue, religious organisations, in the absence of state funding to religious organisations, are more proactive to win 'consumers' since their funding and thus their survival depends on having more 'consumers'.[67] All this accumulates, they argue, in a religious market where there is a religious organisation for every 'consumer need/demand', and where religious organisations are tirelessly recruiting.[68]

The regimes under study in this book, Morocco, Turkey and Jordan, are by no means religiously pluralistic liberal democracies. On the contrary, they are in a constant race with Islamic political movements to control the religious field and often resort to authoritarianism to do so. Nevertheless, a 'religious market' has still flourished in these countries as multiple Islamic movements with diverse interpretations of Islam, political strategies, and electoral paths have emerged outside the control of the state. As these Islamic movements have competed with each other as well as with state establishments for the hearts and minds of everyday Muslims, for 'consumers', a lively 'religious market' has shifted the political centre in these countries towards an open engagement with political Islam. Consequently, regardless of whether individual Islamic movements have succeeded in realising their strategic objectives, collectively their political activism has resulted in a more openly religious socio-political landscape, and thus in the Rise of Islamic Political Movements and Parties.

Notes

1. Jillian Schwedler, 'Review Article: Can Islamists Become Moderates? Rethinking the Inclusion-Moderation Hypothesis', *World Politics*, 63.2 (2011), 347–76.
2. Schwedler, 'Review Article'.
3. Laurence R. Iannaccone, 'Why Strict Churches Are Strong', *American Journal of Sociology*, 99.5 (1994), 1180–211.
4. Clark McCauley and Sophia Moskalenko, 'Mechanisms of Political Radicalization: Pathways Toward Terrorism', *Terrorism and Political Violence*, 20.3 (2008), 415–33.

5. Carrie Rosefsky Wickham, *The Muslim Brotherhood: Evolution of an Islamist Movement* (Princeton, NJ: Princeton University Press, 2013); Shadi Hamid, *Temptations of Power: Islamists and Illiberal Democracy in a New Middle East* (Oxford & New York: Oxford University Press, 2014).
6. Iannaccone, 'Why Strict Churches Are Strong'.
7. McCauley and Moskalenko, 'Mechanisms of Political Radicalization'.
8. Schwedler, 'Review Article'.
9. Carrie Rosefsky Wickham, 'The Path to Moderation: Strategy and Learning in the Formation of Egypt's Wasat Party', *Comparative Politics*, 36.2 (2004), 205–28.
10. Shadi Hamid, 'Arab Islamist Parties: Losing on Purpose?', *Journal of Democracy*, 22.1 (2011), 68–80.
11. Cas Mudde, 'The Populist Zeitgeist', *Government and Opposition*, 39.4 (2004), 542–63.
12. Esen Kirdiş and Amina Drhimeur, 'The Rise of Populism? Comparing Incumbent Pro-Islamic Parties in Turkey and Morocco', *Turkish Studies*, 17.4 (2016), 599–617.
13. Miquel Pellicer and Eva Wegner, 'Socio-Economic Voter Profile and Motives for Islamist Support in Morocco', *Party Politics*, 20.1 (2014), 116–33.
14. Tahar Abou El Farah (2013), 'Le PJD Prépare une OPA sur la Société Civile' ['The PJD Prepares a Takeover on Civil Society'], *La Vie Éco*, 7 June, <http://www.lavieeco.com/news/politique/le-pjd-prepare-une-opa-sur-la-societe-civile-25701.html> (last accessed 30 July 2018).
15. '2012. Mohammed VI: Première Année Islamiste' ['2012. Mohammed VI: Islamists' First Year'] (2013), *Telquel*, 3 January, <http://telquel.ma/2013/01/03/2012-Mohammed-VI-Premiere-annee-islamiste_550-551_5628> (last accessed 30 July 2018).
16. 'The Tussle For Control of Moroccan Media Heats Up' (2012), *Morocco World News*, 14 May, <http://www.moroccoworldnews.com/2012/05/39608/the-tussle-for-control-of-moroccan-media-heats-up/> (last accessed 30 July 2018).
17. 'Maroc: Le PJD Imprime Sa Marque sur L'Audiovisuel Marocain' ['Morocco: The PJD Puts its Mark on Moroccan Audiovisuals'] (2012), *Jeune Afrique*, 12 April, <http://www.jeuneafrique.com/Article/ARTJAWEB20120412161548/pjd-islam-r-formes-libert-de-la-presse-maroc-maroc-le-pjd-imprime-sa-marque-sur-l-audiovisuel-marocain.html> (last accessed 30 July 2018).
18. Mohammed Jaabouk (2012), 'Nouveaux Cahiers de Charges de L'Audiovisuel

au Maroc : Petites Concessions au PJD et Larges Victoires de 2M' ['New Audiovisual Handbook in Morocco: Small Concessions to the PJD and Wide Victories for the 2M Channel'], *Yabiladi*, 28 August, <http://www.yabiladi.com/articles/details/12509/nouveaux-cahiers-charges-l-audiovisuel-maroc.html> (last accessed 30 July 2018).
19. Mohammed Jaabouk (2012), '2M Contre El Khalfi: La Controverse Arrive au Parlement' ['2M Channel against El Khalfi: The Controversy Arrives at the Parliament'], *Yabiladi*, 24 April, <http://www.yabiladi.com/articles/details/10202/contre-khalfi-controverse-arrive-parlement.html> (last accessed 30 July 2018).
20. Zakaria Choukrallah (2015), 'Héritage: Pour le PJD, le CNDH Outrepasse la "Commanderie des Croyants"' ['Legacy: For the PJD, the CNDH Overtakes the "Commander of the Believers"'], *Telquel*, 22 October, <http://telquel.ma/2015/10/22/heritage-pjd-cndh-outrepasse-commanderie-croyants_1467432> (last accessed 30 July 2018).
21. Anonymous interview with a Moroccan journalist by the author, 13 April 2010, Rabat, Morocco.
22. Eva Wegner, *Islamist Opposition in Authoritarian Regimes: The Party of Justice and Development in Morocco* (Syracuse, NY: Syracuse University Press, 2011).
23. Eva Wegner (2004), 'The Contribution of Inclusivist Approaches towards the Islamist Opposition to Regime Stability in Arab States: The Case of the Moroccan Parti de La Justice et Du Développement', *EUI Working Paper RSCAS* <http://cadmus.eui.eu/bitstream/handle/1814/2784/04_42.pdf?sequence=1> (last accessed on 17 July 2018).
24. Wegner, 'The Contribution of Inclusivist Approaches towards the Islamist Opposition to Regime Stability in Arab States'.
25. Rachid Touhtouh (2014), 'Civil Society in Morocco under the New 2011 Constitution: Issues, Stakes and Challenges', *Arab Center for Research and Policy Studies*, 10 September, <https://www.dohainstitute.org/en/ResearchAndStudies/Pages/Civil_Society_in_Morocco_under_the_New_2011_Constitution_Issues_Stakes_and_Challenges.aspx> (last accessed on 17 July 2018).
26. Touhtouh, 'Civil Society in Morocco under the New 2011 Constitution'.
27. Joe Hayns (2017), 'Morocco's Burgeoning Resistance', *Jacobin*, 7 June, <https://www.jacobinmag.com/2017/07/morocco-popular-movement-protest-islam> (last accessed 30 July 2018).
28. Aida Alami (2015), 'Morocco Prepares for Local Elections amid Boycott Calls',

Al Jazeera, 3 September, <http://www.aljazeera.com/news/2015/09/morocco-prepares-local-elections-boycott-calls-150903075800768.html> (last accessed 30 July 2018).

29. Human Rights Watch (2018), 'Morocco/Western Sahara: Events of 2017', *Human Rights Watch*, <https://www.hrw.org/world-report/2018/country-chapters/morocco/western-sahara> (last accessed 30 July 2018).
30. Mohammed Masbah (2015), 'The Ongoing Marginalization of Morocco's Largest Islamist Opposition Group', *Carnegie Endowment for International Peace*, 3 June, <http://carnegieendowment.org/2015/06/03/ongoing-marginalization-of-morocco-s-largest-islamist-opposition-group/i9fo> (last accessed 30 July 2018).
31. Masbah, 'The Ongoing Marginalization of Morocco's Largest Islamist Opposition Group'.
32. Masbah, 'The Ongoing Marginalization of Morocco's Largest Islamist Opposition Group'.
33. Hayns, 'Morocco's Burgeoning Resistance'.
34. Masbah, 'The Ongoing Marginalization of Morocco's Largest Islamist Opposition Group'.
35. Cem Başlevent, Hasan Kirmanoğlu, and Burhan Şenatalar, 'Party Preferences and Economic Voting in Turkey (Now That the Crisis Is Over)', *Party Politics*, 15.3 (2009), 377–91; Burhanettin Duran, 'Türk Dış Politikasinin İç Siyaset Boyutu: 2010 Değerlendirmesi' ['The Domestic Politics Dimension of Turkish Foreign Policy: 2010 Assessment], in Burhanettin Duran, Kemal Inat, and Mesut Özcan (eds), *Türk Dış Politikası Yıllığı* [*Turkish Foreign Policy Yearbook*] (Ankara: SETA, 2011), pp. 15–66.
36. Kirdiş and Drhimeur, 'The Rise of Populism?'.
37. Necmettin Erbakan, *Adil Ekonomik Düzen* [*Just Economic Order*] (Ankara, Turkey: Anadolu Matbaacılık, 1991).
38. Daniel Steinvorth (2012), 'Erdoğan the Misogynist: Turkish Prime Minister Assaults Women's Rights', *Spiegel*, 19 June, <http://www.spiegel.de/international/europe/turkish-prime-minister-erdogan-targets-women-s-rights-a-839568.html> (last accessed 30 July 2018).
39. 'Erdoğan: İçki Içen Alkoliktir' ['Erdoğan: Those who Drink are Alcoholics'] (2013), *Milliyet*, 2 June, <http://siyaset.milliyet.com.tr/erdogan-icki-icen-alkoliktir/siyaset/detay/1717637/default.htm> (last accessed 30 July 2018).
40. 'Sezeryan Kürtajla Cinayet İşlediler' ['Those Who Have Engaged in Cesarean

Sections Have Committed Murder'] (2013), *Hürriyet*, 19 June <http://www.hurriyet.com.tr/gundem/23537027.asp> (last accessed 2 August 2018).
41. 'Erdoğan "dindar Nesil"i Savundu' ['Erdoğan Defends "Pious Generation"'] (2012), *Radikal*, 6 February, <http://www.radikal.com.tr/politika/erdogan-dindar-nesili-savundu-1077899/> (last accessed 30 July 2018).
42. Ahmet Erdi Öztürk, 'Turkey's Diyanet under AKP Rule: From Protector to Imposer of State Ideology?', *Southeast European and Black Sea Studies*, 16.4 (2016), 619–35.
43. Ruşen Çakır (2002), 'AKP Yedi Eğilimi Aynı Potada Eritti' ['AKP Has Melted Down Seven Trends in the Same Pot'], *Vatan*, 2 December, <http://www.gazetevatan.com/akp-yedi-egilimi-ayni-potada-eritti-1219-gundem/> (last accessed 30 July 2018).
44. Robert Michels, *Political Parties: A Sociological Study of the Oligarchical Tendencies of Modern Democracy* ([S.l.]: General Books, 2009).
45. 'Erdogan Slams CHP as Opposition March Nears Istanbul' (2017), *Al Jazeera*, 1 July, <https://www.aljazeera.com/news/2017/07/erdogan-slams-chp-opposition-march-nears-istanbul-170701112203655.html> (last accessed 2 August 2018).
46. Kirdiş and Drhimeur, 'The Rise of Populism?'.
47. 'Erdoğan'dan "Hayır" Diyenlere Terörist, Almanya'ya Nazi Benzetmesi' ['Erdoğan Likens Those Who Say "No" to Terrorists, Germany to Nazis'] (2017), *Cumhuriyet*, 5 March <http://www.cumhuriyet.com.tr/haber/turkiye/691334/Erdogan_dan__Hayir__diyenlere_terorist__Almanya_ya_Nazi_benzetmesi.html> (last accessed 2 August 2018).
48. Ruşen Çakır, *Ayet ve Slogan: Türkiye'de Islamcı Oluşumlar [Verse and Slogan: Islamic Formations in Turkey]* (Istanbul: Metis Yayınları, 2002).
49. Jillian Schwedler, 'Review Article'.
50. Hakan M. Yavuz and Bayram Balcı, *Turkey's July 15th Coup: What Happened and Why* (Salt Lake City, UT: The University of Utah Press, 2018); Ruşen Çakır and Semih Sakallı, *100 Soruda Erdoğan – Gülen Savaşı [Erdoğan – Gülen War in 100 Questions]* (Istanbul: Metis Yayınları, 2014).
51. Stephanie Saul (2016), 'An Exiled Cleric Denies Playing a Leading Role in Coup Attempt', *The New York Times*, 16 July, <https://www.nytimes.com/2016/07/17/us/fethullah-gulen-turkey-coup-attempt.html> (last accessed 30 July 2018).
52. For a discussion, see: Yavuz and Balcı, *Turkey's July 15th Coup*.
53. Ruşen Çakır (2017), 'Nihayet Başlayan İçeriden Eleştiriler Fethullah Gülen'i

Nasıl Etkiler?' ['How Will Internal criticism that at Last Have Started Affect Fethullah Gülen?'], *Medyascope.Tv*, 6 November, <http://rusencakir.com/Nihayet-baslayan-iceriden-elestiriler-Fethullah-Guleni-nasil-etkiler/6600> (last accessed 30 July 2018).

54. Taylor Luck (2013), 'Political Activists Officially Launch Zamzam Social Movement', *Jordan Times*, 5 October, <http://vista.sahafi.jo/art.php?id=31ecfeb10041fa6fbabd7992e1bcffaabc8ad73f> (last accessed 30 July 2018).

55. Tareq Al-Naimat (2014), 'Zamzam and the Jordanian Brotherhood', *Carnegie Endowment for International Peace*, 14 February, <http://carnegieendowment.org/sada/54427> (last accessed 30 July 2018).

56. David Schenker (2013), 'Down and Out in Amman', *Foreign Affairs*, 3 October, <https://www.foreignaffairs.com/articles/middle-east/2013-10-03/down-and-out-amman> (last accessed 30 July 2018).

57. '"Zamzam" Reveals Divisions in Jordan's Muslim Brotherhood' (2012), *Al-Hayat*, 5 December, <http://en.ammonnews.net/article.aspx?articleNO=19384#.W1-NZNhKi-U> (last accessed 30 July 2018).

58. '"Zamzam" Reveals Divisions in Jordan's Muslim Brotherhood'.

59. Neven Bondokji (2015), 'The Muslim Brotherhood in Jordan: Time to Reform', *Brookings Institution*, <https://www.brookings.edu/wp-content/uploads/2016/06/en-muslim-brotherhood-in-jordan.pdf> (last accessed 28 July 2018).

60 Mohammad S. Abu Rumman and Hassan Abu Hanieh, *The 'Islamic Solution' in Jordan: Islamists, the State, and the Ventures of Democracy and Security* (Amman: Friedrich-Ebert-Stiftung, 2013).

61. Osama Al-Sharif (2016), 'Who Are the Winners and Losers in Jordan's Latest Elections?', *Al Monitor*, 28 September, <https://levantpost.wordpress.com/2016/10/11/who-are-the-winners-and-losers-in-jordans-latest-elections/> (last accessed 30 July 2018).

62. Curtis R. Ryan (2016), 'Jordan's Holding Elections Next Week. Here's What to Expect', *The Washington Post*, 16 September, <https://www.washingtonpost.com/news/monkey-cage/wp/2016/09/16/jordans-holding-elections-next-week-heres-what-to-expect/?utm_term=.a66387deae1a> (last accessed 30 July 2018).

63. Joas Wagemakers, *Salafism in Jordan: Political Islam in a Quietist Community* (New York: Cambridge University Press, 2016).

64. Wagemakers, *Salafism in Jordan*.

65. Rodney Stark and Roger Finke, *Acts of Faith: Explaining the Human Side of Religion* (Berkeley, CA: University of California Press, 2000).

66. Stark and Finke, *Acts of Faith*.
67. Stark and Finke, *Acts of Faith*.
68. Stark and Finke, *Acts of Faith*.

BIBLIOGRAPHY

'2002–2014 Sessiz Devrim: Türkiye'nin Demokratik Değişim ve Dönüşüm Envanteri' ['2002–2014 Silent Revolution: Turkey's Democratic Change and Transformation Inventory'] (2015), *Official Website of the AKP*, 1 August, <https://www.akparti.org.tr/site/haberler/sessiz-devrim/77738#1> (last accessed 30 July 2018).

'2012. Mohammed VI: Première Année Islamiste' ['2012. Mohammed VI: Islamists' First Year'] (2013), *Telquel*, 3 January, <http://telquel.ma/2013/01/03/2012-Mohammed-VI-Premiere-annee-islamiste_550-551_5628> (last accessed 30 July 2018).

Abdelwahid, Mustafa, *The Rise of the Islamic Movement in Sudan (1945–1989)* (Lampeter: The Edwin Mellen Press Ltd, 2008).

Abduh, Muhammad (n.d.), 'Laws Should Change in Accordance with the Conditions of Nations and the Theology of Unity', *Oxford Islamic Studies Online* <http://www.oxfordislamicstudies.com/book/islam-9780195154672/islam-9780195154672-chapter-3> (last accessed 10 April 2012).

Abu Faris, Mohammad, *Al-Musharaka fi Al-Wizara fi Al-Anthima Al-Jahiliyya [Participation in the Cabinet of the Jahili (Pre-Islamic/Ignorant) Systems]* (Amman: Dar al-Furqan, 1991).

Abu Hanieh, Hassan, *Women and Politics: From the Perspective of Islamic Movements in Jordan* (Amman: Friedrich-Ebert-Stiftung, 2008).

Abu Latifeh, Atallah, 'Die Muslimbruderschaft in Jordanien zwischen Ideologie und Pragmatischer Anpassung' ['The Muslim Brotherhood in Jordan between

Ideology and Pragmatic Adjustments'] (unpublished Doctoral Dissertation, Freie Universität Berlin Fachbereich Politische Wissenschaft [Freie University Berlin Political Science Department], 1997).

Abu Nowar, Maan, *The Struggle for Independence 1939–1947: A History of the Hashemite Kingdom of Jordan* (Reading: Ithaca Press, 2001).

Abu Rumman, Mohammad S., *The Muslim Brotherhood in the 2007 Jordanian Parliamentary Elections: A Passing 'Political Setback' or Diminished Popularity* (Amman: Friedrich-Ebert-Stiftung, 2007).

Abu Rumman, Mohammad S., and Hassan Abu Haneh, *Jordanian Salafism: A Strategy for the 'Islamization of Society' and an Ambiguous Relationship with the State* (Amman: Friedrich-Ebert-Stiftung, 2010).

——, *The 'Islamic Solution' in Jordan Islamists, the State, and the Ventures of Democracy and Security* (Amman: Friedrich-Ebert-Stiftung, 2013).

Abu Zayd, Nasr, *Reformation of Islamic Thought: A Critical Historical Analysis* (Amsterdam: Amsterdam University Press, 2006).

Adler, Emanuel, 'Constructivism in International Relations: Sources, Contributions, and Debates', in Walter Carlsnaes, Thomas Risse-Kappen, and Beth A. Simmons (eds), *Handbook of International Relations* (London: SAGE, 2013), pp. 112–44.

Ahmad, Irfan, 'Genealogy of the Islamic State: Reflections on Maududi's Political Thought and Islamism', *The Journal of the Royal Anthropological Institute*, 15.1 (2009), 145–62.

Akhavi, Shahrough (n.d.), 'Qutb, Sayyid', *The Oxford Encyclopedia of the Islamic World, Oxford Islamic Studies Online* <http://www.oxfordislamicstudies.com/opr/t236/e0663> (last accessed 10 April 2012).

ᶜAl-Adl Wal Ihsane Annonce Son Retrait du Mouvement du 20 Février: La Fin de la Lune de Miel' [ᶜal-Adl Wal Ihsane Announces Its Withdrawal from the February 20th Movement: The End of the Honeymoon'] (2011), *Aufait*, 19 December <http://www.aufaitmaroc.com/actualites/maroc/2011/12/18/la-fin-de-la-lune-de-miel#.U7UMmqj1uSZ> (last accessed 3 July 2014).

Alami, Aida (2015), 'Morocco Prepares for Local Elections amid Boycott Calls', *Al Jazeera*, 3 September, <http://www.aljazeera.com/news/2015/09/morocco-prepares-local-elections-boycott-calls-150903075800768.html> (last accessed 30 July 2018).

Al-Anani, Khalil, 'Islamist Parties Post-Arab Spring', *Mediterranean Politics*, 17.3 (2012), 466–72.

Al-Ashqar, Omar Suleiman, *Hukm Al-Musharaka fi Al-Wizara wa Al-Majalis*

Al-Niyabiya [The Ruling on Participation in the Cabinet Government and Municipal Councils] (Amman: Dar al-Nafaʾis, 1992).

Aldrich, John H., *Why Parties?: The Origin and Transformation of Political Parties in America* (Chicago, IL: University of Chicago Press, 1995).

Al-Emam, Dana (2014), 'Economists Discuss Muslim Brotherhood's Proposed Economic Strategy', *Jordan Times*, 22 July, <http://www.jordantimes.com/news/local/economists-discuss-muslim-brotherhood%E2%80%99s-proposed-economic-strategy> (last accessed 28 July 2018).

Al-Fodeilat, Mohammad (2012), 'How Jordan's Islamists Came to Dominate Society: An Evolution', *Al Monitor*, 10 September, <https://archive.li/mJ7yq> (last accessed 25 July 2018).

Al-Naimat, Tareq (2014), 'The Jordanian Regime and the Muslim Brotherhood: A Tug of War', *Wilson Center*, <https://www.wilsoncenter.org/sites/default/files/jordanian_regime_muslim_brotherhood_tug_of_war.pdf> (last accessed 28 July 2018).

—— (2014), 'Zamzam and the Jordanian Brotherhood', *Carnegie Endowment for International Peace*, 14 February, < http://carnegieendowment.org/sada/54427> (last accessed 30 July 2018).

Al-Sharif, Osama (2016), 'Who Are the Winners and Losers in Jordan's Latest Elections?', *Al Monitor*, 28 September, <https://levantpost.wordpress.com/2016/10/11/who-are-the-winners-and-losers-in-jordans-latest-elections/> (last accessed 30 July 2018).

Amghar, Samir (2007), 'Political Islam in Morocco', *CEPS Working Document*, <http://aei.pitt.edu/11725/1/1510.pdf> (last accessed 28 July 2018).

Anderson, Lisa, 'Searching Where the Light Shines: Studying Democratization in the Middle East', *Annual Review of Political Science*, 9 (2006), 189–214.

An-Naim, Abdallah Ahmad, *Islam and the Secular State: Negotiating the Future of Shari`a* (Cambridge, MA: Harvard University Press, 2008).

Atacan, Fulya, 'Explaining Religious Politics at the Crossroad: AKP-SP', in Ali Çarkoğlu and Barry Rubin (eds), *Religion and Politics in Turkey* (London & New York: Routledge, 2006), pp. 45–58.

Ayata, Sencer, 'Patronage, Party, and State: The Politicization of Islam in Turkey', *Middle East Journal*, 50.1 (1996), 40–56.

Azem, Ahmad Jamil, 'The Islamic Action Front Party', in Hani Hurani, Jillian Schwedler, and George A. Musleh (eds), *Islamic Movements in Jordan* (Amman: Al-Urdun al-Jadid Research Center & Friedrich Ebert Stiftung, 1997), pp. 95–144.

Bahaji, Kassem, 'Islamism in Morocco: Appeal, Impact and Implications (1969–2003)' (unpublished PhD Dissertation, Political Science, Northern Illinois University, 2007).
Balcı, Bayram, and Hakan M. Yavuz, *Turkey's July 15th Coup: What Happened and Why* (Salt Lake City, UT: The University of Utah Press, 2018).
Bar, Shmuel, *The Muslim Brotherhood in Jordan* (Tel Aviv: The Moshe Dayan Center for Middle Eastern and African Studies, 1998).
Başlevent, Cem, Hasan Kirmanoğlu, and Burhan Şenatalar, 'Party Preferences and Economic Voting in Turkey (Now That the Crisis Is Over)', *Party Politics*, 15.3 (2009), 377–91.
Bayat, Asef, 'Revolution without Movement, Movement without Revolution: Comparing Islamic Activism in Iran and Egypt', *Comparative Studies in Society and History*, 40.1 (1998), 136–69.
——, 'Islamism and Social Movement Theory', *Third World Quarterly*, 26.6 (2005), 891–908.
——, *Making Islam Democratic: Social Movements and the Post-Islamist Turn* (Stanford, CA: Stanford University Press, 2007).
Belal, Youssef, 'Mystique et Politique chez Abdessalam Yassine et Ses Adeptes' ['Mystique and Politics in Abdessalam Yassine and His Followers'], *Archives de Sciences Sociales des Religions* 135 (2006): 165–84.
——, *Le Cheikh et le Calife: Sociologie Religieuse de l'Islam Politique au Maroc* [*The Sheikh and the Caliph: Religious Sociology of Political Islam in Morocco*] (Lyon: ENS Editions, 2011).
Bencheikh, Souleïman (2013), 'Morocco's Cabinet Crisis', *Al Monitor*, 17 July, <http://www.al-monitor.com/pulse/politics/2013/07/morocco-istiqlal-withdrawal-replacement-rni.html#> (last accessed 2 July 2014).
Benchemsi, Ahmed, 'Morocco's Makhzen and the Haphazard Activists', in Lina Khatib and Ellen Lust (eds), *Taking to the Streets: The Transformation of Arab Activism* (Baltimore, MD: Johns Hopkins University Press, 2014), pp. 199–235.
Bloom, Jonathan M., and Sheila S. Blair (n.d.), 'Amman', *The Grove Encyclopedia of Islamic Art and Architecture*, Oxford Islamic Studies Online <http://www.oxfordislamicstudies.com/article/opr/t276/e76> (last accessed on 19 July 2018).
——(n.d.), 'Ankara', *The Grove Encyclopedia of Islamic Art and Architecture*, Oxford Islamic Studies Online <http://www.oxfordislamicstudies.com/article/opr/t276/e79> (last accessed on 19 July 2018).
——(n.d.), 'Rabat', *The Grove Encyclopedia of Islamic Art and Architecture*, Oxford

Islamic Studies Online <http://www.oxfordislamicstudies.com/article/opr/t276/e771> (last accessed on 19 July 2018).

Blyth, Mark, 'Structures Do Not Come with an Instruction Sheet: Interests, Ideas, and Progress in Political Science', *Perspectives on Politics*, 1.4 (2003), 695–706.

Bokhari, Kamran (n.d.), 'Jamaᶜat-I Islami', *The Oxford Encyclopedia of the Islamic World. Oxford Islamic Studies Online* <http://www.oxfordislamicstudies.com/opr/t236/e0408> (last accessed 10 April 2012).

Bondokji, Neven (2015), 'The Muslim Brotherhood in Jordan: Time to Reform', *Brookings Institution,* <https://www.brookings.edu/wp-content/uploads/2016/06/en-muslim-brotherhood-in-jordan.pdf> (last accessed 28 July 2018).

Bonner, Arthur, 'An Islamic Reformation in Turkey', *Middle East Policy*, 11.1 (2004), 84–97.

Boulby, Marion, *The Muslim Brotherhood and the Kings of Jordan, 1945–1993* (Atlanta, GA: Scholars Press, 1999).

—— (n.d.), 'Hussein Ibn Talal of Jordan', *The Oxford Encyclopedia of the Islamic World, Oxford Islamic Studies Online* <http://www.oxfordislamicstudies.com/article/opr/t236/e1040> (last accessed 6 August 2018).

Boudarham, Mohammed (2013), 'Leaders Islamistes. Les Dix Portraits' ['Islamist Leaders: Six Portraits'], *Telquel*, 14 November, <http://telquel.ma/2013/11/14/leaders-islamistes-les-dix-portraits_9487> (last accessed 2 July 2014).

Boussaid, Farid, 'The Rise of the PAM in Morocco: Trampling the Political Scene or Stumbling into It?', *Mediterranean Politics*, 14.3 (2009), 413–19.

Bouyibri, Rochdi, 'Towards a Society that Rejects Violence', in Maâti Monjib (ed.), *Islamists versus Secularists: Confrontations and Dialogues in Morocco – Values, Democracy, Violence, Freedom, Education* (Rabat: IKV PAX, 2009).

Brocker, Manfred, and Mirjam Künkler, 'Religious Parties: Revisiting the Inclusion-Moderation Hypothesis- Introduction', *Party Politics*, 19.2 (2013), 171–86.

'Brotherhood to Take Part in Elections through IAF', *Al Dustur*, 27 August 1993.

Browers, Michaelle, *Democracy and Civil Society in Arab Political Thought: Transcultural Possibilities* (Syracuse, NY: Syracuse University Press, 2006).

Brown, Nathan J. (2006), 'Jordan and Its Islamic Movement: The Limits of Inclusion?', *Carnegie Endowment for International Peace*, <https://carnegieendowment.org/files/cp_74_brown_final.pdf> (last accessed 19 July 2018).

——, *When Victory Is Not an Option: Islamist Movements in Arab Politics* (Ithaca, NY: Cornell University Press, 2012).

Brown, Nathan J. and Amr Hamzawy, *Between Religion and Politics* (Washington, DC: Carnegie Endowment for International Peace, 2010).

Buehler, Michael, 'Revisiting the Inclusion–Moderation Thesis in the Context of Decentralized Institutions: The Behavior of Indonesia's Prosperous Justice Party in National and Local Politics', *Party Politics*, 19.2 (2013), 210–29.

Bulaç, Ali, *Din, Kent ve Cemaat: Fethullah Gülen Örneği [Religion, City and Religious Community: The Example of Fethullah Gülen]* (Istanbul: Ufuk Kitap, 2007).

——, *Göçün ve Kentin Siyaseti -MNP'den SP'ye Milli Görüş Partileri [Politics of Migration and the City–National Outlook Parties from the National Order Party to the Felicity Party]* (Istanbul: Çıra Yayınları, 2009).

——, 'The Most Recent Reviver in the 'Ulama Tradition: The Intellectual 'Alim Fethullah Gülen', in Robert A. Hunt and Yüksel A. Aslandoğan (eds), *Muslim Citizens of the Globalized World: Contributions of the Gülen Movement* (Houston, TX: Tughra Books, 2010), pp. 101–20.

Burgat, François, *Face to Face with Political Islam* (London & New York: I. B. Tauris, 2003).

Burgat, François, and William Dowell, *The Islamic Movement in North Africa* (Austin, TX: University of Texas Press, 1997).

Burke, Edmund III, 'Istiqlal', *The Oxford Encyclopedia of the Islamic World*, Oxford Islamic Studies Online <http://www.oxfordislamicstudies.com/article/opr/t236/e0399> (last accessed 19 July 2018).

Burr, Millard, and Robert Oakley Collins, *Revolutionary Sudan: Hasan Al-Turabi and the Islamist State, 1989–2000* (Leiden: Brill, 2003).

Butko, Thomas, 'Unity Through Opposition: Islam as an Instrument of Radical Political Change', *Peace Research Abstracts*, 42.3 (2005), 33–48.

Campbell, David, *Writing Security: United States Foreign Policy and the Politics of Identity* (Minneapolis, MN: University of Minnesota Press, 1992).

Casanova, José, *Public Religions in the Modern World* (Chicago, IL: University of Chicago Press, 1994).

Castells, Manuel, *The Power of Identity* (Malden, MA: Blackwell, 1997).

Cavatorta, Francesco, 'Neither Participation nor Revolution: The Strategy of the Moroccan Jamiat Al-Adl Wal-Ihsan', *Mediterranean Politics*, 12.3 (2007), 381–97.

——, 'Salafism, Liberalism and Democratic Learning in Tunisia', *The Journal of North African Studies*, 20.5 (2015), 770–83.

Cevizoğlu, Hulki, *Generalinden 28 Şubat İtirafı: Postmodern Darbe [February 28 Confession from its General: Post-Modern Coup]* (Istanbul: Ceviz Kabuğu Yayınları, 2001).

Chandra, Kanchan, *Why Ethnic Parties Succeed: Patronage and Ethnic Head Counts in India* (Cambridge & New York: Cambridge University Press, 2004).

Chhibber, Pradeep, and Mariano Torcal, 'Electoral Strategies, Social Cleavages, and Party Systems in a New Democracy: Spain', *Comparative Political Studies*, 30.1 (1997), 27–54.

Choukrallah, Zakaria (2015), 'Héritage: Pour Le PJD, Le CNDH Outrepasse La "Commanderie Des Croyants"' ['Legacy: For the PJD, the CNDH overtakes the "Commander of the Believers"'], *Telquel*, 22 October, <http://telquel.ma/2015/10/22/heritage-pjd-cndh-outrepasse-commanderie-croyants_1467432> (last accessed 30 July 2018).

Consultative Council of the JSM (2012), 'Closing Communiqué of the Consultative [Shūrā] Council of the Movement Al Adl Wal Iḥsān', *Abdessalam Yassine*, <https://yassine.net/en/2012/12/27/closing-communique-of-the-consultative-shura-council-of-the-movement-al-adl-wal-i%E1%B8%A5san/> (last accessed 28 July 2018).

Cox, Gary W., *The Efficient Secret: The Cabinet and the Development of Political Parties in Victorian England* (Cambridge & New York: Cambridge University Press, 1987).

Çakır, Ruşen, *Ayet ve Slogan: Türkiye'de İslamcı Oluşumlar [Verse and Slogan: Islamic Formations in Turkey]* (Istanbul: Metis Yayınları, 2002).

—— (2002), 'AKP Yedi Eğilimi Aynı Potada Eritti' ['AKP Has Melted Down Seven Trends in the Same Pot'], *Vatan*, 2 December, <http://www.gazetevatan.com/akp-yedi-egilimi-ayni-potada-eritti-1219-gundem/> (last accessed 30 July 2018).

——, 'Milli Görüş Hareketi' ['National Outlook Movement'], in Yasin Aktay (ed.), *Modern Türkiye'de Siyasi Düşünce, Cilt 6: İslamcılık [Political Thought in Modern Turkey, Volume 6: Islamism]* (Istanbul: İletişim Yayınları, 2004), pp. 544–603.

—— (2013), 'Gülen Cemaatinin "Sivil" Kanadı' ['Gülen Religious Community's "Civilian" Wing'], *Vatan*, 13 December, <http://www.rusencakir.com/Gulen-cemaatinin-sivil-kanadi/2332> (last accessed 25 July 2018).

—— (2013), 'Cemaat–Hükümet Meydan Muharebesi: Kim Kazanır?' ['Religious Community–Government Field Battle: Who Would Win'], *Vatan*, 16 December, <http://www.rusencakir.com/Cemaat-hukumet-meydan-muharebesi-Kim-kazanir/2335> (last accessed 28 July 2018).

—— (2017), 'Nihayet Başlayan İçeriden Eleştiriler Fethullah Gülen'i Nasıl Etkiler?' ['How Will the Internal Criticism that Has at Last Started Affect Fethullah Gülen?'], *Medyascope.Tv*, 6 November, <http://rusencakir.com/Nihayet-baslayan-iceriden-elestiriler-Fethullah-Guleni-nasil-etkiler/6600> (last accessed 30 July 2018).

Çakır, Ruşen, and Semih Sakallı, *100 Soruda Erdoğan –Gülen Savaşı [Erdoğan – Gülen War in 100 Questions]* (Istanbul: Metis Yayınları, 2014)

Çalışlar, Oral, *Refah Partisi, Nereden Nereye [Welfare Party, from/to Where]* (Istanbul: Pencere Yayınları, 1995).

Çalışlar, Oral, and Tolga Çelik, *Erbakan—Fethullah Gülen Kavgası: Cemaat ve Tarikatların Siyasetteki 40 Yılı [Erbakan—Fethullah Gülen Fight: The 40 Years of Religious Communities and Orders in Politics]* (Istanbul: Sıfır Noktası Yayınları, 2000).

——, *Islamcılığın Üç Kolu [Three Branches of Islamism]* (Istanbul: Güncel Yayıncılık, 2006).

Çalmuk, Fehmi, 'Necmettin Erbakan', in Yasin Aktay (ed.), *Modern Türkiye'de Siyasi Düşünce, Cilt 6: Islamcılık [Political Thought in Modern Turkey, Volume 6: Islamism]* (Istanbul: Iletişim Yayınları, 2004), pp. 550–67.

Çarkoğlu, Ali, 'Turkey's 2011 General Elections: Towards a Dominant Party System?', *Insight Turkey*, 13.3 (2011), 43–62.

Çarkoğlu, Ali, and Ersin Kalaycıoğlu, *The Rising Tide of Conservatism in Turkey* (New York: Palgrave Macmillan, 2009).

Çavdar, Gamze, 'Islamist New Thinking in Turkey: A Model for Political Learning?', *Political Science Quarterly*, 121.3 (2006), 477–97.

Çınar, Menderes, 'Kemalist Cumhuriyetçilik ve Islamcı Kemalizm' ['Kemalist Republicanism and Islamist Kemalism'], in Yasin Aktay (ed.), *Modern Türkiye'de Siyasi Düşünce, Cilt 6: Islamcılık [Political Thought in Modern Turkey, Volume 6: Islamism]* (Istanbul: Iletişim Yayınları, 2005), pp. 157–77.

Daadaoui, Mohamed, *Moroccan Monarchy and the Islamist Challenge: Maintaining Makhzen Power* (New York: Palgrave Macmillan, 2011).

Dağı, Ihsan, 'Transformation of Islamic Political Identity in Turkey: Rethinking the West and Westernization', *Turkish Studies*, 6.1 (2005), 21–37.

Darif, Muhammad, *Monarchie Marocaine et Acteurs Religieux [Moroccan Monarchy and Religious Actors]* (Casablanca: Afrique Orient, 2010).

De Leon, Cedric, Manali Desai, and Cihan Tuğal, *Building Blocs: How Parties Organize Society* (Stanford, CA: Stanford University Press, 2015).

Della Porta, Donatella, and Mario Diani, *Social Movements: An Introduction* (Malden, MA: Blackwell, 2011).

Doğan, Pınar, and Dani Rodrik, *Yargı, Cemaat ve Bir Darbe Kurgusunun İçyüzü [Judiciary, Religious Community, and Behind the Scenes of a Coup Fabrication]* (Istanbul: Destek Yayınevi).

Driessen, Michael D., 'Public Religion, Democracy, and Islam: Examining the Moderation Thesis in Algeria', *Comparative Politics*, 44.2 (2012), 171–89.

Duran, Burhanettin, 'Türk Dış Politikasinin İç Siyaset Boyutu: 2010 Değerlendirmesi' ['The Domestic Politics Dimension of Turkish Foreign Policy: 2010 Assessment'], in Burhanettin Duran, Kemal Inat, and Mesut Özcan (eds), *Türk Dış Politikası Yıllığı* [*Turkish Foreign Policy Yearbook*] (Ankara: SETA, 2011), pp. 15–66.

Duverger, Maurice, *Political Parties, Their Organization and Activity in the Modern State* (London & New York: Wiley, 1954).

El Affendi, Abdelwahab, *Turabi's Revolution: Islam and Power in Sudan* (London: Grey Seal Books, 1991).

El Azizi, Abdellatif (2006), 'Al Adl Wal Ihsane, L'Internationale Islamiste'['Justice and Spirituality, International Islamist'], *Telquel*, <http://www.telquel-online.com/185/sujet1.shtml> (last accessed 1 June 2010).

El Farah, Tahar Abou (2013), 'Le PJD Prépare une OPA sur la Société Civile' ['The PJD Prepares a Takeover of Civil Society'], *La Vie Éco*, 7 June, <http://www.lavieeco.com/news/politique/le-pjd-prepare-une-opa-sur-la-societe-civile-25701.html> (last accessed 30 July 2018).

El Katiri, Mohammed, 'The Institutionalisation of Religious Affairs: Religious Reform in Morocco', *The Journal of North African Studies*, 18.1 (2013), 53–69.

El Said, Hamed, and James E. Rauch, 'Education, Political Participation, and Islamist Parties: The Case of Jordan's Islamic Action Front', *The Middle East Journal*, 69.1 (2015), 51–73.

El Sherif, Ashraf Nabih, 'Institutional and Ideological Re-Construction of the Justice and Development Party (PJD): The Question of Democratic Islamism in Morocco', *The Middle East Journal*, 66.4 (2012), 660–82.

Emre, Süleyman Arif, *Siyasette 35 Yıl [35 Years in Politics]* (Istanbul: Keşif Yayınları, 2002).

Epstein, Leon D., *Political Parties in Western Democracies* (New Brunswick, NJ: Transaction Books, 1980).

Erbakan, Necmettin, *Adil Ekonomik Düzen [Just Economic Order]* (Ankara: Anadolu Matbaacılık, 1991).

—— (n.d.), 'Erbakan Milli Görüş'ü Tarif Ediyor' ['Erbakan Describes National Outlook'], *National Outlook Movement Germany's Erbakan Page* <http://erbakan.vze.com/> (last accessed 23 September 2009).

'Erdoğan'dan "Hayır" Diyenlere Terörist, Almanya'ya Nazi Benzetmesi ['Erdoğan

Likens Those Who Say "No" to Terrorists, Germany to Nazis']' (2017), *Cumhuriyet*, 5 March <http://www.cumhuriyet.com.tr/haber/turkiye/691334/Erdogan_dan__Hayir__diyenlere_terorist__Almanya_ya_Nazi_benzetmesi.html> (last accessed 2 August 2018).

'Erdoğan "Dindar Nesil"i Savundu' ['Erdoğan Defends "Pious Generation"'] (2012), *Radikal*, 6 February, <http://www.radikal.com.tr/politika/erdogan-dindar-nesili-savundu-1077899/> (last accessed 30 July 2013).

'Erdoğan: İçki İçen Alkoliktir' ['Erdoğan: Those who Drink are Alcoholics'] (2013), *Milliyet*, 2 June, <http://siyaset.milliyet.com.tr/erdogan-icki-icen-alkoliktir/siyaset/detay/1717637/default.htm> (last accessed 30 July 2018).

Escobar, Arturo, and Sonia E. Alvarez, *The Making of Social Movements in Latin America: Identity, Strategy, and Democracy* (Boulder, CO: Westview Press, 1992).

'Erdogan Slams CHP as Opposition March Nears Istanbul' (2017), *Al Jazeera*, 1 July, <https://www.aljazeera.com/news/2017/07/erdogan-slams-chp-opposition-march-nears-istanbul-170701112203655.html> (last accessed 2 August 2018).

Euben, Roxanne L., 'Premodern, Antimodern or Postmodern? Islamic and Western Critiques of Modernity', *The Review of Politics*, 59.3 (1997), 429–59.

European Commission (2003), '2003 Regular Report on Turkey's Progress towards Accession', *EU Publications*, <https://publications.europa.eu/en/publication-detail/-/publication/deffe767-febd-4228-8c07-657380fa3cf/language-en> (last accessed 28 July 2018).

—— (2004), '2004 Regular Report on Turkey's Progress towards Accession', *European Parliament*, <http://www.europarl.europa.eu/meetdocs/2004_2009/documents/sec/com_sec(2004)1201_/com_sec(2004)1201_en.pdf> (last accessed 28 July 2018).

—— (2006), 'Commission Staff Working Document - Turkey 2006 Progress Report', *Access to European Union Law*, <https://eur-lex.europa.eu/legal-content/EN/TXT/?uri=celex%3A52006SC1390> (last accessed 28 July 2018).

Fox, David, and Katrina Sammour (2012), 'Disquiet on the Jordanian Front', *Carnegie Endowment for International Peace*, September 27, <http://carnegieendowment.org/sada/49500> (last accessed 28 July 2018).

Gamson, William A., and David S. Meyer, 'Framing Political Opportunity', in Doug McAdam, John D. McCarthy, and Mayer N. Zald (eds), *Comparative Perspectives on Social Movements: Political Opportunities, Mobilizing Structures, and Cultural Framings* (Cambridge & New York: Cambridge University Press, 1996), pp. 275–90.

Gazeteciler ve Yazarlar Vakfı (2013), 'Gündeme Dair: Gazeteciler ve Yazarlar

Vakfi'ndan Hizmet Hareketi'ne Yönelik Iddialara Cevaplar' ['About Current News: Journalists and Writers Foundation's Response to Accusations against the Hizmet Movement'], *Gazeteciler ve Yazarlar Vakfı [Journalists and Writers Foundation]*, 13 August, <http://gyv.org.tr/Haberler/Detay/2454/> (last accessed 1 July 2014).

Geddes, Barbara, 'How the Cases You Choose Affect the Answers You Get: Selection Bias in Comparative Politics', in James A. Stimson (ed.), *Political Analysis, Vol. 2* (Ann Arbor, MI: University of Michigan Press, 1990), pp. 131–50.

Ghanem, As'ad, and Mohanad Mustafa, 'Strategies of Electoral Participation by Islamic Movements: The Muslim Brotherhood and Parliamentary Elections in Egypt and Jordan', *Contemporary Politics*, 17.4 (2011), 393–409.

Gharaibeh, Ibrahim, *Jama-a Ikhwan Muslimin fi Al-Urdun (1946–1996) [Muslim Brotherhood in Jordan (1946–1996)]*. (Amman: Al-Urdun al-Jadid Research Center, 1997).

——, 'The Political Performance and the Organisation of the Muslim Brotherhood', in Hani Hourani (ed.), *Islamic Movements in Jordan* (Amman: Al-Urdun al-Jadid Research Center, 1997), pp. 47-80.

Gharaibeh, Ruheil (2004), 'Islamists and Political Development in Jordan: A Vision and an Experience', *Al Quds Research Center*, <http://alqudscenter.org/english/pages.php?local_type=128&local_details=2&id1=543&menu_id=19&program_id=6&cat_id=24> (last accessed 12 February 2010).

Goldberg, Jeffrey (2013), 'The Modern King in the Arab Spring', *The Atlantic*, <https://www.theatlantic.com/magazine/archive/2013/04/monarch-in-the-middle/309270/> (last accessed 28 July 2018).

Gözaydın, İştar B., 'The Fethullah Gülen Movement and Politics in Turkey: A Chance for Democratisation or a Trojan Horse?', *Democratization*, 16.6 (2009), 1214–36.

Gramsci, Antonio, *Selections from the Prison Notebooks of Antonio Gramsci* (New York: International Publishers, 1972).

Gunther, Richard, Jose R. Montero, and Juan J. Linz, *Political Parties: Old Concepts and New Challenges* (Oxford & New York: Oxford University Press, 2002).

Gülen, Fethullah, *Toward a Global Civilisation of Love and Tolerance* (Somerset, NJ: Light, Inc., 2004).

Gülen Institute, 'A Brief Biography of Fethullah Gülen', 2010, *Gülen Institute*, <http://www.guleninstitute.org/index.php/Biography.html> (last accessed 10 November 2010).

Gümüşçü, Şebnem, 'Class, Status, and Party: The Changing Face of Political

Islam in Turkey and Egypt', *Comparative Political Studies*, 43.7 (2010), 835–61.

Gürsoy, Yaprak, 'The Final Curtain for the Turkish Armed Forces? Civil-Military Relations in View of the 2011 General Elections', *Turkish Studies*, 13.2 (2012), 191–211.

Hafez, Mohammed M., 'From Marginalisation to Massacres: A Political Process Explanation of GIA Violence in Algeria', in Quintan Wiktorowicz (ed.), *Islamic Activism: A Social Movement Theory Approach* (Bloomington, IN: Indiana University Press, 2012), pp. 37–60.

Hafidh, Hassan (2011), 'Jordan's King, Islamists Meet After Nearly 10-Year Hiatus', *The Wall Street Journal*, 4 February, <https://www.wsj.com/articles/SB10001424052748703652104576121773416123228?mod=ITP_pageone_3> (last accessed 28 July 2018).

Hajjouji, Abdelhakim, 'Education and Values', in Maati Monjib (ed.), *Islamists versus Secularists: Confrontations and Dialogues in Morocco: Values, Democracy, Violence, Freedom, Education* (Rabat: IKV PAX, 2009).

Hale, William M., and Ergun Özbudun, *Islamism, Democracy and Liberalism in Turkey: The Case of the AKP* (Abingdon & New York: Routledge, 2010).

Hamayil, Umar Khrawish, 'Institutional Characteristics of the Jordanian Professional Associations', in Warwick M. Knowled (ed.), *Professional Associations and the Challenges of Democratic Transformation in Jordan: Proceedings and Workshops* (Amman: Al-Urdun al-Jadid Research Center, 2000).

Hamid, Shadi, 'Arab Islamist Parties: Losing on Purpose?', *Journal of Democracy*, 22.1 (2011), 68–80.

——, *Temptations of Power: Islamists and Illiberal Democracy in a New Middle East* (Oxford & New York: Oxford University Press, 2014).

—— (n.d.), 'The Islamic Action Front in Jordan', *The Oxford Handbook of Islam and Politics, Oxford Islamic Studies Online*, <http://www.oxfordislamicstudies.com/article/opr/t9001/e008> (last accessed 28 July 2018).

Hamid, Shadi, and James Liddell (n.d.), 'Hassan II of Morocco', *Oxford Islamic Studies Online* <http://www.oxfordislamicstudies.com/opr/t236/e1035> (last accessed 17 July 2018).

Hamzawy, Amr (2008), 'Party for Justice and Development in Morocco: Participation and its Discontents', *Carnegie Endowment for International Peace*, <http://www.carnegieendowment.org/files/cp93_hamzawy_pjd_final1.pdf> (last accessed 21 July 2018).

Harmel, Robert, Uk Heo, Alexander Tan, and Kenneth Janda, 'Performance,

Leadership, Factions and Party Change: An Empirical Analysis', *West European Politics*, 18.1 (1995), 1–33.

Harmel, Robert, and John D. Robertson, 'Formation and Success of New Parties: A Cross-National Analysis', *International Political Science Review*, 6.4 (1985), 501–23.

Hayns, Joe (2017), 'Morocco's Burgeoning Resistance', *Jacobin*, 7 June, <https://www.jacobinmag.com/2017/07/morocco-popular-movement-protest-islam> (last accessed 30 July 2018).

Hendrick, Joshua D., *Gülen: The Ambiguous Politics of Market Islam in Turkey and the World* (New York: New York University Press, 2013).

—— (n.d.), 'Gülen Movement', *Oxford Islamic Studies Online*, <http://www.oxfordislamicstudies.com/opr/t343/e0178> (last accessed 25 July 2018).

Hermansen, Marcia, 'The Cultivation of Memory in the Gülen Community', in Ihsan Yilmaz (ed.), *Muslim World in Transition: Contributions of the Gülen Movement* (Leeds: Leeds Metropolitan University Press, 2007), pp. 60–76.

Hirschman, Albert O., *Exit, Voice, and Loyalty: Responses to Decline in Firms, Organizations, and States* (Cambridge, MA: Harvard University Press, 1970).

Hourani, Hani, Sa'eda Kilani, Taleb Awad, and Hamed Dabbas, *Islamic Action Front Party* (Amman: Al-Urdun Al-Jadid Research Center, 1993).

Howe, Marvine, *Morocco: The Islamist Awakening and Other Challenges* (New York: Oxford University Press, 2005).

Hug, Simon, *Altering Party Systems: Strategic Behavior and the Emergence of New Political Parties in Western Democracies* (Ann Arbor, MI: University of Michigan Press, 2001).

Hughes, Stephen O., *Morocco under King Hassan* (Reading: Ithaca Press, 2006)

Human Rights Watch (2018), 'Morocco/Western Sahara: Events of 2017', *Human Rights Watch*, <https://www.hrw.org/world-report/2018/country-chapters/morocco/western-sahara> (last accessed 30 July 2018).

Iannaccone, Laurence R., 'Why Strict Churches Are Strong', *American Journal of Sociology*, 99.5 (1994), 1180–211.

Inalcık, Halil, 'Tarihsel Bağlamda Sivil Toplum ve Tarikatlar' ['Civil Society and Religious Orders in Historical Perspective'], in Emin Fuat Keyman and Ali Yaşar Sarıbay (eds), *Global Yerel Eksende Türkiye* [*Turkey within the Global-Local Axis*] (Istanbul: Alfa Yayınları, 2000), pp. 593–616.

Inter-Parliamentary Union Database (n.d.), 'Morocco: Majliss-annouwab (House of Representatives)', *Inter-parliamentary Union*, <http://www.ipu.org/parline-e/reports/2221_arc.htm> (last accessed 10 August 2018).

—— (n.d.), 'Turkey: Türkiye Büyük Millet Meclisi (T.B.M.M) (Grand National Assembly of Turkey)', *Interparliamentary Union*, <http://archive.ipu.org/parline-e/reports/2323_arc.htm> (last accessed 10 August 2018).

—— (n.d.), 'Jordan: Majlis Al-Nuwaab (House of Representatives)', *Interparliamentary Union*, <http://archive.ipu.org/parline-e/reports/2163_arc.htm> (last accessed 10 August 2018).

Interview with Abdelkébir Alaoui M'Daghri (2004), 'Interview–vérité, Abdelkébir Alaoui M'Daghri: J'ai Gagné la Confiance des Islamistes', ['Interview—truth, Abdelkebir M'Daghri Alaoui: I Won the Confidence of the Islamists'], *Telquel*, <http://www.telquel-online.com/archives/150/sujet4.shtml> (last accessed 10 April 2012).

'Islamic Action Front Approves Four-Year Strategy to Increase Membership Base', *Jordan Times*, 9 January 2011.

'Istiqlal Party Quits Morocco's Islamist-Led Government' (2013), *BBC News*, 9 July, <http://www.bbc.com/news/world-africa-23250370> (last accessed 2 July 2014).

Jaabouk, Mohammed (2012), '2M contre El Khalfi: La Controverse Arrive au Parlement' ['2M Channel against El Khalfi: The Controversy Arrives at the Parliament'], *Yabiladi*, 24 April, <http://www.yabiladi.com/articles/details/10202/contre-khalfi-controverse-arrive-parlement.html> (last accessed 30 July 2018).

——,(2012), 'Nouveaux Cahiers de Charges de L'Audiovisuel au Maroc: Petites Concessions au PJD et Larges Victoires de 2M' ['New Audiovisual Handbook in Morocco: Small Concessions to the PJD and Wide Victories for the 2M Channel'], *Yabiladi*, 28 August, <http://www.yabiladi.com/articles/details/12509/nouveaux-cahiers-charges-l-audiovisuel-maroc.html> (last accessed 30 July 2018).

Jalid, Mohamed (2012), 'The Rise of Populists in Moroccan Politics', *Carnegie Endowment for International Peace*, <http://carnegieendowment.org/sada/?fa=50182> (last accessed 2 July 2014).

'Jordan's King Abdullah Swears in Caretaker Government' (2012), *BBC News*, 12 October <http://www.bbc.com/news/world-middle-east-19924672> (last accessed 28 July 2018).

Kalyvas, Stathis, *The Rise of Christian Democracy in Europe* (Ithaca, NY: Cornell University Press, 1996).

Kamal, Mustapha Pasha, 'Predatory Globalization and Democracy in the Islamic World', *The Annals of the American Academy of Political and Social Science*, 581 (2002), 121–32.

Karpat, Kemal H., *The Politicization of Islam: Reconstructing Identity, State, Faith, and Community in the Late Ottoman State* (New York: Oxford University Press, 2001).

Keck, Margaret E., and Kathryn Sikkink, *Activists Beyond Borders: Advocacy Networks in International Politics* (Ithaca, NY: Cornell University Press, 1998).

Khan, Mujeeb R. 'The July 15th Coup: A Critical Institutional Framework for Analysis', in Bayram Balcı and Hakan M. Yavuz (eds), *Turkey's July 15th Coup: What Happened and Why* (Salt Lake City, UT: The University of Utah Press, 2018), pp. 46–77.

Kirdiş, Esen, 'Between Movement and Party: Islamic Movements in Morocco and the Decision to Enter Party Politics', *Politics, Religion & Ideology*, 16.1 (2015), 65–86.

——, 'From Loyal to Hard Opposition: The Political Transformation of the Jordanian Muslim Brotherhood', *Politics, Religion & Ideology*, 17.2/3 (2016), 121–42.

——, 'Immoderation: Comparing the Christian Right in the US and Pro-Islamic Movement-Parties in Turkey', *Democratization*, 23.3 (2016), 417–36.

Kirdiş, Esen, and Amina Drhimeur, 'The Rise of Populism? Comparing Incumbent Pro-Islamic Parties in Turkey and Morocco', *Turkish Studies*, 17.4 (2016), 599–617.

Kitschelt, Herbert P., 'Political Opportunity Structures and Political Protest: Anti-Nuclear Movements in Four Democracies', *British Journal of Political Science*, 16.1 (1986), 57–85.

Kömeçoğlu, Uğur, 'Kutsal ile Kamusal: Fethullah Gülen Cemaat Hareketi' ['Sacred and Public: Fethullah Gülen Religious Community Movement'], in Nilüfer Göle (ed.), *Islam'ın Yeni Kamusal Yüzleri: Islam ve Kamusal Alan Üzerine Bir Atölye Çalışması [New Public Faces of Islam: A Workshop on Islam and Public Space]* (Istanbul: Metis Yayınları, 2000), pp. 148–94.

Krämer, Gudrun, 'Cross-Links and Double Talk? Islamist Movements in the Political Process', in Laura Guazzone (ed.), *The Islamist Dilemma: The Political Role of Islamist Movements in the Contemporary Arab World* (Reading: Ithaca Press, 1995), pp. 39–67.

——, 'The Integration of the Integrists: A Comparative Study of Egypt, Jordan, and Tunisia', in Ghassan Salamé (ed.), *Democracy without Democrats?: The*

Renewal of Politics in the Muslim World (London: I. B. Tauris, 2001), pp. 200–26.

Kriesi, Hanspeter, *New Social Movements in Western Europe: A Comparative Analysis* (Minneapolis, MN: University of Minnesota Press, 1995).

Kumbaracıbaşı, Arda Can, *Turkish Politics and the Rise of the AKP: Dilemmas of Institutionalization and Leadership Strategy* (London & New York: Routledge, 2009).

Kuru, Ahmet T., 'Globalization and Diversification of Islamic Movements: Three Turkish Cases', *Political Science Quarterly*, 120 (2005), 253–74.

——, 'Passive and Assertive Secularism: Historical Conditions, Ideological Struggles, and State Policies toward Religion', *World Politics*, 59.4 (2007), 568–94.

'La Jeunesse d'Al Adl Wal Ihsane Participe aux Protestations du 20 Février 2011' ['The Youth of Al Adl Wal Ihsane Participates in the Protests of 20 February 2011'] (2011), *Al Jamaa*, <http://www.aljamaa.net/fr/document/2484.shtml> (last accessed 3 July 2014).

Lauzière, Henri, 'Post-Islamism and the Religious Discourse of Abd Al-Salam Yasin', *International Journal of Middle East Studies*, 37.2 (2005), 241–61.

Layachi, Azzedine, 'Islam and Politics in North Africa', in John L. Esposito and Emad El-Din Shahin (eds), *The Oxford Handbook of Islam and Politics* (Oxford & New York: Oxford University Press, 2013), pp. 352–78.

Levant, Yves, and Leila Maziane, 'The Republic of Sale (1627–1641/1666); An Alternative Pirate Organization Model?', *Management & Organizational History*, 12.1 (2017), 1–29.

Lijphart, Arend, 'Comparative Politics and the Comparative Method', *American Political Science Review*, 65.3 (1971), 682–93.

Linz, Juan J., and Alfred C. Stepan, *Problems of Democratic Transition and Consolidation: Southern Europe, South America, and Post-Communist Europe* (Baltimore, MD: Johns Hopkins University Press, 1996).

Lipset, Seymour Martin, and Stein Rokkan, *Party Systems and Voter Alignments: Cross-National Perspectives* (New York: Free Press, 1967).

Lucas, Russell E., 'Deliberalization in Jordan', *Journal of Democracy*, 14.1 (2003), 137–44.

——, *Institutions and the Politics of Survival in Jordan: Domestic Responses to External Challenges, 1988–2001* (Albany, NY: State University of New York Press, 2005).

Luck, Taylor (2013), 'Political Activists Officially Launch Zamzam Social

Movement', *Jordan Times*, 5 October, <http://vista.sahafi.jo/art.php?id=31ecfe
b10041fa6fbabd7992e1bcffaabc8ad73f> (last accessed 30 July 2018).

Lupu, Noam, and Rachel Beatty Riedl, 'Political Parties and Uncertainty in Developing Democracies', *Comparative Political Studies*, 46.11 (2013), 1339–65.

Lust-Okar, Ellen, *Structuring Conflict in the Arab World: Incumbents, Opponents, and Institutions* (Cambridge & New York: Cambridge University Press, 2006).

Lust-Okar, Ellen, and Sami Hourani, 'Jordan Votes: Election or Selection?', *Journal of Democracy*, 22.2 (2011), 119–29.

Maddy-Weitzman, Bruce, 'Islamism Moroccan-Style: The Ideas of Sheikh Yassine', *Middle East Quarterly*, 10.1 (2003), 43–51.

Maghraoui, Driss, 'The Strengths and Limits of Religious Reforms in Morocco', *Mediterranean Politics*, 14.2 (2009), 195–211.

Magid, Aaron (2016), 'The King and the Islamists', *Foreign Affairs*, 3 May, <https://www.foreignaffairs.com/articles/jordan/2016-05-03/king-and-islamists> (last accessed 28 July 2018).

Mair, Peter, 'Cleavages', in Richard S. Katz and William J. Crotty (eds), *Handbook of Party Politics* (London: SAGE, 2005), pp. 371–5.

March, James G., and Johan P. Olsen, 'The Institutional Dynamics of International Political Orders', *International Organization*, 52.4 (1998), 943–69.

Mardin, Şerif, 'The Nakshibendi Order of Turkey', in Martin Marty and R. Scott Appleby (eds), *Fundamentalisms and the State: Remaking Polities, Economies, and Militance* (Chicago, IL: University of Chicago Press, 1993), pp. 204–32.

——, *Religion, Society, and Modernity in Turkey* (Syracuse, NY: Syracuse University Press, 2006).

—— (n.d.), 'Nurculuk', *The Oxford Encyclopedia of the Islamic World, Oxford Islamic Studies Online*, <http://www.oxfordislamicstudies.com/opr/t236/e0517> (last accessed 12 April 2012).

'Mardin: Gülen Cemaatini Çözemedim' ['Mardin: I Could Not Figure out the Gülen Religious Community'] (2010), *NTV*, 17 September, <https://www.ntv.com.tr/turkiye/mardin-gulen-cemaatini-cozemedim,9vq9a2cFe0m8KvMU5cpuoQ> (last accessed 24 July 2018).

Marks, Monica, 'Youth Politics and Tunisian Salafism: Understanding the Jihadi Current', *Mediterranean Politics*, 18.1 (2013), 104–11.

'Maroc: Le PJD Imprime Sa Marque Sur L'Audiovisuel Marocain' ['Morocco: The

PJD Puts its Mark on Moroccan Audiovisuals'] (2012), *Jeune Afrique*, 12 April, <http://www.jeuneafrique.com/Article/ARTJAWEB20120412161548/pjd-isl am-r-formes-libert-de-la-presse-maroc-maroc-le-pjd-imprime-sa-marque-sur-l-audiovisuel-marocain.html> (last accessed 30 July 2018).

'M. Arsalan: Le Mouvement a Un Vaste Projet de Société Qui Touche à Toutes Les Catégories et Répond à Tous Les Soucis et Dont Le Centre d'intérêt Est l'Homme [Mr. Arsalan: The Movement Has a Broad Vision of Society That Affects All Classes and Meets All the Worries and Whose Focus Is the Man]' (2009), *Justice and Spirituality Movement's Webpage*, <http://www.aljamaa.net/fr/document/1405.shtml> (last accessed 23 April 2013).

Masbah, Mohammed, 'The Party Just In (and Developing)' (2012), *Carnegie Endowment for International Peace*, <http://carnegieendowment.org/sada/2012/07/03/party-just-in-and-developing/d31e> (last accessed 2 July 2014).

—— (2013), 'In Yassine's Footsteps', *Carnegie Endowment for International Peace*, <http://carnegieendowment.org/sada/2013/01/10/in-yassine-s-footsteps/f0nj> (last accessed 3 July 2014).

—— (2013), 'The PJD's Balancing Act', *Carnegie Endowment for International Peace*, <http://carnegieendowment.org/sada/2013/05/01/pjd-s-balancing-act/g1uy> (last accessed 2 July 2014).

—— (2014), 'Morocco's Slow Motion Reform Process', *Stiftung Wissenschaft und Politik*, <http://www.swp-berlin.org/en/publications/swp-comments-en/swp-aktuelle-details/article/moroccos_slow_motion_reform_process.html> (last accessed 19 July 2018).

—— (2015), 'The Ongoing Marginalization of Morocco's Largest Islamist Opposition Group', *Carnegie Endowment for International Peace*, 3 June, <http://carnegieendowment.org/2015/06/03/ongoing-marginalization-of-morocco-s-largest-islamist-opposition-group/i9fo> (last accessed 30 July 2018).

McAdam, Doug, *Political Process and the Development of Black Insurgency, 1930–1970* (Chicago, IL: University of Chicago Press, 1999).

McAdam, Doug, Sidney G. Tarrow, and Charles Tilly, *Dynamics of Contention* (Cambridge & New York: Cambridge University Press, 2001).

McCarthy, John D., Mayer N. Zald, and Doug McAdam, 'Introduction', in Doug McAdam, John D. McCarthy, and Mayer N. Zald (eds), *Comparative Perspectives on Social Movements: Political Opportunities, Mobilizing Structures, and Cultural Framings* (Cambridge & New York: Cambridge University Press, 1996), pp. 1–22.

McCauley, Clark, and Sophia Moskalenko, 'Mechanisms of Political Radicalization: Pathways Toward Terrorism', *Terrorism and Political Violence*, 20.3 (2008), 415–33.

McEneaney, Kyle (2008), 'Interview with Nadia Yassine of the Moroccan Justice and Charity Group', 18 August, *Carnegie Endowment for International Peace*, <https://carnegieendowment.org/sada/20813> (last accessed 21 July 2018).

Mecham, R. Quinn, 'From the Ashes of Virtue, a Promise of Light: The Transformation of Political Islam in Turkey', *Third World Quarterly*, 25.2 (2004), 339–58.

——, *Institutional Origins of Islamist Political Mobilization* (Cambridge & New York: Cambridge University Press, 2017).

Mercan, Faruk, *Fethullah Gülen* (Istanbul: Doğan Egmont Yayıncılık ve Yapımcılık A.Ş., 2009).

Merone, Fabio, and Francesco Cavatorta, *Salafism after the Arab Awakening* (Oxford & New York: Oxford University Press, 2017).

'Mezardakiler Bile Referandum Için Kaldırılmalı' ['Even those in the Grave Shall be Woken Up for the Referendum'] (2010), *Cumhuriyet*, 1 August, <http://www.cumhuriyet.com.tr/haber/diger/167646/_Mezardakiler_bile_referandum_icin_kaldirilmali_.html> (last accessed 4 August 2018).

Michels, Robert, *Political Parties: A Sociological Study of the Oligarchical Tendencies of Modern Democracy* ([S.l.]: General Books, 2009).

Migdal, Joel S., *State in Society: Studying How States and Societies Transform and Constitute One Another* (New York: Cambridge University Press, 2007).

'Milli Nizam Partisi: Program ve Tüzük' ['National Order Party: Programme and Regulations'] (1970), *Türkiye Büyük Millet Meclisi Resmi İnternet Sitesi [Official Website of the Grand National Assembly of Turkey]*, <http://www.tbmm.gov.tr/develop/owa/e_yayin.eser_bilgi_q?ptip=SIYASI%20PARTI%20YAYINLARI&pdemirbas=197600505> (last accessed 25 July 2018).

Mohsen-Finan, Khadija, and Malika Zeghal, 'Opposition Islamiste et Pouvoir Monarchique au Maroc: Le Cas du Parti de La Justice et Du Développement' ['Islamist Opposition and Monarchical Power in Morocco: The Case of the Party for Justice and Development'], *Revue Française de Science Politique*, 56 (2006), 79–119.

Mudde, Cas, 'The Populist Zeitgeist', *Government and Opposition*, 39 (2004), 542–63.

Munson, Henry, *Religion and Power in Morocco* (New Haven, CT: Yale University Press, 1993).

Müller, Wolfgang C., and Kaare Strøm, *Policy, Office, or Votes?: How Political Parties in Western Europe Make Hard Decisions* (Cambridge & New York: Cambridge University Press, 1999).

Nasr, Seyyed Vali Reza, *Forces of Fortune: The Rise of the New Muslim Middle Class and What It Will Mean for Our World* (New York: Free Press, 2009).

——(n.d.), 'Mawdudi, Sayyid Abu al-Ala', *The Oxford Encyclopedia of the Islamic World*, <http://www.oxfordislamicstudies.com/opr/t236/e0517> (last accessed 12 April 2012).

Olidort, Jacob (2015), 'The Politics of "Quietist" Salafism', *Brookings Institution*, <https://www.brookings.edu/wp-content/uploads/2016/07/Brookings-Analysis-Paper_Jacob-Olidort-Inside_Final_Web.pdf> (last accessed 25 July 2018).

Ottaway, Marina, and Meredith Riley (2006), 'Morocco: From Top-Down Reform to Democratic Transition?', *Carnegie Endowment for International Peace*, <http://www.carnegieendowment.org/files/cp71_ottaway_final.pdf> (last accessed 21 July 2018).

Ozzano, Luca, 'The Many Faces of the Political God: A Typology of Religiously Oriented Parties', *Democratization*, 20.5 (2013), 807–30.

Ozzano, Luca, and Francesco Cavatorta, 'Introduction: Religiously Oriented Parties and Democratization', *Democratization*, 20.5 (2013), 799–806.

Öniş, Ziya, 'The Triumph of Conservative Globalism: The Political Economy of the AKP Era', *Turkish Studies*, 13.2 (2012), 135–52.

Öniş, Ziya, and Emin Fuat Keyman, 'A New Path Emerges', *Journal of Democracy*, 14.2 (2003), 95–107.

Özdalga, Elizabeth, 'Secularizing Trends in Fethullah Gülen's Movement: Impasse or Opportunity for Further Renewal?', *Middle East Critique*, 12.1 (2003), 61–73.

Öztürk, Ahmet Erdi, 'Turkey's Diyanet Under AKP Rule: From Protector to Imposer of State Ideology?', *Southeast European and Black Sea Studies*, 16.4 (2016), 619–35

Panebianco, Angelo, *Political Parties: Organization and Power* (Cambridge & New York: Cambridge University Press, 1988).

Pape, Robert A., 'The Strategic Logic of Suicide Terrorism', *The American Political Science Review*, 97.3 (2003), 343–61.

Patel, David Siddhartha (2015), 'The More Things Change, the More They Stay the Same: Jordanian Islamist Responses in Spring and Fall', *Brookings Institution*, <https://www.brookings.edu/wp-content/uploads/2016/07/Jordan_Patel-FINALE.pdf> (last accessed 28 July 2018).

Pellicer, Miquel, and Eva Wegner, 'Socio-Economic Voter Profile and Motives for Islamist Support in Morocco', *Party Politics*, 20.1 (2014), 116–33

'Prof. İsmail Kara ile Gülen Cemaati–AKP Hükümeti Savaşı Üzerine Söyleşi' ['A Conversation about the Gülen Religious Community–AKP Government War with Prof. Ismail Kara'] (2014), *Ruşen Çakır*, 27 December 2014, <http://rusencakir.com/Prof-Ismail-Kara-ile-Gulen-cemaati-AKP-hukumeti-savasi-uzerine-soylesi-tam-metin/4039> (last accessed 25 July 2018).

Pruzan-Jørgensen, Julie E. (2010), 'Islamist Movement in Morocco: Main Actors and Regime Responses', *Academia*, <http://www.academia.edu/1892070/Islamist_Movement_in_Morocco_Main_Actors_and_Regime_Responses_DIIS_Report_2010_April_2010> (last accessed 21 July 2018).

Qutb, Sayyid, *Milestones* (Indianapolis, IN: American Trust, 1990).

Raissouni, Ahmed, interview by Al Hassan Al Sarat (2006), 'Raissouni: Religious Scholars Should Participate in Governments, Parliaments', *The Muslim Brotherhood's Official English Website*, 24 November, <http://www.ikhwanweb.com/article.php?id=2999> (last accessed 21 July 2018).

Reus-Smit, Christian, *The Moral Purpose of the State: Culture, Social Identity, and Institutional Rationality in International Relations* (Princeton, NJ: Princeton University Press, 1999).

Robbins, Michael, and Lawrence Rubin, 'The Rise of Official Islam in Jordan', *Politics, Religion & Ideology*, 14.1 (2013), 59–74.

Roberts, Kenneth M., 'Populism, Political Conflict, and Grass-Roots Organization in Latin America', *Comparative Politics*, 38.2 (2006), 127–48.

Robinson, Glenn E., 'Defensive Democratization in Jordan', *International Journal of Middle East Studies*, 30.3 (1998), 387–410.

Roy, Olivier, *The Failure of Political Islam* (Cambridge, MA: Harvard University Press, 1994).

——, *Globalized Islam: The Search for a New Ummah* (New York: Columbia University Press, 2004).

Ryan, Curtis R., *Jordan in Transition: From Hussein to Abdullah* (Boulder, CO: Lynne Rienner Publishers, 2002).

——, 'Islamist Political Activism in Jordan: Moderation, Militancy, and Democracy', *The Middle East Review of International Affairs*, 12.2 (2008), 1–13.

—— (2012), 'The Implications of Jordan's New Electoral Law', *Foreign Policy*, 13 April, <https://foreignpolicy.com/2012/04/13/the-implications-of-jordans-new-electoral-law/> (last accessed 28 July 2018).

—— (2016), 'Jordan's Holding Elections Next Week. Here's What to Expect',

The Washington Post, 16 September, <https://www.washingtonpost.com/news/monkey-cage/wp/2016/09/16/jordans-holding-elections-next-week-heres-what-to-expect/?utm_term=.a66387deae1a> (last accessed 30 July 2018).

Saaf, Abdallah, and Abdelrahim Manar Al Slimi (2008), 'Morocco 1996–2007: A Decisive Decade of Reforms?', *Arab Reform Initiative*, <https://www.arab-reform.net/en/node/914> (last accessed 21 July 2018).

Sartori, Giovanni, *Parties and Party Systems: A Framework for Analysis* (Cambridge & New York: Cambridge University Press, 1976).

Sater, James N., 'Parliamentary Elections and Authoritarian Rule in Morocco', *The Middle East Journal*, 63.3 (2009), 381–400.

Saul, Stephanie (2016), 'An Exiled Cleric Denies Playing a Leading Role in Coup Attempt', *The New York Times*, 16 July, <https://www.nytimes.com/2016/07/17/us/fethullah-gulen-turkey-coup-attempt.html> (last accessed 30 July 2018).

Schenker, David (2013), 'Down and Out in Amman', *Foreign Affairs*, 3 October, <https://www.foreignaffairs.com/articles/middle-east/2013-10-03/down-and-out-amman> (last accessed 30 July 2018).

Schwedler, Jillian, 'Islamic Identity: Myth, Menace, or Mobilizer?', *SAIS Review*, 21.2 (2001), 1–17.

——, *Faith in Moderation: Islamist Parties in Jordan and Yemen* (Cambridge & New York: Cambridge University Press, 2007).

——, 'Review Article: Can Islamists Become Moderates? Rethinking the Inclusion-Moderation Hypothesis', *World Politics*, 63.2 (2011), 347–376.

—— (n.d.), 'Jordan', *Oxford Islamic Studies Online*, <http://www.oxfordislamicstudies.com/opr/t236/e0422> (last accessed 28 July 2018).

Seniguer, Haoues, 'Genèse et Transformations de l'Islamisme Marocain à Travers les Noms. Le Cas du Parti de La Justice et Du Développement' ['Genesis and Transformations of Moroccan Islamism through Party Names: The Case of Justice and Development Party'], *Mots: Les Langages du Politique* 103 (2013): 111–20.

Sewell, William H., 'A Theory of Structure: Duality, Agency, and Transformation', *American Journal of Sociology*, 98.1 (1992), 1–29.

'Sezeryan Kürtajla Cinayet İşlediler' ['Those Who Have Engaged in Cesarean Section Have Committed Murder'] (2013), *Hürriyet*, 19 June <http://www.hurriyet.com.tr/gundem/23537027.asp> (last accessed 2 August 2018).

Shahin, Emad Eldin, *Political Ascent: Contemporary Islamic Movements in North Africa* (Boulder, CO: Westview Press, 1997).

Shambayati, Hootan, and Esen Kirdiş, 'In Pursuit of "Contemporary Civilization": Judicial Empowerment in Turkey', *Political Research Quarterly*, 62.4 (2009), 767–80.

Sharon-Krespin, Rachel, 'Fethullah Gülen's Grand Ambition Turkey's Islamist Danger', *Middle East Quarterly*, 16.1 (2009), 55–66.

Shaw, Stanford Jay, and Ezel Kural Shaw, *History of the Ottoman Empire and Modern Turkey: Volume 2, Reform, Revolution, and Republic: The Rise of Modern Turkey 1808–1975* (Cambridge & New York: Cambridge University Press, 1977).

Sidner, Sara, and Ashley Fantz (2012), 'Thousands Rally for Political Change in Jordan', *CNN*, 5 October <http://edition.cnn.com/2012/10/05/world/jordan-protest/> (last accessed 28 July 2018).

Simons, Marlise (1998), 'Morocco Finds Fundamentalism Benign but Scary', *The New York Times*, 9 April, <http://go.galegroup.com/ps/i.do?id=GALE%7CA150212737&v=2.1&u=tel_a_rhodes&it=r&p=AONE&sw=w&asid=145102eaefd295e95ab765797b517033> (last accessed 9 November 2014).

Sinno, Abdulkader H., and Ahmed Khanani, 'Of Opportunities and Organization: When Do Islamic Parties Choose to Compete Electorally?', in Mohamed Abdel Rahim M Salih (ed.), *Interpreting Islamic Political Parties* (New York: Palgrave Macmillan, 2009), pp. 29–49.

Skocpol, Theda, 'Bringing the State Back In: Strategies of Analysis in Current Research', in Peter B. Evans, Dietrich Rueschemeyer, and Theda Skocpol (eds), *Bringing the State Back In* (Cambridge & New York: Cambridge University Press, 1985), pp. 3–37.

——, *States and Social Revolutions: A Comparative Analysis of France, Russia and China* (Cambridge & New York: Cambridge University Press, 2015).

Sokhey, Sarah Wilson, and A. Kadir Yildirim, 'Economic Liberalization and Political Moderation: The Case of Anti-System Parties', *Party Politics*, 19.2 (2013), 230–55.

Solaker, Gulsen (2016), 'Turkish Appeals Court Overturns "Ergenekon" Coup Plot Convictions', *Reuters*, 21 April, <https://www.reuters.com/article/us-turkey-coup-trial/turkish-appeals-court-overturns-ergenekon-coup-plot-convictions-idUSKCN0XI1WS> (last accessed 2 August 2018).

Somer, Murat, 'Moderation of Religious and Secular Politics, a Country's Centre and Democratization', *Democratization*, 21.2 (2014), 244–67.

Stark, Rodney, and Roger Finke, *Acts of Faith: Explaining the Human Side of Religion* (Berkeley, CA: University of California Press, 2000).

Steinvorth, Daniel (2012), 'Erdoğan the Misogynist: Turkish Prime Minister

Assaults Women's Rights', *Spiegel*, 19 June, <http://www.spiegel.de/international/europe/turkish-prime-minister-erdogan-targets-women-s-rights-a-839568.html> (last accessed 30 July 2018).
Stepan, Alfred C., 'Religion, Democracy, and the "Twin Tolerations"', *Journal of Democracy*, 11.4 (2000), 37–57.
Stepan, Alfred, and Juan J. Linz, 'Democratization Theory and the Arab Spring', *Journal of Democracy*, 24.2 (2013), 15–30.
Şener, Nedim, *Ergenekon Belgelerinde Fethullah Gülen ve Cemaat [Fethullah Gülen and His Religious Community in Ergenekon Documents]* (Istanbul: Destek Yayınevi, 2014).
Şık, Ahmet, *Paralel Yürüdük Biz Bu Yollarda [We Walked Parallel on these Roads]* (Istanbul: Postacı Yayınevi, 2014).
Tamimi, Azzam, *Rachid Ghannouchi: A Democrat within Islamism* (Oxford & New York: Oxford University Press, 2001).
Tanıyıcı, Saban, 'Transformation of Political Islam in Turkey: Islamist Welfare Party's Pro-EU Turn', *Party Politics*, 9.4 (2003), 463–83.
Tarrow, Sidney G., *Democracy and Disorder: Protest and Politics in Italy, 1965–1975* (Oxford & New York: Oxford University Press, 1989).
——, *Power in Movement: Social Movements and Contentious Politics* (Cambridge & New York: Cambridge University Press, 1998).
Tepe, Sultan, 'Moderation of Religious Parties: Electoral Constraints, Ideological Commitments, and the Democratic Capacities of Religious Parties in Israel and Turkey', *Political Research Quarterly*, 65.3 (2012), 467–85.
Tezcür, Güneş Murat, 'The Moderation Theory Revisited: The Case of Islamic Political Actors', *Party Politics*, 16.1 (2009), 69–88.
——, *Muslim Reformers in Iran and Turkey: The Paradox of Moderation* (Austin, TX: University of Texas Press, 2011).
The Jakarta Post (2011), 'NU Leaders Cannot Hold Political Posts', *The Jakarta Post*, 20 June, <https://web.archive.org/web/20110624120742/http://www.thejakartapost.com/news/2011/06/20/nation%E2%80%99s-largest-muslim-group-laments-%E2%80%98waning-influence%E2%80%99.html> (last accessed on 19 July 2018).
Thelen, Kathleen, 'Historical Institutionalism in Comparative Politics', *Annual Review of Political Science*, 2 (1999), 369–404.
'The Tussle For Control of Moroccan Media Heats Up' (2012), *Morocco World News*, 14 May, <http://www.moroccoworldnews.com/2012/05/39608/the-tussle-for-control-of-moroccan-media-heats-up/> (last accessed 30 July 2018).

Tilly, Charles, *Contention and Democracy in Europe, 1650–2000* (Cambridge & New York: Cambridge University Press, 2004).
Tilly, Charles, and Sidney G. Tarrow, *Contentious Politics* (Boulder, CO: Paradigm Publishers, 2007).
Touhtouh, Rachid (2014), 'Civil Society in Morocco under the New 2011 Constitution: Issues, Stakes and Challenges', *Arab Center for Research and Policy Studies*, 10 September, < https://www.dohainstitute.org/en/ResearchAndStudies/Pages/Civil_Society_in_Morocco_under_the_New_2011_Constitution_Issues_Stakes_and_Challenges.asp> (last accessed on 17 July 2018).
Tozy, Mohamed, 'Champ et Contre Champ Político-Religieux Au Maroc' ['The Religious Field and Its Counter-Field in Morocco'] (unpublished PhD Dissertation, Université de Droit, d'Économie et des Sciences d'Aix-Marseille, Faculte de Droit et de Science Politique, 1984).
——, *Monarchie et Islam Politique au Maroc [Monarchy and Political Islam in Morocco]* (Paris: Presses de la Fondation Nationale des Sciences Politiques, 1999)
——(1999), 'Qui Sont les Islamistes au Maroc' ['Who Are the Islamists in Morocco'], *Le Monde Diplomatique*, <http://www.monde-diplomatique.fr/1999/08/TOZY/12315> (last accessed 21 July 2018).
Turam, Berna, *Between Islam and the State: The Politics of Engagement* (Stanford, CA: Stanford University Press, 2007).
Turgut, Pelin (2010), 'The Turkish Imam and His Global Educational Mission', *Time Magazine*, 26 April, <http://content.time.com/time/magazine/article/0,9171,1969290,00.html> (last accessed 25 July 2018).
Volpi, Frédéric, *Political Islam Observed: Disciplinary Perspectives* (New York: Columbia University Press, 2010).
Volpi, Frédéric, and Ewan Stein, 'Islamism and the State after the Arab Uprisings: Between People Power and State Power', *Democratization*, 22.2 (2015), 276–93
Wagemakers, Joas, 'Contesting Religious Authority in Jordanian Salafi Networks', in Marko Milosevic and Kacper Rekawek (eds), *Perseverance of Terrorism: Focus on Leaders* (Amsterdam: IOS Press, 2014), pp. 111–25.
——, *Salafism in Jordan: Political Islam in a Quietist Community* (Cambridge & New York: Cambridge University Press, 2016).
Wardi, Mohammed Taha, *Islamists and the Outside World: The Case of Abdessalam Yassin and Al Adl Wal Ihsan* (Ifrane: Al Akhawayn University Press, 2003).
Ware, Alan, *Political Parties and Party Systems* (Oxford & New York: Oxford University Press, 1996).
Wegner, Eva (2004), 'The Contribution of Inclusivist Approaches towards the

Islamist Opposition to Regime Stability in Arab States: The Case of the Moroccan Parti de La Justice et Du Développement', *EUI Working Paper RSCAS* <http://cadmus.eui.eu/bitstream/handle/1814/2784/04_42.pdf?sequence=1> (last accessed on 17 July 2018).

——, *Islamist Opposition in Authoritarian Regimes: The Party of Justice and Development in Morocco* (Syracuse, NY: Syracuse University Press, 2011).

Wegner, Eva, and Miquel Pellicer, 'Islamist Moderation without Democratization: The Coming of Age of the Moroccan Party of Justice and Development?', *Democratization*, 16.1 (2009), 157–75.

Weyland, Kurt Gerhard, *Bounded Rationality and Policy Diffusion: Social Sector Reform in Latin America* (Princeton, NJ: Princeton University Press, 2006).

Wickham, Carrie Rosefsky, *Mobilizing Islam: Religion, Activism, and Political Change in Egypt* (New York: Columbia University Press, 2002).

——, 'The Path to Moderation: Strategy and Learning in the Formation of Egypt's Wasat Party', *Comparative Politics*, 36.2 (2004), 205–28.

——, *The Muslim Brotherhood: Evolution of an Islamist Movement* (Princeton, NJ: Princeton University Press, 2013).

Wiktorowicz, Quintan, 'Civil Society as Social Control: State Power in Jordan', *Comparative Politics*, 33.1 (2000), 43–61.

——, 'The Salafi Movement in Jordan', *International Journal of Middle East Studies*, 32.2 (2000), 219–40.

——, *The Management of Islamic Activism: Salafis, the Muslim Brotherhood, and State Power in Jordan* (Albany, NY: State University of New York Press, 2001).

Wiktorowicz, Quintan, and Karl Kaltenthaler, 'The Rationality of Radical Islam', *Political Science Quarterly*, 121.2 (2006), 295–319.

Willis, Michael J., *The Islamist Challenge in Algeria: A Political History* (New York: New York University Press, 1997).

——, 'Between Alternance and the Makhzen: At-Tawhid Wa Al-Islah's Entry into Moroccan Politics', *Journal of North African Studies*, 4.3 (1999), 45–80.

——, 'Morocco's Islamists and the Legislative Elections of 2002: The Strange Case of the Party That Did Not Want to Win', *Mediterranean Politics*, 9.1 (2004), 53–81.

——, *Politics and Power in the Maghreb: Algeria, Tunisia and Morocco from Independence to the Arab Spring* (New York: Columbia University Press, 2012).

Wittes, Tamara Cofman, 'Three Kinds of Movements', *Journal of Democracy*, 19.3 (2008), 7–12.

Woodward, Mark R., Dale F. Eickelman, Charles C. Stewart, Rafiuddin Ahmed,

John R. Bowen, Fred R. von der Mehden and Char Simons (n.d.), 'Popular Religion', *The Oxford Encyclopedia of the Islamic World, Oxford Islamic Studies Online* <http://www.oxfordislamicstudies.com/article/opr/t236/e0642> (last accessed 21 July 2018).

World Bank (n.d.), 'World Bank Open Data', *World Bank*, <http://data.worldbank.org/> (last accessed 12 August 2018).

Yalçın, Soner, *Hangi Erbakan [Which Erbakan]* (Ankara: Başak Yayınları, 1999).

Yassine, Abdessalam, *Winning the Modern World for Islam* (Iowa City, IA: Justice and Spirituality Publishing, 2000).

——, *The Muslim Mind on Trial: Divine Revelation versus Secular Rationalism* (Iowa City, IA: Justice and Spirituality Publishing, 2003).

——(2013), 'Two-Fold Renewal', *Abdessalam Yassine*, <https://yassine.net/en/2013/05/02/two-fold-renewal/> (last accessed 21 July 2018).

—— (2013), 'The Last Testament of Imam Abdessalam Yassine', *Abdessalam Yassine*, <https://yassine.net/en/2013/05/04/the-last-testament-of-imam-abdessalam-yassine/> (last accessed 28 July 2018).

Yassine, Nadia (2005), 'Presentation of the Justice and Spirituality Association: A Great Hello to All the Militants!', *Nadia Yassine*, <http://www.nadiayassine.net/en/page/10364.htm> (last accessed 29 March 2009).

——(2008), 'Only the Combined Efforts of All Forces of the Nation Can Get Morocco Out of the Crisis', *Nadia Yassine,* <http://www.nadiayassine.net/en/page/12400.htm> (last accessed 19 April 2009).

Yassine, Nadia, interview by Emmanuel Martinez (2008), 'Féminisme Islamique' ['Islamic Feminism'], *Le Journal Des Alternatives*, 28 September, <http://journal.alternatives.ca/spip.php?article4140> (last accessed 24 July 2018).

Yaşar, Emin, 'Dergâh'tan Parti'ye, Vakıftan Şirkete Bir Kimliğin Oluşumu ve Dönüşümü: Iskenderpaşa Cemaati' ['Identity Formation and Transformation from Lodge to Party, from Foundation to Company: The Iskenderpaşa Congregation'], in Yasin Aktay (ed.), *Modern Türkiye'de Siyasi Düşünce, Cilt 6: Islamcılık [Political Thought in Modern Turkey, Volume 6: Islamism]* (Istanbul: Iletişim Yayınları, 2004), pp. 321–40.

Yavuz, Hakan M., 'Neo-Nurcular: Gülen Hareketi' ['The Neo-Nurcus: The Gülen Movement'], in Yasin Aktay (ed.), *Modern Türkiye'de Siyasi Düşünce, Cilt 6: Islamcılık [Political Thought in Modern Turkey, Volume 6: Islamism]* (Istanbul: Iletişim Yayınları, 2004), pp. 295–307.

——, *Secularism and Muslim Democracy in Turkey* (Cambridge & New York: Cambridge University Press, 2009).

——, *Toward an Islamic Enlightenment: The Gülen Movement* (Oxford & New York: Oxford University Press, 2013).

——, 'The Three Stages of the Gülen Movement: From Pietistic Weeping Movement to Power-Obsessed Structure', in Bayram Balcı and Hakan M. Yavuz (eds), *Turkey's July 15th Coup: What Happened and Why* (Salt Lake City, UT: The University of Utah Press, 2018), pp. 20–45.

Yavuz, Hakan M. and Bayram Balcı, 'Introduction: The Gülen Movement and the Coup', in Bayram Balcı and Hakan M. Yavuz (eds), *Turkey's July 15th Coup: What Happened and Why* (Salt Lake City, UT: The University of Utah Press, 2018), pp. 1–19.

Yavuz, Hakan M., and Rasim Koç, 'The Turkish Coup Attempt: The Gülen Movement vs. the State', *Middle East Policy* 23.4 (2016), 136–48.

Yıldırım, A. Kadir, *Muslim Democratic Parties in the Middle East: Economy and Politics of Islamist Moderation* (Bloomington, IN: Indiana University Press, 2017).

Yükleyen, Ahmet, and Aziz Abba, 'Religious Authorization of the Justice and Spirituality Movement in Morocco', *Politics, Religion & Ideology*, 14.1 (2013), 136–53.

'"Zamzam" Reveals Divisions in Jordan's Muslim Brotherhood' (2012), *Al-Hayat*, 5 December, <http://en.ammonnews.net/article.aspx?articleNO=19384#.W1-NZNhKi-U> (last accessed 30 July 2018).

Zeghal, Malika, 'Participation without Power', *Journal of Democracy*, 19.3 (2008), 31–6.

——, *Islamism in Morocco: Religion, Authoritarianism, and Electoral Politics* (Princeton, NJ: Markus Wiener Publishing, 2009).

——(n.d.), 'Yasin, Abdessalam', *The Oxford Encyclopedia of the Islamic World, Oxford Islamic Studies Online*, <http://www.oxfordislamicstudies.com/article/opr/t236/e0983> (last accessed 21 July 2018).

Zeghal, Malika, and Henry Munson (n.d.), 'Morocco', *The Oxford Encyclopedia of the Islamic World. Oxford Islamic Studies Online*, <http://www.oxfordislamicstudies.com/article/opr/t236/e0544> (last accessed 21 July 2018).

Zemni, Sami, 'Moroccan Post-Islamism: Emerging Trend or Chimera?', in Asef Bayat (ed.), *Post-Islamism: The Changing Faces of Political Islam* (New York & Oxford: Oxford University Press, 2013), pp. 134–56.

Zerhouni, Saloua, 'The Moroccan Parliament', in Ellen Lust-Okar and Saloua Zerhouni (eds), *Political Participation in the Middle East* (Boulder, CO: Lynne Rienner Publishers, 2008), pp. 217–38.

INTERVIEWS

Anonymous interview with a veteran parliamentarian from the NOM by the author, 18 June 2009, Ankara, Turkey.

Anonymous interview with a veteran Turkish journalist by the author, 2 July 2009, Istanbul, Turkey.

Anonymous interview with a former Executive Committee Member of the JMB by the author, 7 February 2010, Amman, Jordan.

Anonymous interview with a former Deputy from the IAF by the author, 8 February 2010, Amman, Jordan.

Anonymous interview with a loyalist member of the Jordanian Senate by the author, 9 February 2010, Amman, Jordan.

Anonymous interview of a Jordanian scholar by the author, 10 February 2010, Amman, Jordan.

Anonymous interview of a Jordanian journalist by the author, 11 February 2010, Amman, Jordan.

Anonymous interview with a JMB leader by the author, 15 February 2010, Amman, Jordan.

Anonymous interview with a high-ranking leader of the JMB by the author, 16 February 2010, Amman, Jordan.

Anonymous interview with a Jordanian scholar by the author, 17 February 2010, Amman, Jordan.

Anonymous interview with a former Executive Committee Member of the JMB by the author, 21 February 2010, Amman, Jordan.

Anonymous interview with a leading member of the JMB/IAF by the author, 23 February 2010, Amman, Jordan.

Anonymous interview with a former Deputy of the IAF by the author, 24 February 2010, Amman, Jordan.

Anonymous interview with a leading member of the JMB/IAF by the author, 25 February 2010, Amman, Jordan.

Anonymous interview with a former Deputy of the IAF by the author, 1 March 2010, Amman, Jordan.

Anonymous interview with a journalist from the Islamist daily *Assabeel* by the author, 9 March 2010, Amman, Jordan.

Anonymous interview with a former member of the JMB and IAF by the author, 10 March 2010, Amman, Jordan.

Anonymous interview with a Moroccan journalist by the author, 13 April 2010, Rabat, Morocco.

Anonymous interview with a PJD minister by the author, 15 April 2010, Rabat, Morocco.

Anonymous interview with a Moroccan scholar of political Islam by the author, 16 April 2010, Rabat, Morocco.

Anonymous interview with a PJD minister by the author, 19 April 2010, Rabat, Morocco.

Anonymous interview with a high-ranking leader of the MUR by the author, 21 April 2010, Rabat, Morocco.

Anonymous interview with a Moroccan researcher of political Islam, 21 April 2010, Rabat, Morocco.

Anonymous interview with a parliamentarian from the PJD by the author, 28 April 2010, Rabat, Morocco.

Anonymous interview with a former member of the Islamic Youth's preaching wing and current PJD leader by the author, 3 May 2010, Rabat, Morocco.

Anonymous interview with a high-ranking member of the JSM by the author, 4 May 2010, Rabat, Morocco.

Anonymous interview with a member of JSM's youth branch by the author, 10 May 2010, Casablanca, Morocco.

Anonymous interview with a veteran Moroccan scholar of political Islam by the author, 10 May 2010, Casablanca, Morocco.

Anonymous interview with a member of JSM's board of guidance by the author, 13 May 2010, Rabat, Morocco.

Anonymous interview with a high-ranking leader from the JSM by the author, 14 May 2010, Rabat, Morocco.

Anonymous interview with a high-ranking NOM leader by the author, 29 May 2010, Istanbul, Turkey.

Anonymous interview with a high-ranking leader of the Gülen-linked Journalists and Writers Foundation by the author, 1 June 2010, Istanbul, Turkey.

Anonymous interview with a researcher at the Journalists and Writers Foundation, 1 June 2010, Istanbul, Turkey.

Anonymous interview with an official at the Journalists and Writers Foundation, 1 June 2010, Istanbul, Turkey.

Anonymous interview with a founder of the NOM by the author, 5 June 2010, Bolu, Turkey.

A NOTE

Earlier versions of the themes addressed in this book were partially published in:

Kirdiş, Esen, 'Between Movement and Party: Islamic Movements in Morocco and the Decision to Enter Party Politics', *Politics, Religion & Ideology*, 16 (2015), 65–86. Permission provided by the publisher Taylor & Francis Ltd, http://www.tandfonline.com.

Kirdiş, Esen, 'From Loyal to Hard Opposition: The Political Transformation of the Jordanian Muslim Brotherhood', *Politics, Religion & Ideology*, 17 (2016), 121–42. Permission provided by the publisher Taylor & Francis Ltd, http://www.tandfonline.com.

Kirdiş, Esen, 'Immoderation: Comparing the Christian Right in the US and Pro-Islamic Movement-Parties in Turkey', *Democratization*, 23 (2016), 417–36. Permission provided by the publisher Taylor & Francis Ltd, http://www.tandfonline.com.

Kirdiş, Esen, 'Same Context, Different Political Paths: Two Islamic Movements in Turkey', *International Area Studies Review*, 19 (2016), 249–65. Permission provided by the publisher Sage Publishing, http://journals.sagepub.com/.

Kirdiş, Esen, and Amina Drhimeur, 'The Rise of Populism? Comparing Incumbent Pro-Islamic Parties in Turkey and Morocco', *Turkish Studies*, 17 (2016), 599–617. Permission provided by the publisher Taylor & Francis Ltd, http://www.tandfonline.com.

Kirdiş, Esen, 'Wolves in Sheep Clothing or Victims of Times? Discussing the

Immoderation of Incumbent Islamic Parties in Turkey, Egypt, Morocco, and Tunisia', *Democratization*, 25 (2018), 901–18. Permission provided by the publisher Taylor & Francis Ltd, http://www.tandfonline.com.

INDEX

Abbadi, Mohamed, 133, 173; *see also* Justice and Spirituality Movement
Abduh, Muhammad, 56
Adalet Partisi see Justice Party
Adalet ve Kalkınma Partisi see Justice and Development Party
adil düzen see just order
agency-based explanations, 15, 16, 17, 21–2
Al-Adl wal Ihsane see Justice and Spirituality Movement
Albani, Nasir al-Din, 55, 97, 99, 100, 153; *see also* Quietist Salafis
Al-Banna, Hassan, 66
Al-Halabi (al-Halaby), Ali Hasan, 150, 153; *see also* Quietist Salafis
Al-Turabi, Hassan, 91
Anavatan Partisi see Motherland Party
Arabiyat, Abdullatif, 88; *see also* Jordanian Muslim Brotherhood
Arab Spring, 22, 36, 125, 129, 130–3, 150–1, 169
Arsalane, Fathallah, 129, 134, 173; *see also* Justice and Spirituality Movement

Benkirane, Abdelilah, 60, 61, 171; *see also* Party for Justice and Development

Commander of the Believers, 9–10, 36, 65, 69, 72, 134, 155; *see also* Moroccan regime
comparative method, 5–14
Cumhuriyet Halk Partisi see Republican People's Party

Demirel, Süleyman, 74, 75; *see also* Justice Party
Democratic Left Party, 138
Democrat Party, 74
Demokrat Parti see Democrat Party
Demokratik Sol Parti see Democratic Left Party
Directorate of Religious Affairs (*Diyanet*), 41, 79, 175; *see also* laicism
Doğru Yol Partisi see True Path Party

Erbakan, Necmettin, 75, 76, 77, 79, 84, 138, 174–5; *see also* National Outlook Movement
Erdoğan, Recep Tayyip, 140; *see also* Justice and Development Party
European Union (EU), 141, 142, 174, 175

Farhan, Ishaq, 88; *see also* Jordanian Muslim Brotherhood
Fazilet Partisi see Virtue Party
February 20 Movement (F20M), 130, 131, 132, 133, 140, 141, 142, 170, 172, 173; *see also* Moroccan regime
February 28 Process, 140, 141; *see also* Turkish regime
Felicity Party, 136, 141; *see also* National Outlook Movement

Ghannouchi, Rachid, 179
Gharaibeh, Ruheil, 178; *see also* Islamic Action Front Party

grassroots movements, 55, 56–7, 58–9, 124–5, 168–70
Gül, Abdullah, 142, 176; *see also* Justice and Development Party
Gülen, Fethullah, 54, 77, 79, 80, 81, 82, 83, 84, 141, 144, 177; *see also* Gülen Movement (GM)
Gülen Movement (GM)
  growth, 138–9
  history of, 79–81
  ideology of, 81–2
  organisation of, 82–3, 177
  reasons for non-participation, 83–5
  relations with the regime, 143–4, 176–7
  transnationalisation, 139–40
  see also Gülen, Fethullah

Haraka Attawhid Wal Islah see Movement for Unity and Reform (MUR)
Hizb al-Adala wa Tanmia see Party for Justice and Development (PJD)

ideological priorities, 18
immoderation, 124, 146, 178
inclusion-moderation hypothesis, 4, 123, 169
Independence Party, 39, 40, 131, 132
Islamic Action Front Party (IAF)
  electoral performance of, 145
  formation of, 96–7
  in opposition, 145–50
  organisation of, 92, 147–9
  relations with the regime, 145–7
  see also Gharaibeh, Ruheil; Jordanian Muslim Brotherhood; Thneibat, Abdel Hamid
Islamic movements–regime relations, 19–20, 125–6
Islamic movements vs Islamic political parties, 4–5
Islamic Youth, 12, 14, 59–61, 62, 63, 65, 67, 74, 77, 90; *see also* Muti, Abdulkarim
Islamist vs Islamic, 3
Istiqlal Party *see* Independence Party

Jabhat al-ᶜAmal al-Islami see Islamic Action Front Party
Jama'at al-Ikhwan al-Muslimin fi al-Urdun see Jordanian Muslim Brotherhood
Jihadi Salafism, 98
Jordanian Muslim Brotherhood (JMB)
  changes in, 151–3, 178–9

growth, 87–8
hardliners vs reformists, 90–1, 92–5
history of, 86–90
ideology of, 90–1
in coalition, 89, 145–6
organisation of, 92, 96–7, 178–9
reasons for participation, 92–5
see also Arabiat, Abdullatif; Farhan, Ishaq; Islamic Action Front Party
Jordanian regime
  history of, 44–5
  King Abdullah II, 147, 151
  King Hussein, 8
  Palestinians, 87, 99, 147, 148, 179
  party system in, 46
  relations with Islamic movements, 45–6, 154
  response to the Arab Spring, 151
  role of religion in, 9–10
  socio-economy of, 46–7
  state–society relations in, 8
July 15 coup (2016), 1–2, 177
just order, 135, 140, 173; *see also* National Outlook Movement
Justice and Development Party (AKP)
  electoral performance of, 137
  formation of, 140–1
  incumbency of, 141–2, 143, 174
  organisation of, 175–6
  relations with the regime, 141–2
  see also Erdoğan, Recep Tayyip; Gül, Abdullah
Justice and Spirituality Movement (JSM)
  alliances, 129–30, 173–4
  history of, 65–6, 69
  ideology of, 66–7
  organisation of, 67–8, 133–4, 173
  participation in F20M, 131–2
  reasons for non-participation, 69–72
  relations with the regime, 68–9, 71–2, 172–3
  transnationalisation, 129
  see also Abbadi, Mohamed; Arsalane, Fathallah; Yassine, Abdessalam; Yassine, Nadia
Justice Party, 74, 75, 84, 134, 135, 137; *see also* Demirel, Süleyman

Kemalists, 7, 8, 9, 13, 41, 78, 144; *see also* Turkish regime
Kotku, Mehmed Zahit, 73–4, 75, 79, 85, 137; *see also* Nakşibendi Order

laicism, 9, 10, 41, 42, 44, 76, 77, 81, 135, 136, 140, 142, 174; *see also* Directorate of Religious Affairs

Makhzen, 37–8, 64, 69, 70, 72, 76, 127, 130, 132, 170; *see also* Moroccan regime
Mawdudi, Sayyid Abu al-Ala, 69
menu of options, 14–17, 18–21, 33–5, 36, 55, 85, 101–2, 123, 126, 127
Milli Görüş Hareketi see National Outlook Movement
Milli Nizam Partisi see National Order Party
Milli Selamet Partisi see National Salvation Party
Milliyetçi Hareket Partisi see Nationalist Action Party
Moroccan regime
  history of, 35–6
  King Hassan II, 6–8, 39, 65, 69
  King Mohammed VI, 39, 130
  loyal opposition in, 37, 39–40, 63, 71, 170
  party system in, 39–40
  relations with Islamic movements, 36
  response to the Arab Spring, 130
  role of religion in, 8–9, 134–5
  socio-economy of, 38–9
  state–society relations in, 6–7
  ulama, 36, 134, 135
  see also Commander of the Believers; February 20 Movement; *Makhzen*
Motherland Party, 138
Mouvement de l'Unicité et de la Réforme see Movement for Unity and Reform
Movement for Unity and Reform (MUR)
  history of, 60–1, 62, 64–5
  ideology of, 61
  organisation of, 61–2
  reasons for participation, 62–4
  see also Party for Justice and Development (PJD)
Muti, Abdulkarim, 59, 60, 74; *see also* Islamic Youth

Nakşibendi Order, 54, 73, 74, 76, 78, 85, 138; *see also* Kotku, Mehmed Zahit
National Order Party, 79, 135, 136; *see also* National Outlook Movement
National Outlook Movement (NOM)
  changes in, 137–8
  electoral performance of, 137
  history of, 73–6, 78–9

ideology of, 76–7
in coalition, 136–7
in opposition, 135–8
organisation of, 77
reasons for participation, 77–9
see also Erbakan, Necmettin; Felicity Party; just order; National Order Party; National Salvation Party; Virtue Party; Welfare Party
National Rally of Independents (RNI), 131
National Salvation Party, 135, 136; *see also* National Outlook Movement
Nationalist Action Party, 143
non-participation
  benefits of, 34–5, 49
  consequences of, 19
  costs of, 34, 35, 49
  definition of, 14
Nursi, Said, 81, 84, 85

organisational needs, 18
Othmani, Saadeddine, 60, 61, 171; *see also* Party for Justice and Development
Ottoman Empire, 7, 32, 40
Ottomanism, 76, 77

Parti de la Justice et du Développement see Party for Justice and Development
participation
  benefits of, 33, 34, 49
  consequences of, 19
  costs of, 33–5, 49
  definition of, 14
Party for Justice and Development (PJD)
  electoral performance of, 127
  formation of, 64–5
  in opposition, 127–9
  incumbency, 130–1, 132–3, 170–2
  organisation of, 128–9, 171–2
  relations with the regime, 127–8
  see also Benkirane, Abdelilah; Movement for Unity and Reform (MUR); Othmani, Saadeddine

Quietist Salafis
  growth, 150
  history of, 97–8, 149
  ideology of, 98
  organisation of, 99, 150, 153
  politicisation of, 98–9, 180
  reasons for non-participation, 100–1
  relations with the regime, 149, 179–80

Quietist Salafis (*see also*)
  see also Albani, Nasir al-Din; Al-Halabi (al-Halaby), Ali Hasan; Shaqra, Muhammad Abu
Qutb, Sayyid, 59, 60, 66, 69, 90, 91

Rassemblement National des Indépendants see National Rally of Independents (RNI)
Refah Partisi see Welfare Party
Republican People's Party, 135, 136, 143

Saadet Partisi see Felicity Party
Shaqra, Muhammad Abu, 153; *see also* Quietist Salafis
Socialist Union of Popular Forces (USFP), 39, 40, 64
structural explanations, 14–17
structure–agency debate, 6, 20–1

Thneibat, Abdel Hamid, 154; *see also* Islamic Action Front Party
True Path Party, 138
Turkish regime
  centre–periphery debate, 43
  history of, 40–1
  National Security Council, 140, 142
  party system in, 41–2
  relations with Islamic movements, 41
  role of religion in, 9
  socio-economy of, 42–3
  state–society relations in, 7–8
  see also February 28 Process; Kemalists; laicism

Union Socialiste des Forces Populaires see Socialist Union of Popular Forces

vanguard (Islamic) movements, 55–6, 57–8, 59, 123–4, 155, 167–8
Virtue Party, 136, 137, 140; *see also* National Outlook Movement

Yassine, Abdessalam, 54, 65–70, 79, 129–30, 133; *see also* Justice and Spirituality Movement
Yassine, Nadia, 67, 70, 71, 72, 129; *see also* Justice and Spirituality Movement

Welfare Party, 136, 137, 138, 140; *see also* National Outlook Movement

EU representative:
Easy Access System Europe
Mustamäe tee 50, 10621 Tallinn, Estonia
Gpsr.requests@easproject.com